Here is a bold, new interpretation
of the military conduct of the Civil
War that sheds new light on the
cultural and intel'ectual life of ante
bellum America.
the prevailing vie
ginia campaigns s
military skills led
victories. The union armies, he
argues, defeated themselves by
assuming Southern superiority.
Northerners saw in the South,
which they defined as an area ruled
by aristocracy, many values that
they believed were lacking in their
own newly developing bourgeois
and commercially oriented society.
Too, they held inflated notions
about the martial capacity of their
foe and their leaders enforced this
view.

Even after the war, the Southern
military tradition bewitched Northerners. Grant's hammering tactics
and Sherman's destruction made
Northerners guilty and led them to
believe that they had not outfought
the South but only trampled them
down by numbers. Thus the idea of
the Lost Cause was born and the
romantic myth of the South was

reinforced in a harsh Northern
workaday world. Only in our day
have the historical layers been
stripped away to yield harsher
truths and reality.

Michael C. C. Adams is Assistant
Professor of History, Northern
Kentucky University

Our Masters the Rebels

Our Masters the Rebels

A Speculation on
Union Military Failure in the East
1861-1865

MICHAEL C. C. ADAMS

HARVARD UNIVERSITY PRESS
Cambridge, Massachusetts
and London, England
1978

Publication of this book has been aided by a grant from the Andrew W. Mellon Foundation.

LIBRARY OF CONGRESS CATALOGING IN PUBLICATION DATA

Adams, Michael C. C., 1945–
    Our masters the rebels.

    Includes bibliographical references and index.
    1. United States—History—Civil War, 1861–1865—
Campaigns and battles. 2. United States—History—
Civil War, 1861–1186—Influence. I. Title.
E470.A2   973.7'3012   78–17107

ISBN 0–674–64643–6

For ALBERT EDWARD ADAMS
and L. OWEN GREGORY

Preface

The trouble with General George B. McClellan, said President Lincoln, was that he had "the slows." So, it seemed, did nearly every Northern commander during the first two years of the Civil War. It would be untrue to say that all the poor performers were on the Union side in the conflict, but it does seem that the national forces had more than their share of sluggish officers. A list might include Henry W. Halleck, Don Carlos Buell, Rosecrans, John Charles Fremont, George B. McClellan, and George Gordon Meade, to name only some at the level of army command.

Numerous authors have tried to explain the phenomenon. Some have found the answer in individual personality failings, others in a West Point training that emphasized wars of movement and position rather than head-on conflict. I would like in this book to try a different approach, one that stresses the psychological dimension of the problem. I suggest that a number of Northern soldiers, and civilians for that matter, doubted their ability to whip the rebels. They felt inferior to the enemy and hence their actions lacked the flair and the drive that confidence supplies.

Why should this have been? The North, at least in quantitative terms, had the stronger team. It possessed more men, more money, greater industrial capacity, better transportation facilities of all kinds. The South, in choosing to fight a conventional war against a stronger opponent, should have appeared as the loser from the beginning. But it is here that the psychological element enters: men do not necessarily act on what is objectively true but on what they perceive as the truth. And it was easy for some people to see the Southerner as a superior martial figure.

There were two popular conceptions of Southern character in the antebellum period. One was the abolitionist portrait of the planter as a savage slaveocrat; the other was the more common and more romantic depiction of the South as a place of pillared mansions, courtly manners, and smiling black servants. Neither image was very accurate but both were tremendously influential. And they shared a common theme in suggesting that the Southerner was drawn to violence. The slaveocrat was supposed to maintain the peculiar institution through the use of whips, chains, pistols, and bowie knives. The gentleman of the romantic picture was sensitive to honor and would defend his reputation on the dueling field. He was seen as a gentleman and an officer; so it was assumed that West Point had a special attraction for the planter class.

On the other side, the North was often characterized as a commercial, industrial civilization. In recent times, or at least until Vietnam, it was assumed that the most industrially advanced nations would also be the strongest in war. In the mid-nineteenth century industrial capitalism was too young to have entirely proved itself and to be quite respectable. It was widely believed that the capitalist ethic would prove inimical to the masculine values of courage and self-sacrifice. The reasoning is very clear: the profit motive is essentially selfish and is thus diametrically opposed, at least in theory, to the soldierly virtues of disinterested service and duty. It was also said that the North was more democratic than the South and, in that age, democracy was assumed to be corrosive of the social discipline required by a warlike people.

It was these common views that, I believe, lay at the basis of what may be loosely termed the inferiority complex of some Northerners in the Civil War. Such a complex must have handicapped the North in realizing its military potential. The exploration of this theme involves a major reinterpretation of a whole era and I would not attempt to offer the last word on the subject here. Rather, I am suggesting a fresh line of thought for further study. The nature of the material precludes final analysis at this point. Consider that the actors in the drama were in a war situation where expressions of pessimism could be interpreted as treason. Also, their sentiments often included a rejection of the popular faith in democracy. Naturally, they were reluctant to state explicitly their views in writing. Particularly was this true of professional soldiers, whose training and background made difficult the admission of inferiority feelings. As a result, the piecing together of a pattern requires a vast amount of research and the documentation of certain areas will require the labor of others in the field.

I have told the story for the area where inferiority feelings were most pronounced: the war in Virginia. Lack of confidence was greatest in the east for a number of reasons. Industrialism and business capitalism, assumed to be indices of military weakness, were most advanced in the northeast. Also, here were representatives of old Northern families that had once held power in the nation but whose leadership had been questioned in more democratic times. Uncertain of their status and disturbed by the trend of society, these people were susceptible to inferiority feelings. The bulk of Union soldiers drawn from this class saw service in Virginia and hence added to the self-doubt there. Finally, as a factor producing unease in the east, we should note the high esteem accorded to Virginians as the foremost examples of Southern honor and manliness.

There was a good amount of self-doubt in the Union armies of the west particularly during the first two years of the war. But conditions were not so acute. The men of the northwest tended to be less self-critical than those of the east, seeing themselves as closer to the traditional rural values of America. In fact, they often shared in Southern dislike of New England "Yankee" moral corruption. They felt less awe of the South, or at least of the Confederate southwestern armies they had to face and, correspondingly, were accorded more respect by their opponents than were the Union armies in Virginia. To conclude, those Union soldiers with the least confidence faced the rebels with the most self-esteem—in Virginia.

Leo Marx and his colleagues suggested in *Studies in American Culture* (1960) that not all the traits of a culture are overt or obvious. There exist others, equally part of the whole, but not openly acknowledged by their owners. In exposing these covert aspects, a great deal of speculation is sometimes necessary. This can be dangerous but the danger is far outweighed by the rewards of further illuminating the nature of a society. In this context, an examination of Northern attitudes toward the South reveals much about American covert culture in the nineteenth century.

The South has often been defined as peculiar or un-American; it has performed a function as scapegoat for American failings, pointing up the supposed virtues of other regions. It is well known that in the antebellum period it was criticized as backward, even barbaric, as behind the egalitarian, improving spirit of the age. At the same time, the idea of the South served another, equally important purpose. For example, critics of democracy, afraid to avow their sentiments openly, resorted to indirection. By praising the supposedly aristocratic social structure of the South they could implicitly condemn the prevailing spirit of egalitarianism. The fact that the South was less aristocratic than people thought does not alter the essential point: the South was used, in the realm of the mind, as a vehicle for the expression of ideas running counter to the American mainstream.

The fact that the Southerner served as a sort of covert hero for many Americans was first pointed out by that unusually stimulating critic W. J. Cash. He was followed by William R. Taylor, who examined the subtle dialogue between North and South through a study of antebellum fiction, but his work ends in 1860. So far, only George M. Fredrickson, in his *Inner Civil War,* has attempted to deal at all with the period of the war. His interest is not entirely in the South and he is concerned only with a small group of intellectuals. By offering a complete treatment of the Civil War, I hope to contribute to the intellectual history of the time. Specifically, I believe that in a time of crisis Northern society revealed, at least among the well-bred and the professional, a significant lack of faith in democracy and industrial capitalism.

Finally, a word on terminology. The words North and South, when applied to sectional groupings, are capitalized throughout to signify that these are the principal units discussed. By the same token, east and west are not capitalized as these represent subgroups of the major areas. The term South refers broadly to those states lying below the Mason–Dixon line, though it would be historically inaccurate to use this as a hard-and-fast rule. Kentucky, for example, is treated as illustrating points about North and South.

I would like to thank the following for their contributions: Marcus Cunliffe, my graduate school adviser, who generously shared with me his many ideas on American history; Maldwyn Jones, Paul C. Nagel, Robert K. Wallace, Rupert Wilkinson, and T. Harry Williams, all of whom read and commented upon the manuscript at some stage in its evolution; T. D. Clark, Clement Eaton, Holman Hamilton, and the late A. Kirwan, who added to my knowledge of the South; Aida Donald of Harvard University Press; Jan Vaal, my administrative assistant, who cheerfully gave me long hours of help, and, last but never least, my wife, Joan, without whose unfailing moral support, professional insights, and practical assistance, this project probably could not have been completed.

Contents

"The rebels are masters, taking our leaders by the nose."

Adam Gurowski, *Diary*, April 1861

I

North and South

The Antebellum Debate over Character

Their civilization is a mermaid—lovely and languid above, but ending in bestial deformity.

    —*Harper's Weekly*

Are there any gentlemen among the Yankees?

    —Comment of a Kentucky
    "hillbilly" in Charles Fenno
    Hoffman, *A Winter in the
    West*

If there had been no Union reverses in the Civil War there could have been no talk of Southern military superiority in that conflict. The battlefield experience was therefore crucial. First Bull Run was particularly important as this Federal reverse came at the beginning of the war and set a tone for what was to follow. But the germ idea of Southern martial superiority was born neither at Bull Run nor in the defeats that followed. Some essential ingredients were present in American thinking before the war. Northerners drew on them to explain the failure at Bull Run. Thus, this battle did not so much create the idea as give it immediate meaning and significance. From then on, it was a powerful factor working to limit Northern military confidence, particularly in the east.

To understand these developments we must begin in the antebellum period and with a particular concept in the thought of the time—the idea that the typical Northerner and Southerner differed significantly in character. This belief in difference was basic to much that was said on the military theme. Of course, many observers thought that the people of the two areas were much alike and those who did talk of variations in character often stressed that Americans of all regions still shared many traits in common. Philip Schaff, who came to America from Switzerland, found that certain manners and customs of the Old World were perpetuated among the settlers. In Virginia, for example, could be seen an "English gentleman of the age of Elizabeth and the later Stuarts" or "in New England, the Puritan of the times of Cromwell and Baxter." But he stressed that over the diversity there brooded "a higher unity, and that in the chaos of peoples the traces of a specifically American character may be discerned."[1]

Nevertheless, the concept of differences was a potent one, potent enough that James Johnston Pettigrew, a distinguished Southerner, could compare his relief on leaving Austria, a country he disliked, to "leaving the Yankee land on the way to the South." The idea of foreignness was stated even more boldly by a writer for the *Charleston Mercury* who maintained that "not for an hour since the first white man set his foot on American soil have the people of the United States been one people." Politically

2

and socially, he said, the South was as distinct from the North as from France or England.[2]

To recreate the characterizations of American society is a large task and hence the subject will be dealt with in two chapters. Here, an attempt will be made to paint the dominant images on a broad canvas. The South, it will be suggested, was portrayed as a land of aristocracy, possessing the best and worst traits of that form of society. The Southerner at his best was described as a cultivated, chivalric gentleman. But it was also noted that his refinement sometimes seemed to hide a harsher strain. For example, Southern elegance was possible only at the expense of black slaves. The North was seen as more advanced in terms of material development and political freedom. But for this, too, it seemed a price had to be paid. The atmosphere of the North appeared to suggest industrial drabness and a certain lack of couth, particularly among the new men of the middle class.

To begin with Southern ideas, numerous writers have pointed out that in the decades following the War of 1812 Southern spokesmen moved steadily from a nationalist standpoint to a defense of State Rights. They came to see themselves as representing a minority group within the nation. The transition might be symbolized by Calhoun's change from championship of nationalistic legislation to a concern for sectional protection. A leader of the War Hawks in 1812, he was, by 1828, challenging the power of the Federal government in his "South Carolina Exposition." This suggestion of Southern change is, of course, a generalization and like all generalizations subject to overstatement. The South never entirely developed a group consciousness. Different economic, social, and geographical blocs, with varying views and interests, existed within the region until the end of the antebellum period. And many people continued to see themselves as American rather than Southern.[3]

Still, it remains true that during this period leading Southern spokesmen, in politics and literature, came increasingly to talk of a difference in character and interests between themselves and the people above the Mason–Dixon line. A number of factors accounted for this inward-looking search for a unique identity. At one level, it was part of a more general

eagerness on the part of Americans and Europeans to define what was peculiar about this "new" nation of America.[4]

A more important reason for Southern introspection was the need to
justify the existence of slavery. At the time of the Revolution some Southerners believed slavery to be an unprofitable, undesirable institution which
they hoped might quickly die away. But with the opening of new lands to
the west that were suitable for cotton culture and the development of the
cotton gin, which allowed the plant to be processed quickly by unskilled
labor, slavery received a new lease of life. More than before, Southerners
saw slavery as an economic necessity. But, for the sake of appearances if
not for conscience, they also had to rationalize it as a positive social good.
The extent to which Southerners felt the contradiction between slavery and
the principles enunciated during the Revolution is still not clear but one
thing is certain: even before the abolitionist attacks from the North, Southerners began the defense of slavery as a social system that provided unique
benefits, both for the slave whom it placed under the fatherly care of a superior race and for the master who was given the freedom from toil necessary to the creation of a superior culture. The development of the argument was given much additional impetus by outside attacks during the
thirties and after. As Northern criticisms became more intense, Southerners tended to close ranks on the slavery issue and to withdraw intel-
lectually and emotionally within their borders.[5]

Related to the slavery issue was that of territorial expansion. The attempts made to keep slavery out of the territories also helped breed in some
Southerners a sense of difference from the rest of the nation—a feeling of
outside threat to their well-being, which caused them to think of solidarity
within the section. People began to think of an independent South reaching down into Latin America. Expansion was not only an economic but
a political issue for it seemed clear to radical Southerners that unless the
balance of slave and free states was kept equal, the South would be persecuted by a political majority opposed to its interests.[6]

The shape of this opposition they felt could be discerned in the struggle over the tariff, which they believed was kept deliberately high to protect the growing industry of the northeast at the expense of the agricultural
regions. In 1832 South Carolina came close to secession over this issue.
(It should be remembered again that these comments are of a general nature. Resentment of the tariff did not hold true for all the South. In
Kentucky, for example, there was much feeling in favor of protection,
which helped the local hemp and rope industries. South Carolina could
not get any other state to join it in nullification.)[7]

In less obvious ways also, some Southerners resented what they saw as

Northern economic domination. Historians still do not agree on whether slavery was a profitable institution but, whether it was or not, some planters believed they should have been getting better returns on their crops. Most of their products were shipped across the Atlantic in Northern or European ships and the whole of the coastal trade was dominated by Northern shipowners. Northern factors handled Southern imports. Southerners resented these people in the way that the middle man is usually mistrusted. The British geologist, G. W. Featherstonhaugh, found that the South Carolina planters held in contempt the Northern merchants "whom they consider to be by the nature of their avocations, incapable of rising to their level." This dislike was most intense among those who owed money to the merchant. The planter, "perceiving himself therefore the debtor and quasi slave of the man he despises, his pride, his interest, and his passions, all combine to raise his indignation."[8]

There was a genuine distaste for capitalistic enterprise that went beyond self-interest. In particular, the emerging industrial order of the North appeared to pose a threat to stable society. Workers in large industrial cities lost the community ties and values fostered in smaller towns and rural areas; long hours away from home at the factory loom meant that family links were weakened. Writers like George Fitzhugh feared that the alienation of labor inherent in the factory system would lead to class warfare. In the squalid industrial districts he saw the seeds of revolution.[9]

Perhaps those most troubled by economic considerations were planters of the Tidewater regions, who saw wealth and power move away from them as the South expanded westward into fresh cotton and tobacco lands. There was a sense of decay, of degeneration, and of nostalgia for the past. This blended with the romantic movement in literature to produce both the Gothic tales of Edgar Allan Poe—stories of living death and putrefaction—and a rose-colored vision of how life had been in the Tidewater during her colonial heyday. Their imaginations touched by the writings of Walter Scott and other leading Romantics, novelists produced a spate of books about the booted and spurred Cavaliers of the Old Dominion. This preoccupation with the past coincided with the need of other Southerners for a comprehensive rationale of their situation (which would defend slavery and the Southern way of life while also attacking Northern faults) to produce the Cavalier and Yankee theory of American origins.[10]

In its most elaborate form the Cavalier and Yankee thesis posed a view of the North and South as being radically different in character because of separate racial origins. Northerners, it was said, were descended from the Saxons of England. These were conquered by William of Normandy in 1066 and they became the lower class of laborers and artisans. Centuries later this group gave rise to the Puritans who settled New England and from there sent out their influence across the North. Southerners were descended from William's barons, who spawned the Cavaliers of Charles I, enough of whom came to the Southern colonies to form an artistocracy there. The Yankee, molded by his Puritan background and the bleak New England climate, was cold and hypocritical. As befitted his traditional status as a tradesman, he was good at striking advantageous bargains, was tricky and clever, but without the breeding to turn this into true brilliance. Southerners, as aristocrats, were chivalric, generous by nature, less concerned with money than with honor.[11]

This picture was not only pleasing to the romantic imagination; it was an excellent justification of all things Southern. If the South was not keeping pace with the economic growth of the North, it was because this growth was not desirable. Change was dominated by the Yankee, who, in his thirst to make money, would thrust aside traditional values such as noble-mindedness and generosity. In the capitalistic society of the North the only standard of measurement was profit. Northern charges that slavery was a remnant of feudal barbarism could be met with the claim that apparent Southern backwardness was actually Southern wisdom. By removing the constant pressure of work from the shoulders of the master, so ran the argument, slavery left him free to cultivate the artistocratic qualities lacking in acquisitive Yankee society. Nor were the blacks unhappy, said Southerners. The planter's sense of noblesse oblige kept him from abusing his people, who were not only his workers but his wards. He would look after them when they were old whereas the Northerner, whose only concern was profit, would turn a worker out from his factory to starve once he was no longer productive.[12]

This interpretation of American character was, in the words of W. J. Cash, "a nearly perfect defense-mechanism," for it shifted the blame for society's ills away from the slaveholder to the business-industrial leaders of the North. Of course, not all Southerners were familiar with the Cavalier and Yankee thesis in this, its most refined form. Many people would not have known a Saxon from a Norman and, for that matter, would not have cared to know. The full depiction of a Cavalier society seems to have been restricted to Southern writers, politicians, editors, and so on. But in one form or another, the idea of difference was widespread in Southern society. It was a common assumption that all Yankees were traders or mechanics and that there were no gentlemen in the North. The representation of Southerners as planter aristocrats became so popular, especially among outsiders, that the outlines of pillared mansions still obscure the realities of Southern history.

As a definition of Southern society, the Cavalier argument was very misleading. To begin with, it missed out the vast bulk of Southern people, who were written off as white trash, dirt eaters, or devoted peasants rather being seen as resembling the serfs on a feudal manor. However, though research shows that clay eating may have been more prevalent than historians suspected, the bulk of Southerners were neither trash nor upperclass planters; they were of the middling sort. Frank L. Owsley showed a number of years ago that the majority of the population was comprised of middle class farmers and small planters, lawyers, and other professional types. He estimated that the majority owned their own land, grew their own food, and made their own clothing. They were usually not wealthy but they lived a decent life. Despite the common idea that these people had no power or influence, Owsley maintained that in politics the middling man "could nearly always rise to local leadership" and exercised a powerful influence through the ballot box. He noted that "the significance of the role of the plain folk in politics may be partly evaluated from some of the provisions of the new state constitutions adapted under popular pressure between 1830 and 1860. Universal white male manhood suffrage, the popular election of virtually all county and state officers, and the abolition of property qualifications for office holding in most cases were good examples."[13]

Owsley's conclusions tend to be borne out by later writings. Clement Eaton estimates from the 1860 census returns that only 46,274 persons out of approximately 8,000,000 could be classed as "planters" by virtue of owning 20 slaves. Of these, only 2,292 held 100 slaves or more. The only area in which there appears to be substantial disagreement is regarding the question of how far the plain folk identified with the planters and accepted their values. Eaton decided that "though the great mass of Southerners could not live like the privileged planters with their numerous slaves, they absorbed something of the spirit and sense of values of the Southern gentry." Peter F. Walker, on the other hand, in a case study of the city of Vicksburg on the eve of Civil War, found that the professional classes did not particularly desire to emulate the planters or rise into their ranks. At any rate, the debate need not concern us. Whatever the case, the important point is that the outside world received an impression of the South as gentry-dominated and Southerners were themselves prone to think of their culture as superior to that of the North.[14]

A second gross inaccuracy in the planter legend was that it portrayed the planter class as static—as a hereditary aristocracy closed to entrance from below. In fact, Southern society was relatively fluid: a number of those who were most influential in propagating the myth of a planter South were newly arrived members of the upper class seeking social acceptance or were fallen aristocrats looking back to an earlier period when their families had been at the top. So far as the contrast with the North is concerned, it is true that there was more commercial and industrial development above the Mason–Dixon line and that a society may be characterized through these, its most advanced elements. But the degree of disparity can be exaggerated. Louisville and Lexington, in the slaveholding state of Kentucky, had more textile factories in 1820 than the state of Maine. In the North, agriculture was still the primary occupation at the end of the antebellum period: the average man was not a mechanic or a captain of industry—he was, like the Southerner, a farmer of moderate means.[15]

Jane H. Pease, a recent student, argues that the most cherished of Southern claims—to less concern with profit and loss, more hospitality and generosity with money—may not be true. She speculates that lavish entertainment of house guests appears to have been an American rather than a Southern phenomenon. Likewise, when Americans traveled abroad their expense accounts tended to be similar. Northern abolitionists in Europe spent as much on personal comfort as did Southerners. And Northerners made certain that they were well catered to at their spas and resort areas.[16]

To conclude, the South did have its fine planter families who lived in splendid style and they controlled a disproportionate share of the wealth, as does any upper class. But they were not the whole South and they were not typical of the average inhabitant. Even the majority of the well-to-do did not live in pillared Greek mansions but in unpretentious farmhouses. One obvious reason for this was that the agricultural methods of the period used up land at an incredible rate, so it was hardly worth building a fine house when a move was in the offing to fresh lands in the west.[17]

If the plantation image with its Cavalier gentry involved a large distortion of Southern realities, how were Southern spokesmen able to use it so much without an uncomfortable awareness of its inadequacy? A prime factor was ignorance. In an age when accurate statistical method was not the rule, Southerners were not always clear about the actual breakdown of their social groupings. J. B. De Bow, who pioneered the use of census returns to estimate the social strata of the South, wrote, "I am not aware that the relative number of these two classes [slaveholders and non-slaveholders] has ever been ascertained in any of the States." Moreover, once the stereotypes of Southern classes had been established, it was difficult to see beyond them, no matter what statistics were available. Hinton Rowan Helper, a Southern advocate of abolition, attempted a statistical method in his book *The Impending Crisis of the South: How to Meet It.* Yet he still described all the non-slaveholders as dirty and degraded. "Poverty, ignorance, and superstition, are the three leading characteristics of the non-slaveholding white of the South," he wrote. "Many of them grow up to the age of maturity, and pass through life without ever owning as much as five dollars at any one time."[18]

Again, there was enough of a grain of truth in the Cavalier idea for the romantic imagination to fix upon and turn into a seeming reality. Statistics show that the population of Virginia doubled during the period of the English Commonwealth. Presumably, at least some of these immigrants were followers of Charles I. Then too, while most of the Virginia aristocracy of the eighteenth century was descended from middle or lower class origins, enough younger sons of the gentry did go to the colonies to give a shade of verity to the Cavalier idea. And certainly, by the eighteenth century, Virginia had developed a native aristocracy of wealth and power. It was not difficult to project the image of this colonial society onto the newly arrived planters of the nineteenth century.[19]

The fact that New England was settled in part by Puritans and took its original character from them made it easy to cast the Northerner as a lineal descendant of Cromwell's Roundhead troopers. New England's commercial success was not difficult to portray as an unhealthy concern with material success, and for those educated or interested enough to read the works of Fitzhugh, the trend of modern industrial society must have seemed appalling enough. But for the average Southerner, the stereotype of the Northerner as a man devoured by the desire to make money owed most to the phenomenon of the Yankee peddler who traveled the South and west during the antebellum period selling clocks, pins, nutmegs, and the like.[20]

These traders quickly gained an unenviable reputation as cunning and unprincipled men who would cheat and swindle for a little more profit. It was said that they sold wooden nutmegs and would foist clocks without works on unknowing rustics. One early student of frontier life described the peddlers as shrewd New Englanders of Puritan descent who "could 'calculate,' with the most absolute certainty, what precise stage of advancement and cultivation, was necessary to the introduction of every article of merchandise their stock comprised." John Bernard, a European visitor, was told in the Carolinas that the approach of a New England trader created more havoc than a tornado. At his appearance, the people "bar doors and windows, while many even double lock drawers, to prevent a conjuration over the counter by which the money seems to leap out of the till into the peddler's pocket."[21]

Many such tales were not true but were made up to provide amusement. Yet stories and rumors can become a substitute for reality. Tales about, or experience with, Yankee tradesmen were the only contacts many Southerners had with Northern culture and so they easily came to see the whole society as corrupt and vulgar. Of course, stereotypes flourished for other reasons than ignorance. William R. Taylor, a leading student, believes that many who used Cavalier and Yankee images did not believe in them as realities. Rather, they were a convenient vehicle for the criticism of certain trends in American life—trends which troubled Northerners also.[22]

The Cavalier and Yankee thesis was in many ways abusive of Northern character, particularly of the northeast. Hence it is surprising to find that for the greater part of the antebellum period many Northerners, including a large number from New England and the Atlantic states, who commented on Southern manners spoke highly of the planter class. Why did they accept the Southern picture? Why did they not point out, for instance, that the vast majority of Southerners did not even belong to the slaveholding class?

One reason was that Northerners had even less means than Southerners of gauging just how many people were planters or fitted the picture of the cultivated gentleman. Newspapers and magazines carried information about the South but much of this was biased by editorial opinion or was based on the impressionistic sketches of travelers. Typical of much published material was a passage from a Methodist journal in which it was said that "Southern society, then, and always had these two extremes—the high-toned gentlemen whose favorite political idea has been that of aristocracy and absolutism, and a miserable rabble without enterprise and wretched in the extreme."

Abolitionist propaganda formed another medium for the dissemination of data about the South but it was hardly objective and, even while highly critical of the slaveholders, it accepted almost entirely the common assumption that the planters were the only important element in the South.[23]

Those who actually visited the South rarely achieved a greater degree of accuracy, for they took their preconceptions with them. And the fact that they could travel such distances often meant that they were of a social and economic class that would restrict its sojourns to the homes of planters. Relatively few had the time or interest to accurately observe the common folk. A Massachusetts traveler who visited the region in 1850 brought back a stereotyped picture of the Southerner as "high-spirited, chivalrous, quick to resent an insult, too proud to give one, ready to fight for his lady-love or his country! prone to high living and horse-racing, but at home courteous and hospitable as becomes a true country gentleman."[24]

Even unusually perceptive critics were unable to get beyond the conventional view. Frederick Law Olmsted, whose observations of Southern life were more piercing than most, still described the non-slaveholding whites as shiftless types who would not work because labor was for slaves. And by the time Alexis de Tocqueville, that most vaunted of European visitors, reached Kentucky he was sufficiently imbued with the prevalent views to write, "There, work is not only painful: it's shameful, . . . To ride, to hunt, to smoke like a Turk in the sunshine: there is the destiny of the white. To do any other kind of manual labour is to act like a slave. The whites, to the South of the Ohio, form a veritable aristocracy." This was a gross exaggeration. Most of the crops grown in the state were not conducive to slave cultivation and there were few large plantations. Where slaves were used, their numbers were usually small and they worked in the fields alongside the master and his family. If Kentucky did have a "veritable aristocracy" it was restricted largely to the Bluegrass area.[25]

Southerners who traveled north were often of the upper classes, so that their appearance confirmed existing images. And the Southerners with whom the North was most familiar, congressmen in the national capital, tended to be less representative of Southern society than were politicians at the local level. The border states of Kentucky and Virginia seemed to enjoy a particularly high level of representation, including men of the caliber of Henry Clay, John J. Crittenden, and the Breckinridge family. Mrs. Frances Trollope, a visiting Englishwoman, was much impressed by the Virginians. On entering the House of Representatives she was mortified to find the congressmen "sitting in the most unseemly attitudes, a large majority with their hats on, and nearly all, spitting to an excess that decency forbids me to describe." Among the crowds were a few "distinguished by not wearing their hats, and by sitting on their chairs like other human beings, without throwing their legs above their heads." These, Mrs. Trollope discovered, were all Virginians.[26]

If lack of precise evidence partly accounted for outside acceptance of the gentleman image of Southern life, there were also more positive factors at work. The idea of aristocracy made a direct appeal to Northerners at a number of levels. Romantic interest in the past was as marked in the North as in the South. There was excitement in the idea of having a native-grown aristocracy below the Mason–Dixon line. It might not be quite as interesting as the knights of Norman England or the Highlanders of Scotland but it at least added a touch of color to the American scene. Northerners wanted to be wooed by the charm of the South and to visit, in imagination if not in fact, the pillared homes where genial blacks entertained under the shade of magnolia trees. Sentimental lithographs of the South were eagerly bought in the North. So great was the fascination that Frank Wilkie, a Northern sketch artist, believed it influenced many boys to join the Union army in 1861. They were, he said, "romantic dreamers who caught glimpses in the distance of dark-eyed women with raven hair . . . who enjoyed in anticipation the languid delights of the orange groves, the flowering hedges, the beauty of the magnolia blossoms, and the genial air of the 'sunny South.' "[27]

Nor were all the people who fell under the spell adventure-starved farm boys. N. P. Willis, a New York editor who visited New Orleans in 1852, was intrigued by the elusive Creole ladies, "these wonders of the adorable gender." He was also impressed by the manners of the planters who had, he thought, that "air of conscious superiority which can never be assumed, but which is prized above all other traits by the high-born in Europe."[28]

It seemed rather splendid to visit a Southern plantation and pretend that one had been "dropped down in the midst of the smooth green lawns and old oaks and all the domestic comforts of an English country seat . . . I can hardly conceive myself now in America," wrote Henry Barnard, a Northern educator. Similarly, A. De Puy Van Buren from Battle Creek, Michigan, felt that "the planter also, may be considered a lord in possession of a large estate, and his slaves are his vassals. And, like your English gentleman of landed possessions, he loves the chase, keeps a parliament of hounds, and the requisites for the hunt." A life of lordly ease was quite pleasant, thought Edwin Hall, a traveler from Maine, who found that in the house of a planter "everything is done for me. I have nothing to do and find it really convenient to be waited on."[29]

The North had an aristocracy of its own. In New England, for example, lived some of the oldest and best descended families in America. But this aristocracy did not appeal to everyone. It seemed too ascetic, too bookish. Harriet Martineau thought there was a good deal of religious cant among the New Englanders. Josiah Gorgas, an army officer who was originally from Pennsylvania but who was very attracted to the South, looked on a tour of duty in Maine as something of an exile. He wrote that "the manners and habits of the people are so uncongenial here that one cannot help sighing after the frankness of Southern manners." The pleasures available were "but a sorry compensation for the rustle of leaves, the voice of birds, and the beauty and odor of flowers" to be found in the South.[30]

In this fashion Northerners helped propagate the myth of a planter South. It would be absurd to say that all these people exaggerated their accounts of Southern society but they did over-generalize from acquaintance with a small portion of the community. Perhaps, too, they saw in the South only what they wanted to see—the idea of a Cavalier South met a need for romantic color, it titillated the fancy.

The image of the Southern gentleman was also admired, even envied, for more serious and subtle reasons. The planter could be seen as an example of social values worthy of imitation in the North. To get at this point it is necessary to examine a belief held by certain Northerners that both the individual and society were degenerating. This anxiety was most acute among, but was not restricted to, the old pre-industrial upper class of gentleman merchants, bankers, lawyers, the landed gentry, clergymen of the Anglican and other older denominations, professors. They were usually men of established background and breeding, or closely identified with such.

The fear of degeneracy can be seen most clearly in the writings of some cultivated New Englanders who felt that the New England way had lost vitality and was a narrow, inadequate thing. They saw themselves as both critics and victims of the trend. Some suggested that New England was dogged by the gloomy legacy of Puritanism. Nathaniel Hawthorne, who was haunted by the part an ancestor had played in the seventeenth-century Salem witch trials, intimated in *The House of the Seven Gables* that New Englanders were imprisoned by the sense of past sin and guilt. Others felt that the problem was as much physical as mental. John William De Forest, a New England writer, suggested that the rigorous climate had a destructive effect on health. He recalled that many women of his acquaintance were "thin-lipped, hollow-cheeked, narrow-chested, with only one lung and an intermittent digestion, . . . a sad example of what the New England east winds can do in enfeebling and distorting the human form divine."[31]

There was criticism, too, of the traditional stress on solely intellectual endeavor. It was charged that the development of the mind had been achieved at the expense of the body so that weak, dyspeptic types were produced. Francis Walker, a New England soldier and educational reformer, recalled in his 1893 Phi Beta Kappa address at Harvard that the antebellum undergraduate had been self-conscious, introspective, and moody. He would, said Walker, have mistrusted his calling had he found himself engaged in bodily exercise and "not infrequently mistook physical lassitude for intellectuality, and the gnawings of dyspepsia for spiritual cravings."[32]

To compensate for this apparent neglect of the body, certain New Englanders took a pioneer course in physical development. Among them was Richard Henry Dana who, as a Harvard undergraduate, shipped before the mast on a California-bound brig "to cure, if possible, by an entire change of life, and by a long absence from books, with plenty of hard work, plain food, and open air, a weakness of the eyes, which had obliged me to give up my studies." Dana lost his ailment and gained a lifelong interest in the sea. Francis Parkman, taking the Oregon Trail as an overland route to bodily vigor, was less fortunate. Without the rugged constitution which the trip demanded, he was to suffer physical distress for much of his life.[33]

It is difficult to determine whether these New Englanders were a particularly unhealthy breed. So far as climate is concerned, was a Boston winter more debilitating than a New Orleans summer? Again, it is true that intensive study must have ruined weaker types but there were also men like Henry David Thoreau and Thomas Wentworth Higginson, hardy specimens by any standards. And the fact that New England officers were to stand up as well as any others to the rigors of civil war seems to imply that the physical degeneration had not gone deep. One suspects therefore that behind the anxiety about health and academic routine were other, less tangible but equally real, concerns. In a mood of deep dissatisfaction with America, these people were hypercritical of their own seeming inability to take hold of the situation and change it. What troubled them, it may be suggested, was the spirit of the modern age, exemplified primarily in popular democracy.[34]

It is now generally understood among historians that the American Revolution did not bring sweeping democratic changes: wealth and power remained at the top. But the rhetoric of equality used during the Revolution had planted a seed that flowered in the years following. As early as 1807, New Jersey established white manhood suffrage and Maryland followed in 1810. The frontier, with its leveling influence, encouraged the trend: every state added to the Union after the War of 1812 made provision for white manhood suffrage. Business added a further stimulus as new men, rising to wealth through financial or industrial expertise, pushed for a place in the power structure. Even factory workers, thrown together by mutual need, demanded a share in decisions. Of course, this did not mean that there was immediately a revolutionary change in the style of American government but it did mean that the established upper classes increasingly had to share power with, or at least be responsive to, the people.[35]

It was difficult for many of us to understand, until recent disillusioning developments, that a broad, encompassing democracy may not be seen always and everywhere as the ideal form of government. Nineteenth-century Americans of breeding and class often did not wish to see in Congress politicians thrown up by the rough-and-tumble democracy of the west. Abraham Lincoln, the "rail splitter," was to them embarrassingly uncouth and not at all the classical image of the republican statesman. Similarly, they had no desire to rub shoulders with the newly rich industrialists and speculators, who often appeared vulgar and ostentatious in their attempts to ape aristocracy.[36]

The point may be illustrated through a brief glimpse at developments in New York state. According to Dixon Ryan Fox, one student of the period, New York became committed to the doctrine of political democracy between 1821 and 1824. To some gentlemen who had been making gloomy predictions for years about the instability of republics, this liberalizing force foreshadowed disaster. They warned that the newly enfranchised masses would soon want the property and positions of their betters. These predictions appeared to be fulfilled when, toward the end of the decade, New York workers began to press for better conditions of work and opportunity.[37]

In upstate New York, James Fenimore Cooper became embroiled with the locals who tried to use his lands as a picnic ground. The newspaper attacks made on him as a result of his stand he considered to be the work of demagogues and in 1838 he published *The American Democrat* as a plea for Americans to allow a place for gentlemen, to accept enlightened leadership, and not to allow themselves to be drawn into demagoguery and anarchy. If this disgraceful business of ruling by mobs should continue, he said, "even those well affected to a popular government, will be obliged to combine with those who wish its downfall, in order to protect their persons and property, against the designs of the malevolent." Strong enough warning that gentlemen might be driven to consider a dictatorship, a theme we will return to.[38]

If Cooper did not particularly wish to rub shoulders with the masses, neither did many others. In the 1831 New York mayoral election, the voters for the first time were allowed to express directly their choice for the office. The friends of the winner, instead of congratulating him, expressed sympathy at his misfortune in being elected by the suffrage of the masses. Later, the unhappy fellow had to lock his doors against a crowd that wished to celebrate the victory. Frances Seward, wife of the New York politician William H. Seward and from a family of good estate, was not able to keep out the people. "The canaille," as she put it, tore up the house during the festivities attending Seward's election to the governorship. Again, in 1839, the Whig rank and file came to cover her carpets with mud and tobacco juice. "O the beauties of democracy," she cried.[39]

Rather than submit to what they saw as the indignities of democratic politics—the log-rollings, picnics, and hand shakings that accompanied electioneering—many gentlemen simply withdrew from public life into private business. Francis Grund, a European visitor, was told in New York that only blackguards were successful in politics and that America was past the age when respectable people could take an interest in public affairs. And John MacGregor, a British lawyer, wrote after visiting America, "Every gentleman . . . abjures politics; and, in proportion to his sense, appears anxious to assure you he is not a politician."[40]

However, if gentlemen abstained from politics, then the very people who were despised as being incapable of governing were left in control. Thus the problem was compounded, as *Harper's Weekly,* a journal of the "respectable" classes in New York, pointed out in a series of anguished articles toward the end of the antebellum period. According to *Harper's,* democratic government was not functioning. There was a corruption abroad in American life, a greed eating at the roots of private and public morality. Signs of disquietude were evident in the very first issue, which appeared on January 3, 1857. It carried a piece on the recent presidential election that bubbled with enthusiasm over the unparalleled display of freedom and intelligence at the polls (Buchanan, a conservative Democrat and a mannerly gentleman had been elected). But, the writer asked, how long was this grand spectacle to last, for already the Union was threatened by local jealousies, by extremists North and South, and by intense love of gain—the peculiar vice of the age.[41]

By the seventeenth of the month *Harper's* had gone over entirely to a pessimistic position. There was not enough public spirit left to carry on a popular form of government, concluded a review of the venality in New York's political machinery. At the root of the trouble lay prosperity, the vice of the age, which had turned the best men of the city away from the thankless obligations of public service to more remunerative pursuits. In their absence, unscrupulous professional politicians had come to power.

The report of Orr's committee on improbity in Congress provoked another *Harper's* tirade on the business-mindedness of the Northern upper classes, while the commercial depression of 1857 served to convince the magazine that its crisis mentality was justified. The calamity appeared to have been caused by speculative fever, a product of the haste to be rich. The following years saw little cause for encouragement so that by April of 1860, when there was apparently even more corruption than usual in the New York state legislature, the *Weekly* could see only two alternatives for the future. Either respectable people would begin to use their franchise to elect the right men or there would be revolution. The climate would be ripe for dictatorship.[42]

Such were some of the issues that troubled conservatives in New York state. The situation certainly appeared to be a bleak one, with greed and selfishness eating at the very fiber of national life. This was particularly frightening for a republic because it was believed that republics, in which most men had a say in the government, were much more dependent on a healthy public spirit than were monarchies or aristocracies, which could continue to function so long as the ruling clique remained pure. Americans, like Europeans, were products of a classical education and history seemed to show that nearly all previous republics had succumbed to venality. Then, said the books, anarchy and despotism followed.[43]

It is not essential for our purposes to establish whether the fears of corruption were justified: the main concern here is to trace belief. But one or two comments might be illuminating. So far as politics are concerned, there certainly was much wrong. The increasing use of gimmicks as in the notorious "Log Cabin" campaign did not speak well of the sincerity of the politicians or the intelligence of the people. Indeed, the illiteracy of many of those with the vote almost forced a drop in sophistication on the public platform. There was graft in politics, encouraged by the growing spoils system which rested essentially on the buying and selling of public office for political favor. Yet the extent of change could be exaggerated. Those who looked back upon the revolutionary fathers as being ideal statesmen were using rose-colored spectacles. If nineteenth-century New Yorkers did not like to be jostled at the polls, neither had Tories enjoyed being set upon by mobs of ruffians directed by the Sons of Liberty. And if there was greed in Congress, many a colonial office holder had been more interested in the emoluments than the obligations of his work. Essentially, what these gentlemen objected to was not mobs but mobs in the hands of the people: democracy itself was their bane.[44]

What about the apparently universal spirit of gain which caused so much worry? This is a difficult question to deal with because there has been greed in all ages and it is a hard quality to quantify. Also, our understanding of the Victorian consciousness is not sufficiently advanced that we can plumb all the depths of those very complex people. Certainly, in a land bountifully supplied with natural resources and possessing the work ethic necessary for their exploitation, the accumulation of vast wealth was a dream not beyond reach and it would naturally have a large place in men's thinking. Perhaps many did go money-mad. More likely, however, the greed was not as serious as the apprehension of it. For this was a time of great technological change and men were not quite sure how far from the familiar the machine might take them. Hence, their attitude to the machine was ambivalent. Like our own society, confronted with its waste and yet not wishing to give up its expensive habits, men hoped that the machine would help them conquer the environment yet wondered if it would rob them of healthful contact with nature, the mother of mankind. Greater productivity would alleviate want but would abundance at the same time sap the old heroic qualities of courage and endurance?[45]

These questions troubled Victorian Britain and they troubled Americans. This was a young nation seemingly in need of strong men to build its frontiers and protect it against the jealousies of old-world powers: it could not afford luxury. Some felt they saw the onset of weakness in the foolish way the nouveaux riches tried to ape European taste instead of cultivating a native and more wholesome style. This type was flayed by the New York playwright Anna Cora Mowatt in *Fashion,* produced during 1845. In one scene a bluff farmer called Trueman (not a frontiersman but an eastern farmer of settled habits who represents traditional values) tells the head of one such family whose ostentation has nearly ruined them: "You must sell your house and all these gew-gaws, and bundle your wife and daughter off to the country. There let them learn economy, true independence, and home virtues instead of foreign follies. As for yourself, continue your business—but let moderation in future be your counsellor."[46]

Finally, there was the possibility that the power released by technology might fall into diabolical rather than benevolent hands. In a recent, brilliant study, Leonard L. Richards pointed out that one reason the abolitionists so alienated "gentlemen of property and standing" was that they used the new techniques of mass production in printing to get their message to groups previously outside politics. Thus, they appealed to women and children and were hated for it. The abolitionists were, concludes Richards, "the cutting edge of a far-reaching change."[47]

In other words, people lived in a fast-moving world which, because of its unknown quality, magnified both hopes and fears. It produced visions of the millennium and a mentality that saw the shadow of doom behind every successful businessman. Because the forces at work were large and perplexing, it was not easy to find ways of handling them. *Harper's* argument that corruption could be stanched if the best men returned to politics was too simplistic. The solution to problems was not always clear and hence opponents of change were often on different sides of the party lines. The presidency of Andrew Jackson is a good example. The Democrats believed they were defending America against control by large capital and hoped to take the nation back to an earlier and better style. The Whigs also felt they were championing traditional values, seeing in their opponents the ugliness of democracy. Taken as typical of Jackson and his followers was an inaugural affair at which rude crowds trampled through the White House and made a shambles. Margaret Bayard Smith, wife of a prominent Philadelphia banker, heard in the distance the sound of Paris mobs in the Tuileries and at Versailles. The people, she feared, would prove ferocious, cruel, and despotic tyrants who might end all rule and rulers.[48]

Another good example of the confusion was that certain gentlemen, finding politics objectionable, turned to the moral crusade against slavery as an outlet for energy. In doing this they ran head on into their own class, which saw abolitionism as a vicious radical product of the age. Anyway, even assuming that conservatives could gain unanimity, they would make little headway so long as a majority was opposed to them—unless they were willing to consider a dictatorship. Some were. European visitors commented upon the frank attraction exerted by the idea of aristocracy on the upper circles in the old, established areas. Harriet Martineau found in Boston "some few who openly desire a monarchy; and a few more who openly insinuate the advantages of a monarchy, and the distastefulness of a republic. It is observable that such always argue on the supposition that if there were a monarchy, they should be the aristocracy."[49]

To others, such talk was absurd because, before the Northern gentleman could do anything, he must rejuvenate himself. Disgusted by politics, so the argument went, they had withdrawn into business pursuits. They too put private gain before public good. William Ellery Channing, a leading New England divine, undoubtedly included the Brahmins in the indictment when he said, "Our present civilization is characterized and tainted by a devouring greediness of wealth: . . . The passion for gain is everywhere sapping pure and generous feeling." This brings us back to the nagging fear of degeneration among the New Englanders and to the suggestion that a sense of frustration and guilt about their lessened role in public life stood back of their morbid self-criticism.[50]

It was partly to find a way of reinvigorating his class and preparing them to regain their position of power that Parkman had taken his somewhat unfortunate trip along the Oregon Trail. He had hoped to find a model of masculinity in the pioneers of the west but his experience had been disappointing. He admired the rugged qualities of the men he met, but they were, after all, rather base material from which to create a blue-print for gentlemen. The seeming robustness of the English gave some New Englanders food for thought. The islanders had, said Emerson, "great vigor of body and endurance. Other countrymen look slight and undersized beside them, and invalids. They are bigger men than the Americans. I suppose a hundred taken at random out of a street would weigh a fourth more than so many Americans."[51]

As Parkman was later to see, an equally good model could be found in the Southern planter, at least as he appeared in stereotyped image. In com-mon conception he was, like the English country gentleman, a hearty fel-low who enjoyed a life of healthy outdoor activity, including hunting and fishing. Such types were not likely to suffer from the melancholy appar-ently encouraged by a New England education. Erasmus Darwin Keyes, a New England-born army officer, was concerned like Hawthorne by the Puritan legacy. He observed that the fear of undefined evil had destroyed the drive of numbers of the best men. In their youth they had been made afraid by "gloomy dogmas" and weighed down by a "mysterious account-ability of a dark and dismal character." Keyes was therefore amazed when, happening to be in the Senate gallery, he heard John J. Crittenden of Ken-tucky speak. The Kentuckian appeared as though he had never been made afraid of life; he had a strength of character, thought Keyes, lacking in Northerners.[52]

This sense of confidence was also noticed by Timothy Flint, a New England minister who preached in the aristocratic Bluegrass region of Ken-tucky during the 1830s. He found in the people "an ardor of character, courage, frankness, generosity." Their good star was self-confidence, "a perfect command of all they knew," which enabled them to take a step "before the tardy, bashful and self-criticizing young man from the North had made up his mind." It was perhaps with his native New Englanders in mind that Flint recommended, in the preface to the life of a Kentucky pioneer, that people pay attention to "the adventures and daring of such men." He continued: "They read a lesson to shrinking and effeminate spirits, the men of soft hands and fashionable life whose frames the winds of heaven are not allowed to visit too roughly."[53]

It is noteworthy that the Southerner is here being held up tentatively as an example of wholesome character. He is a man to be envied if not to be imitated. In the earlier discussion of Northern involvement with the planter image, it was in the context of a rather harmless toying with romantic themes. Now a more serious interest is apparent. The planter intrigued because, with his seeming boldness, he appeared able to retain leadership of his society whereas the Northern gentleman did not: to most Northerners, Southern society was divided between a more or less heredi- tary aristocracy holding the power, and a downtrodden peasantry. Some Northerners sensed an almost hypnotic ability in Southern politicians to command obedience. Witness the comments of Addison G. Proctor, a rep- resentative of Kansas at the 1860 Republican convention. Years later, he recalled meeting the leader of the Kentucky delegation. Though the por- trait must have been embellished with time, the delegate had clearly left a deep impression: "As he stood posed there, ready, he was the ideal Kentucky Colonel with all the mannerisms of that element so well pictured in our literature. A fascinating man handsome to look upon, faultlessly dressed, keen, bright and emotional. We could not keep our eyes off as he stood like a waiting orator charged with a volcanic mission."[54]

There was another important reason for taking note of the planter. According to Southern propaganda, the slaveholder was immune to the cur- rent greed of wealth. He owned slaves not simply for the economic bene- fits involved but because the freedom from labor gave him time to cultivate noble qualities lacking in more acquisitive societies. Many Northerners took Southerners at their own estimate, seeing in the South a healthy anti- dote to materialism. Southerners were hospitable fellows who would rather talk on the porch than run in the sun for dollars.[55]

Henry Benjamin Whipple, a rector from New York on a health trip to Georgia, noted that "the people of the southern states are generally much more hospitable than northerners, and this difference must be attributed mainly to the fact that they are not such a money loving people. You do not see that low mean cupidity, that base selfishness so striking a character- istic of one portion of our restless Yankee brethren." And Amelia M. Murray, an Englishwoman, thought that she could even detect an improve- ment in facial expression as she moved south. In the North, she said, pur- suit of "almighty dollars" made countenances "haggard, anxious, melan- choly, restless, sickly."[56]

Of course, such distinctions between North and South involved a great deal of distortion. Northerners were so blinded by the highly colored literature about the plantation so popular then that they missed some basic points of similarity. The old Southern gentry had also lost influence: its sense of loss helped stimulate the Cavalier legend. New men were con- stantly rising through business or farming skills; indeed the speculative fever raged as fiercely in the South as in the North, as a book like *The Flush Times of Alabama and Mississippi* points out. The author, Joseph G.

Baldwin, went to the southwest while it was still in a relatively early stage of development and, as a lawyer, profited from the large number of cases involving speculation in land. The South was undergoing democratic changes too, as I pointed out earlier. Many Southern politicians rose from humble means—indeed, what Northerners saw as the inbred habit of command of a hereditary aristocracy may often have been the strong will of a self-made man. But to say that Northerners were often wrong does not alter what, for our purposes, is the important fact—that people believed Southerners to be in some ways enviably situated and to possess some superior qualities of character lacking in their Northern counterparts.[57]

However, the idea of the planter as a person to be envied was only taken so far; as people were ambivalent to the machine, so they were toward slaveholding society. In the works of the upper class, there are approving remarks made about much in Southern society, but there are fewer unequivocal suggestions that the North should adopt wholesale the social structure of the slaveholding states. One reason for this might be fear. Talk of aristocratic leadership was not popular among large sectors of the public. When in 1853 Charles Eliot Norton, a Boston Brahmin, issued a book arguing that the mass of people were too ignorant to control their own destiny and must be guided by the few whose background fitted them to lead, he felt obliged to publish anonymously. How much more dangerous it would have been to promote boldly a system in which the majority of whites as well as blacks were thought to be kept in abject poverty and subjection.[58]

It is probable, however, that fear was not the main motive. In most cases it appears that total acceptance of the so-called Southern system was prevented by genuine aversion to certain aspects of the Southern image. The Northern gentleman, while wishing to be accepted as a leader, did not actually wish to reduce his fellows to a position of miserable peonage. George Templeton Strong, an aristocratic New York lawyer, was turned away from the South by the sectional incidents of the fifties. He was no lover of the "people" and despised what he saw as the money-worshiping ethic of the Northern middle class. But he found no panacea in the South, which he viewed as a society based on exploitation and cruelty. After Representative Preston Brooks of South Carolina whipped Charles Sumner on the floor of the Senate, Strong wrote that Northerners believed the South had produced "a high-bred chivalric aristocracy, . . . with grave faults, to be sure, but on the whole, very gallant and generous, . . . Whereas I believe they are, in fact, a race of lazy, ignorant, coarse, sensual, swaggering, sordid, beggarly barbarians, bullying white men and breeding little niggers for sale."[59]

Others noted the ugly features of plantation life. Most obviously, it was based on the entire subjection of one race by another. The point was made by Herman Melville in *The Confidence Man.* The setting of the book was a steamboat and the central theme was the revelation of the essential character of the passengers. One of these was a Southern planter, a man of immaculate, elegant dress. On one hand he wore a white glove and the other, though bare, was hardly less pure in color. The strange thing was that while the soot from the steamer's chimneys lay in a fine covering on the rails and other fixtures, this man's hands and clothing remained spotless. It was noticed that the man in white avoided touching anything. In short, "A certain negro body servant, . . . did most of his master's handling for him; having to do with dirt on his account." In other words, Southern elegance was only possible at the expense of the black. The point was made less subtly by others. Thomas Colley Grattan, visiting the South, found the manners in Virginia and Maryland to be preferable to those in New York and New England. Or rather, this would have been the case, he said, were it not for the presence of slavery.[60]

It was not the simple existence of slavery that troubled some people, for they agreed with Southern spokesmen that the black was an inferior and ought to be placed in tutelage to the white race. But they were shocked by the reports of cruelty to slaves which invariably seeped through, despite the bland assurance of slaveowners that the blacks were better off than Northern wage earners. Thus the Pulzkys, a European family staying in America, heard from a Mr. R. that the planters "were men of generous hospitality, amiable and most pleasant companions, but the slaves on their plantations were often ill-treated, especially by the planter's children, who are accustomed from infancy to give free vent to all their passions."[61]

The most vociferous critics of Southern civilization were the abolitionists. Their target was the slaveholder whom they referred to not as a gentleman but as a "slaveocrat." That the average slaveholder was a man who lived by violence was argued in the majority of abolitionist writings. Theodore Weld and his assistants culled hundreds of cases of cruelty to slaves from Southern newspapers and published them in *Slavery as It Is: Testimony of a Thousand Witnesses* (1839). There were also the reports of runaways, who could give personal evidence of Southern cruelty. Frederick Douglass, a former slave, stated in his *Narrative* that even the most tender-hearted white woman developed a "tiger-like" fierceness when placed in absolute control of another human being. In a preface to the book, William Lloyd Garrison painted his own picture of the slaveocracy maintaining its sway with "whips, chains, thumb-screws, paddles, blood-hounds, overseers, drivers, patrols."[62]

It seemed this violence carried over into relations between whites. Visitors to the South filled their diaries and letters with descriptions of duels, stabbings, street fights, and gougings they witnessed or heard about. Most of these will be dealt with in Chapter 2 but it may be noted here that disapproval of Southern violence intensified toward the end of the antebellum period when the tightening of sectional tensions brought heated clashes between men of North and South. Reports of pro-slavery atrocities in Kansas produced anger and shock. Many of these reports were one-sided and contained gross exaggerations, but they inflamed a public unaware of the distortions. A typical piece of anti-Southern re-porting turned the dismantling of two free-soil presses and the burning of a hotel in Lawrence into "the sack of Lawrence," performed to the tune of pillage and slaughter. One-time Missouri Senator David Atchison, who was present at the scene, was cast as a "slaveocrat" on the abolitionist model and was misreported as saying to his men—"Ruffians! draw your daggers and bowie-knives, and warm them in the heart's blood of those damned dogs that dare defend that damned breathing hole of hell."[63]

Finally, there was the John Brown raid on Harper's Ferry, which produced a period of hysterical reaction in the South during which North-erners were dismissed from their posts and even subjected to physical out-rage. There were so many acts of violence during this period that William Lloyd Garrison could fill a substantial pamphlet entitled *The New Reign of Terror in the Slaveholding States for the Year 1859–60.* Catherine Cooper Hopley, a British teacher, noted the reaction among her Northern friends. They "had always taken pains to assure me that 'the Southerners are the best part of our population, so liberal, so honorable, so kind-hearted, and hospitable.'" The preaching of the abolitionists had been largely ignored by these people. But their attitude quickly changed after the John Brown raid. "Suddenly," said Miss Hopley, " 'those good Virginians,' 'those fine old Virginian families' became transformed into 'brutes' and 'tyrants.' "[64]

Yet the image of the Southerner as a gentleman with some admirable qualities was not lost. Whatever his faults he still seemed to teach lessons for the age. If he was tyrannical, he was still upright; he would not bend his principles to chase a dollar; he put honor before advancement, even before life itself. Thus, there remained ambivalence in the Northern attitude. Finding both good and bad points in the planter, estimates were often a compound of distaste and approval. The point was illustrated in an 1862 issue of *Harper's Weekly*. On one page appeared a sketch by Alfred R. Waud of the First Virginia Cavalry at a halt in Maryland. The artist accompanied his sketch with laudatory comments on the aristocratic lineage and bearing of the troops. But on another page of the magazine was an editorial picture of rebel guerillas sacking a western town. The soldiers were caricatured as satanic beasts engaged in various forms of sadistic violence.[65]

Ambivalence can be found in earlier writings. Even those who were highly critical of slavery sometimes found it difficult to cast the Southerner in the role of chief American villain. The Northerner—or more specifically, the capitalist merchants and mill owners—often seemed more dangerous. Harriet Beecher Stowe, scion of a distinguished New England family, pointed out, in the most famous piece of anti-slavery literature, *Uncle Tom's Cabin*, the kind of inhuman abuses that were possible under a system allowing one man complete control over the body of another. But she let the Southerners off comparatively lightly, recognizing that many of them were trapped by a problem for which they had no answer. And she made the most evil character in the book, the disgusting and cruel Simon Legree, a native of her own New England.[66]

The play *The Octoroon*, which opened successfully in New York during December of 1859, employed the same structural device. Though written by Dion Bouccicault, an Irishman who first went to America in 1853, *The Octoroon* used popular American types and received nationwide praise for its treatment of slavery and the North–South issue. Though the piece was critical of the peculiar institution, the villain was again a New England Yankee deformed by lust and greed.[67]

The problem people had in casting the gentry of the South in unflattering roles would have been appreciated by a young Northerner who in the same year traveled to Mississippi. He recognized that the South could present different faces to the outsider. "It is said," he wrote, "the South, like Calypso, has a smile for every one of her defects." It was the smile that appealed to this young man, for he took employment in the South, saying, "I like her warm-heartedness and hospitality. I like her beautiful climate. I like her fine country."[68]

2

The Plantation and the Garrison

The Idea of a Martial South before the Civil War

It is a law of nature common to all mankind, which no time shall annul or destroy, that those who have more strength and excellence shall bear rule over those who have less.

— DIONYSIUS

He [the slaveholder] treats his equals as his inferiors, and is as overbearing and insolent to them as to his slaves. The pistol, the bowie knife, the bludgeon, are his constant companions, and the emblems of his social condition.

— THE REVEREND T. B.
TURNER in *The Trumpet and Universalist Magazine*

In the last chapter, an attempt was made to explore the ideas and assumptions behind the popular antebellum belief that the North and South were different in character. Now, the perspective must be sharpened to get at the military significance of this theme. It will be argued that the characterizations of the South made it appear more violent and warlike than the North. The idea of a martial South was in currency even before the Mexican War though the theme is often a difficult one to trace in antebellum thought because wars only played a minor role in most people's lives and hence they were not always interested in commenting on the military resources of the two sections. Only in the Civil War setting would they realize the significance of qualities that had appeared innocuous enough in peacetime. For example, wealthy young men of the Old South had a reputation as fine, bold riders. But it took the war to translate this reputation into a legend of Southern invincibility in the cavalry arm. What we have by 1860, then, is a sketch or outline which will be colored in during the following years.

Note that what we are talking about here is an image and that this does not necessarily correspond to the reality. In the latter part of the chapter, evidence will be brought forward that casts doubt on the idea that Southerners were *in fact* more violent or warlike. They may not have been superior in terms of, say, the ability to shoot or ride. Their one advantage was that their enemy feared they were better. The real Southern superiority was a psychological one.

With regard to antebellum attitudes, two general points that might affect the military confidence of North and South may be noted. First, whether people approved or disapproved of the Southerner, they took him very seriously. The Northerner, pictured as a Yankee in his counting house or grinding out wooden nutmegs, could be a figure of fun or contempt. But the Southerner, portrayed as a planter gentleman or slaveocrat, appeared as a person to be reckoned with, even to be feared. This awe of the Southerner could have military significance.

Second, though it is now assumed, or at least was until Vietnam, that the most industrially advanced countries necessarily have the strongest fighting forces, this was by no means the case in the nineteenth century. All nations, including Britain, were close enough to a rural arrangement of society to associate martial qualities with the gentry and countrymen who had formed the backbone of fighting forces for centuries. Those closest to the soil were assumed to have the most stake in it. Industrial workers, pictured as consumptive wretches, were considered to be less desirable as army material. The South, defined as a rural society, might thus have appeared to have a military advantage over the North with its large commercial and industrial sectors.

Moving from the general to the specific, what were the qualities expected of the soldier and how did Southern life appear to encourage them? In an age when military technology was still relatively primitive the basic skills of the fighting man were few in number. The soldier in the ranks was supposed to be well disciplined and versed in military routine. He needed sufficient courage to receive a bayonet charge or remain steady before killing volleys of musketry. He had to be able to handle a musket and, in the cavalry, ride a horse. Officers were expected, at least in theory, to have a working knowledge of tactics and strategy and to possess superior leadership qualities together with a high sense of personal honor.[1]

These attributes of the soldier paralleled to a large degree traits people said were instilled in Southern men. There was a paramilitary air about the planter as described by his contemporaries. People had little doubt that Southerners were well endowed with the key military requisite of courage or the will to fight. To travelers it appeared to be manifested almost daily in violent encounters. The planter appeared to be highly sensitive about his personal reputation, as befitted one who was a gentleman. Affairs of honor were more frequent in the South than in the North, said Harriet Martineau, because slaveholders feared the stigma of cowardice. And Henry Cogswell Knight, a student of regional peculiarities in speech and manners who visited New Orleans during the 1820s, thought that the citizens found the most trivial of excuses to demonstrate their courage. He declared that contrived affronts such as " 'How dared you to spit as I was passing?'—'How dared you to pass as I was spitting?' or 'You shall not sneeze where I am!' " afforded sufficient pretext for a fight.[2]

Things had apparently not changed by the 1840s when James Silk Buckingham, an English parliamentarian, visited the area. Despite an anti-slavery bias, Buckingham found much to like in the Southern people. The professional classes of Charleston, for example, he thought, "have a more liberal education, and more gentlemanly deportment, than is general with the same classes in the north." But he was shocked by Southern violence which he attributed, like the abolitionists, to the encouragement of despotic temper inherent in slavery. Unrestricted power over the bondsmen had bred a "universal irritability of temper, impatience of contradiction, and constant readiness to avenge every imaginary insult with instant and deadly punishment of the offender." He estimated that there were five times more "affrays, duels, street-fights, shootings, stabbings, and assassinations" than in the North.[3]

An almost identical analysis was given by another English person, Frances Anne Kemble, whose American husband owned a plantation. "The gentry of the Southern states," she wrote, "are pre-eminent in their own country for that species of manner which, contrasted with the breeding of the Northerners, would be emphatically pronounced 'good' by Englishmen. Born to inhabit landed property, they are not inevitably made clerks and countinghouse men." But she was also worried that slavery would damage the character of her children by making them tyrannical. "Think of learning to rule despotically your fellow creatures before the first lesson of self-government has been well spelled over." The pernicious effect of slavery seemed apparent to her in the casualness with which Southerners fought and killed each other. When a Dr. Hazzard killed a Mr. Wylly, Miss Kemble was astonished to hear that there was little chance of the murderer being convicted. "What a savage horror," she exclaimed. "And no one seems to think anything of it, more than of a matter of course."[4]

"If a young man feels offended with another, he does not incline to a ring and a fair stand-up set-to, like a young Englishman; he will not attempt to overcome his opponent by logic; he will not be content to vituperate, or to cast ridicule upon him; he is compelled straightway to strike him down with the readiest deadly weapon at hand." So wrote Frederick Law Olmsted, who visited the South two decades after Miss Kemble. Olmsted was originally from New England. His interest in the slave states had been stimulated by a discussion with William Lloyd Garrison, which made him wish to see them for himself. He became a shrewd critic, noticing much that was missed by his contemporaries. But like them, he devoted many pages of his books to cataloging Southern ferocity. In southeast Texas, for instance, he was disturbed one night by a fellow traveler who had drawn a pistol and was threatening to shoot someone whose shouting had prevented him from going to sleep.[5]

This apparently rampant spirit of violence might be frowned upon in peacetime but it would appear in a different light when men were preparing for battle. In such a situation, the South would seem to have a large advantage. Compare the portrait of the militant Southerner—the kind of man Olmsted said asked at dinner about the number of fights that day as casually as one would ask about the arrival of a steamboat in the North—with the sketch of the retiring, consumptive New Englander drawn in Chapter 1.[6]

It followed from his supposed fondness for fighting that the Southerner would be proficient in the use of firearms, another basic skill needed by the soldier. Many travelers agreed that arms were universally carried in the South. Even Southern Congressmen were believed to carry guns as a part of their normal working gear, and they occasionally threatened to use them on Northern colleagues. When not fighting, Southerners might improve their aim by hunting, a sport thought to be more popular in the South than the North, because of its rural image. The planters, as country gentlemen, were assumed to enjoy the chase, and the poor whites, refusing to work because labor was for slaves, would naturally turn to hunting for subsistence and recreation. Visitors reported that both gentry and cabin dwellers were expert with the rifle, an important piece of furniture in their homes. Olmsted reported that while steaming down the Red River a man shot a bird at a range of 200 feet, an impressive display of marksmanship. And Frederick Hawkins Percy, on route up the Mississippi, wrote that "there were some gentlemen on board who had a most disgusting and brutal method of amusing themselves. Armed with rifles, they stationed themselves upon the hurricane deck, and shot ducks and birds, when there was not the slightest possibility of obtaining them."[7]

The military usefulness of this skill was always appreciated in America. Southern backwoodsmen and their long rifles were credited with a major role in stopping the British at New Orleans. A song nationally popular during Jackson's presidency celebrated the accuracy and daring of Kentucky hunters who "dropped 'em" in the Louisiana swamps. Southerners consolidated this reputation in the years that followed. In January 1861, a citizen soldier from New York, watching the practice shooting of South Carolina troops, said it was the finest he had seen. This comment, published in the *Atlantic Monthly* for April 1861, the month when South Carolinians attacked Fort Sumter, might have given Northerners indigestible food for thought.[8]

The Southern sporting bent also seemed to find expression in a love of horse breeding and riding. Kentucky, which, according to one visitor, was "the land, by reputation, of 'red horses, bowie-knives, and gouging,'" was esteemed a mecca for horse fanciers. "Everybody rides in Virginia and Kentucky, master, man, woman, and slave, and they all ride well," wrote Captain Frederick Marryat. Horseback riding was popular apparently in the newer parts of the South also. A young Northerner reported enthusiastically that he had toured a good deal of Mississippi on horseback. Apart from its being "cavalierish," he said, the condition of the roads made this form of transportation a necessity. Less impressed was a sober Philadelphia Quaker on business in Natchez, who wrote that he had been permitted to see "the *chivalric gentry* . . . dashing about here on highbred horses." At other times they might be found recounting their fights and bear hunts or drinking mint juleps through straws. The interesting point is that this description foreshadows the later image of swashbuckling rebel troopers swinging into line behind "Jeb" Stuart for another raid on the Yankees. The Confederate cavalry owed some of its powerful mystique to this picture of the hell-for-leather gentry.[9]

Finally, there is the question of discipline; the capacity to accept and administer the dictates of military authority. Viewed from one aspect, the Southern environment might seem well suited to prepare men for the highly structured life of the army. It will be recalled that white society in the slaveholding states was widely thought to be divided into only two major classes: a large body of ignorant, downtrodden poor people and a small aristocracy of planters holding dictatorial power. The existence of an important middle class was hardly recognized.[10]

When war came, it would be assumed that this civilian structure was duplicated in Confederate military organization. The poor whites would form the bulk of the common soldiers. They would experience few difficulties in adjusting to military routine because, according to this argument, they were already used to a climate of subservience and control. They would simply be changing civilian masters for military commanders. The gentry would become officers and members of elite units such as the cavalry. Like the poor people, their role would come easily because they were used to command. Such was the impression of John William De Forest, a Northerner who visited Charleston in 1860. The facial expressions of military officers and state legislators convinced him that South Carolina was an oligarchy, allowing no plebeians in high places. The physiognomy of these men was good, often commanding, he said, "and almost invariably distinguished by a fearless, open-eyed frankness, in some instances running into arrogance and pugnacity." He remembered two "whose faces would help an artist to idealize a Lacedaemonian general, or a baron of the Middle Ages." Such people were clearly leaders of men.[11]

Others also noted the easy attitude of command which the best planters appeared to possess. A parallel could be drawn between the running of a plantation and a military command where all authority centered at the top. Some felt that this made Southerners better officer material than other Americans. Herman Melville concluded from his experience aboard an American man-of-war that Southerners were superior officers to Northerners and were more respected by the men. The reason for this, he said, was that their position in civilian life made them more accustomed to command and "hence, quarter-deck authority sits more naturally on them."[12]

Southern writers tended to argue that their planters had a special relationship with the military. The slaveholders, after all, were supposed to be born into the English aristocratic tradition and part of that tradition was that only three professions were suitable for a gentleman. They were, as Daniel Robinson Hundley, a Southern author, listed them in 1860: planting or gentleman farming, politics, and the military. Southerners in the regular army sometimes antagonized their Northern colleagues by their arrogant assumption that any officer and gentleman, be he from Texas or Maine, would be Southern in sentiment. Northern officers even fell into this way of thinking. As late as February 1861, less than two months before Sumter, Oliver Otis Howard received a letter from a Northern officer urging him to accept a professorship in North Carolina. The letter stated: "As an officer of the army, I presume, of course, that you entertain no views on the peculiar institution which would be objectionable to a Southern community." Some officers suspected that the common equation between the South and the military led to the unfair preferment of men from Dixie. At least one Northerner resigned his commission on those grounds, saying, "I have lost all ambition to be connected with the service where politics and prejudice ruled, and where the fact that a man was not born in the South was a bar to promotion."[13]

Southerners were generally seen as natural-born soldiers but there was one type who might seem a military liability. This was the slaveholder in whom the high temper supposedly produced by absolute power on the plantation knew no bounds—a man who was dangerous to himself and society in his absolute lack of self-control. If in most cases the plantation experience appeared to produce honor, courage, and leadership qualities, it seemed to work an opposite effect on weak characters, who slipped into gambling, drunkenness, and bestiality. The problem had long troubled responsible Southerners. As early as 1785, Thomas Jefferson had written candidly that "there must doubtless be an unhappy influence on the manners of our people produced by the existence of slavery among us. The whole commerce between master and slave is a perpetual exercise of the most boisterous passions." Many years later, a Southerner chided a slaveholding relative with the remark, "You slaveholders have lived so long on your plantations with no one to gainsay or contradict you, . . . that you expect to govern everybody and have it all your own way."[14]

Such people might endanger the discipline and hence the safety of an army. In the spring of 1861, as a serious clash with Union troops approached, the problem began to agitate some thoughtful Southerners. Mary Boykin Chesnut, whose husband was on General Beauregard's staff, wrote that the Confederacy was not preparing for war. People did nothing but talk, she complained, while there was the "rash, reckless, headlong, devil-may-care, proud, passionate, unruly raw material" of any army waiting to be made into soldiers.[15]

The importance of this point as a psychological factor affecting the confidence of either side should not be overstated. The anxious Southerners were in a small minority but in the North the idea that the rebels might incur a discipline problem was hardly thought of. Most Union soldiers who commented during the war on the discipline of the two armies believed that the enemy had the advantage. They did frequently picture the rebel cavalry as a bunch of wild spirits but in this branch of the service a certain devil-may-care attitude was not considered out of place.

The overall picture that emerges from the antebellum period is of a Southerner well-versed in the skills of riding, shooting, and personal combat. The position with regard to discipline was ambivalent but even here the situation did not appear entirely disadvantageous. By comparison, the North might seem to produce less capable military types, for this region was stereotyped as the precinct of the capitalist, whose primary motivation was profit. Even the best classes, alienated by democratic politics, appeared to have turned from public duty to private gain. Such a society of self-seekers would hardly seem capable of producing the Spartan qualities of the soldier.

Given the premise that nonagrarian pursuits were inimical to manly qualities, it was logical to assume that the rot was worst in the northeast, where commerce and industry were most concentrated. As one moved west, the air became more pure. Consequently, Southerners sometimes qualified their strictures on Yankeedom to exclude the farmers of the northwest, for whom they might have a certain respect. Similarly, westerners often shared Southern contempt for eastern "nutmeg sellers." New England, the fount of Puritanism and a mercantile, industrial leader, was seen as the heartland of Yankeedom. And it is indicative of the correlation that was thought to exist between capitalist growth and the loss of masculine values that the military prestige of this area declined after the Revolution and that of the South went up. The reputations of the two regions are therefore worth examining in some detail.

To begin with the South, the patriots of this region had won some noteworthy successes in the Revolution and had placed some proud names on the roll of Ameircan heroes. But it was with the men of Massachusetts that the lighting of the revolutionary flame was associated. No Southern action could parallel Lexington and Concord. For a long time, Southerners were willing to give New England abundant credit for its performance. As late as 1830, William Gilmore Simms wrote that "the Yankee is the man, who first hung out the banner of liberty . . . and determined to be free." However, as Southern spokesmen became more sectional in viewpoint, this generosity was lost. They increasingly stressed the military accomplishment of their own people, pointing, for instance, to the War of 1812, in which the Southern states, along with the northwest, were credited with springing to arms against Britain while the northeast stood idly by.[16]

Much noise was also made about the South's role in the Mexican War, which many Southerners came to see as their special triumph. Isaac W. Hayne, South Carolina's attorney general, felt "peculiarly gratified that South Carolina has sustained herself." Since the Nullification Crisis, he said, people had spoken lightly of South Carolina's courage and patriotism. They had called her traitor. But now that label must pass to where it rightfully belonged—Massachusetts, which had deplored the war.[17]

In general terms, Southerners boasted that their race, of the Norman or Cavalier stock, had always held a virtual monopoly of the world's martial talent. Such claims naturally bruised Northern sensibilities. Thus Congressman William H. Bissell of Illinois, stung by the comments of the Virginian James A. Seddon on the bravery and chivalry of the South during the Mexican War, denounced the "proneness of our Southern friends to exaggerate all their capabilities." At the same time, there were Northerners willing to credit the South with abundant military achievement. Erasmus Darwin Keyes, a defensive New England-born army officer charged that "the prattlers of both sections" were guilty of making every hero of the Mexican War into a Southerner. Such a prattler was, presumably, the Reverend Philo Tower, anti-slavery minister from New England, who stopped in the midst of an attack on the slaveholders of

South Carolina to praise their gallantry in Mexico. The whites of the South were, he said, "a fine, manly race," whose valor was "attested upon a hundred battle-fields."[18]

This comment is especially interesting, coming from an anti-slavery man. It suggests a fact, unnoticed by previous historians, that even those who openly opposed the slaveholder were reluctantly drawn to respect him. Such ambivalence affected Olmsted, who disliked those Southerners "whose whole life seems to be absorbed in sensualism and sickly excitements" and whose conversation centered on "street encounters, filibustering schemes, or projects of disunion or war." Yet he had to admit that they were "gentlemen, in the sense that they are familiar with the forms and usages of the best society," and that they were brave. "They are especially ambitious of military renown," he wrote, "and in the Mexican War they volunteered almost to a man."[19]

Especially awed by the sense of Southern masculine strength was Jacob Burnet, a resident of Cincinnati, who spent some time analyzing the manners of the people across the river in Kentucky. Here, he said, you might meet a man of the Middle Ages. "Send him to Mexico and humanity is capable of no crime from which he would turn or at which he would shudder. Take him to Boston and his manner will be as pleasing as his conversation will be original." Another man, "slight as a girl, might be safely trusted to lead any corps in any battle." Of the people in general he remarked, "These men, common as they look, are not common men; . . . Such men as these won the battle of Buena Vista, and will rule the world, if they choose to."[20]

So much for the reputation of the South. Meanwhile, the military prestige of New England had declined. The process really began with the reluctance of some of her citizens to endorse the second war against Britain. The men who had fired the first shots of the Revolutionary War were now dubbed " 'damned blue-light,' and 'blue-bellies,' who were too good to fight for their country." Again, the objections made to the Mexican War by New England abolitionists meant that her contributions were vengefully ignored when chroniclers came to write the story of American victory. For example, New England was not mentioned in J. Frost's *The Mexican War and Its Warriors*, published in 1849.[21]

The way in which the seeming reluctance of New England to fight could be coupled with the capitalist image to produce a composite picture of Northern degeneration was well illustrated by a little algebra text for Southern students, produced in 1857 by D. H. Hill, a Southern army man turned professor. In the book, students were asked to solve mathematical problems which drew upon New England "treason" in the War of 1812, the cheating supposedly done by Yankee nutmeg sellers, and the blunder of an Indiana regiment at Buena Vista which nearly lost the battle. The lesson taught was about a civilization without ethics, patriotism, or courage.[22]

Not all the criticisms of New England's manliness originated among outsiders. A cross-section of prominent men within the area shared a conviction that their people, particularly the educated and wealthy, lacked spine. Some, it will be recalled, attributed the problem to education. Oliver Wendell Holmes suggested that in reaching for scholarly excellence the Brahmin caste "has exchanged a certain portion of its animal vigor for its new instincts." The student drawn from this class was "commonly slender,—his face is smooth, and apt to be pallid,—his features are regular and of a certain delicacy." Such people, we may add editorially, would hardly seem the type to withstand the rigors of a military campaign, with their "compromised and lowered vitality."[23]

However, Holmes refrained from being too hard on this sort, for he too was of the Brahmin caste and had a bent toward the intellectual. He reserved his sharpest criticism for the nouveau riche. Of this class he remarked, "Its thorough manhood, its high-caste gallantry, are not so manifest as the plate-glass of its windows and the more or less legitimate heraldry of its coach-panels." These people lacked pluck, he thought, and he gave as the reason their wealth, which saved the younger sons from the necessity of finding gentleman's employment in the military. "It is very curious to observe," he concluded, "of how small account military folks are held among our Northern people."[24]

So also thought Francis Parkman, who had gone out west in search of strength. To this tough-minded conservative, his contemporaries were deficient in the lusty war spirit. He was particularly incensed by the New England pacifist movement, which had a reasonable membership among the people of Parkman's own class. The almost obsessive intensity with which this Brahmin sought a more martial atmosphere may be glimpsed through a passage he wrote while sailing on a British man-of-war from Gibraltar to Malta. Like Emerson, he was struck by the comparative robustness of the English. "No one cants here of temperance reform," he said, "or of systems of diet—eat, drink, and be merry is the motto everywhere, and a stronger and hardier race of men than those around me now never laughed at the doctors. Above all there is no canting of peace. A wholesome system of coercion is manifest in all directions—thirty-two pounders looking over the bows—piles of balls on deck—muskets and cutlasses hung up below." How different, he thought, from the "feeble consumptive wretch at home, who when smitten on one cheek literally turns the other likewise—instead of manfully kicking the offender into the gutter."[25]

The most consistently voiced questions about New Englanders' manliness came, however, from a diverse group of abolitionists who had little use for soldiers in general but who were especially vituperative about the New England military establishment. In some cases their distaste for soldiers was grounded in pacifism but it was also a product of anger at specific acts involving the military. For if they were to have soldiers at all, these radicals wished them to be anti-slavery heroes—men who, like the patriots of 1776, would fight in the cause of liberty. But the military men of the 1840s and 50s did not seem to be cut from this revolutionary pattern.[26]

First of all, New England men served in the Mexican War, which many anti-slavery people saw as part of a gigantic plot to strengthen and extend the influence of slavery at the expense of America's neighbors. Thus, Charles Sumner accused the United States of forcing Mexico into a conflict which, he said, *"is a War to strengthen the 'Slave Power.'"* (Ironically, the New England soldiers were thus snubbed by both slaveholders and abolitionists.) Rubbing salt into the abolitionist wound was the use of state and Federal troops to help carry out the Fugitive Slave Acts. Inevitably, the result of this was contempt for soldiers who appeared to be the tools of slaveholders, used to oppress the righteous and protect the evil. In his essay "Slavery in Massachusetts," Henry David Thoreau gave a merciless lashing to the New England military. After noting the use made of soldiers to help return blacks to bondage he thundered, "Is this what all these soldiers, all this *training*, have been for these seventy-nine years past? Have they been trained merely to rob Mexico and carry back fugitive slaves to their masters?" His verdict on the Massachusetts soldier was that "the best you can say in this connection is that he is a fool made conspicuous by a painted coat."[27]

The abolitionists were equally scathing about the mass of New England civilians who refused to join their crusade. Thus, while their opponent was supposed to be the Southern slaveholder, they often seemed to reserve their greatest contempt for their own people. Theodore Parker charged that the courage of revolutionary New England had been lost. On November 11, 1850, he wrote that in his study were two trophies from the War of Independence. One was the musket his grandfather had carried at Lexington; the other was a gun captured from the Royal forces. They were momentoes, he intimated, of a struggle against tyranny. But now, he said, the position was reversed, for there was tyranny in Boston, where the safety of fugitive slaves could not be guaranteed. He was forced to seek asylum for two runaways in Britain.[28]

Similar thoughts troubled the poet James Russell Lowell. He dreamed that the spirit of Miles Standish came to him and berated New Englanders for cowardly compromising with the slave power. " 'Tis shame," said Standish, "To see your spirit of Seventy-six/Drag humbly in the traces/ With slavery's lash upon her back." It is significant that although Lowell was a member of the Massachusetts Peace Society he chose as his moral example Miles Standish, the professional soldier among the Mayflower Pilgrims.[29]

Inevitably, critics took the path of attributing New England's fall in standards to the corrupting influence of the commercial spirit. New Englanders, they said, might still profess a devotion to the principles of '76 but their real god was the dollar: they would ignore slavery to preserve their lucrative Southern trade. For example, in a letter of October 23, 1846, the anti-slavery leader Gerrit Smith accused Massachusetts of being the servant of party and mammon. So also thought John Greenleaf Whittier. In 1846, the same year that war was declared on Mexico, he wrote a poem expressing concern about the inroad of materialism on New England character. Men were needed, he said, to voice opposition to the slave power. But where were they to be found, for the old free spirit of Boston seemed stilled by the mercenary clamor of merchants and bankers? Was only the dollar real in Massachusetts wondered the poet?

> Beats her Pilgrim pulse no longer?
> Sits she dumb in her despair?
> Has she none to break the silence?
> Has she none to do and dare?[30]

Small wonder with heroes in such short supply that in New England, and indeed throughout the North, opponents of slavery were exhilarated when John Brown attempted revolution at Harper's Ferry. The tremendous admiration expressed for Brown may be cited as evidence of a growing Northern hostility toward the South. Yet it can also be seen as an index of abolitionist frustration with the Northern people. Many words of praise for Brown implied a rebuke to the seemingly craven and corrupt who had refused to sacrifice for freedom. "I wish," wrote Thoreau, "I could say that Brown was the representative man of the North. He was a superior man. He did not value his bodily life in comparison with ideal things."[31]

In Brown's acts Thoreau and like-minded men saw a new hope for the future: perhaps through his example others would find the courage to devote themselves to principle. Within two years these hopes would appear to be fulfilled, for Northern volunteers would be marching South to the tune of "John Brown's Body." The early war days of 1861 would be a time of rejoicing for many abolitionists and they would profess a new faith in the rectitude of the North. But their earlier distrust of Northern motives and manliness, particularly their resentment of the military, could not be laid aside so easily. Bitter mistrust of the professional soldier would return to trouble their thinking through much of the war period.

The trend of antebellum ideas was favorable to the development of a belief in Southern martial superiority. On the one hand, the military ability of the North was thrown into question by doubts as to whether a capitalistic society, symbolized by New England, could long sustain the manly virtues. On the other, the Southerner was coming to be seen as particularly warlike in character. Many of the writers had no military interest and hardly any of them conceived that the notions they peddled would influence men during a civil war. But what was said in the antebellum period made it almost inevitable that the North, defeated in the first major battle of the war, would appear as the less competent of the two combatants.

It would not be necessary, to document the impact of the martial South idea, to determine whether the South, in the antebellum period, did *in fact* develop a more violent and warlike culture. But the perspective can be sharpened by asking if the North might have had real cause to fear that she faced a superior foe. The question is an elusive one as it is difficult to evaluate objectively such qualities as the ability to ride. Most of the issues must be dealt with later, in the chronological framework of the war and in specific instances where hard data on the two sides is available. But some general lines of thought may be advanced here. The conclusion they point to is that the variations between North and South were greatly exaggerated. Where differences existed, they seem to have been of degree rather than of kind and would not have materially affected military performance.

The idea that the South was more warlike rested partially on the assumption that Northern manhood was corrupted by money lust. Quantitative evidence for this is hard to find. Northerners were attuned to the profit motive, but schemes for the improvement of Southern agriculture, dreams of a Southern economic empire, concern about cash returns on cotton sales, and the deliberate exploitation of cheap slave labor, all suggest that Southerners shared the capitalist instinct. In the Civil War, the Northern wealthy appear to have sacrificed as much or as little as their opposite numbers in the Confederacy. Harold Faulkner notes in his economic history of America, "To picture the life of those who remained at home in the North as a mad scramble for wealth to be spent in extravagant living while the 'boys in blue' were fighting and dying for the Union would be far from correct." Even those who lived high, he says, gave liberally to soldiers' aid programs, and the like.[32]

A more tangible method of assessing military potential is to compare antebellum enrollment in military organizations and institutions. John Hope Franklin, in *The Militant South, 1800–1861,* argued that in the South "growing interest in military education, preoccupation with military activities, and many other phases of everyday life reflected a warm attachment to things of a militant nature." Among the areas he dealt with were enlistments in military companies and support for military academies, including West Point. In both cases, he felt that Southerners showed more martial enthusiasm than Northerners. However, most of Franklin's evidence was based on a study of the South alone. Investigation of the Northern states suggests that military organizations had appeal here also. For instance, few Southern volunteer companies can have been superior in training or equipment to the New York 7th Regiment or the Massachusetts 6th. At a military review in Massachusetts, held on September 24, 1859, about 6,000 troops were present and they were watched by an estimated 50,000 spectators.[33]

Franklin's thesis has been given detailed rebuttal by Marcus Cunliffe, who examined manifestations of the martial spirit in America as a whole. He thought it was true that Southern cities "had their clusters of brightly uniformed volunteer companies. But these were rivaled, and outmatched in number and variety, by equivalent companies in the North." On military schools he notes that "though the majority were established in the South, a fair proportion were Northern" and "most of the nation's militia periodicals were published in the North." Finally, and most significantly, Cunliffe questions the assertion, made during the antebellum period and generally accepted by later writers, that Southerners had a special tie with the United States army. A statistical analysis of the number of Northern and Southern cadets graduated from West Point between 1820 and 1860 revealed that 64 percent were from the North. New York and Pennsylvania headed the list with 317 and 187 graduates respectively. Nor, says Cunliffe, is it true that Southerners tended to remain in the army longer than their Northern colleagues. Summarizing the figures collected by

Ezra J. Warner, a recent military historian, he shows that in 1860 the South only had a preponderance of officers in the cavalry. Perhaps, we may add, Southerners were favored for this arm because of their reputation as riders. If this were the case, it could mean not only that the South got more than its share of seasoned cavalry leaders in 1861 but that some Northern officers may have become used to thinking of their people as inferior in the saddle. This possible psychological handicap is worth bearing in mind. But the main point is that other than in this one instance, the officer corps was not a Southern preserve.[34]

Even if there were not a connection between the plantation and the officer corps, it could still be argued that the South had a stronger military tradition because it contributed more to the national wars. But here too the picture needs modification. While supporters of the 1812 War, such as Henry Clay and Richard M. Johnson of Kentucky, liked to cast themselves as disinterested patriots, their state actually stood to make material gains from a misunderstanding with Britain. A boycott of British goods would encourage developing Kentucky textile industries. Also, Kentuckians wished to expand west into regions disputed with Britain. New England, on the other hand, had little to gain from a fight with a nation whose powerful navy might destroy its merchant shipping, a key pillar of the economy. Enthusiasm for the war, or the lack of it, was thus as much a product of self-interest as of disinterested patriotism or military ardor. Anyway, New England forces seem, in the end, to have fought as well as any in a war where the performance was generally mediocre. And there were few victories more creditable than that of New England Captain Oliver Hazard Perry, who smashed a British fleet on Lake Erie.

What about Northern participation in the Mexican War? Viewed from their own standpoint, abolitionists had just cause to condemn a war that they believed would extend slavery. Moreover, their opposition obscured the fact that many Northerners did fight in Mexico—not only men from the northwest but from New England also. New York sent more men than Georgia, Virginia, or South Carolina. The contributions of the Northern states are all the more remarkable when it is remembered that problems of transportation made it logical to draw mainly on the Southern states, which were geographically closest to Mexico.[35]

In more general terms, students of aggressive expansionism in the nineteenth century have pointed out that Americans shared the impulse to extend the boundaries of their country, be it to the west, north, or south. Albert K. Weinberg demonstrates that the same argument of defense against foreign aggression was used by Americans who wished to take Louisiana in the south and Oregon in the north. Americans of all areas felt a militant urge to carry republican institutions to adjacent countries. Winfield Scott's biographer, Charles Winslow Elliot, notes that in 1837 the general had to be sent up to the Canadian border to smooth over tensions created by Americans giving aid and comfort to Canadian rebels. He writes that "Republican sympathy for the supposedly tyrannized masses in Canada was easily excited. The heritage of hatred for Great Britain and the old dream of conquest and annexation [the unsuccessful attempt to take Canada in the War of 1812] were still unforgotten in northern New York, Vermont, Ohio, and Michigan." These were Northern, not Southern, states.[36]

About a year earlier, Northern newspapers had carried emotional appeals to their citizens to aid the Texans to gain freedom from Mexico. In New York, on November 12, 1835, over 2,000 people met at Tammany Hall to pledge their loyalty to Texas. A little later, 210 volunteers left from the city. Boston sent a company of dragoons. The volunteers who gathered in New Orleans were, according to Walter Lord, a student of Texas history, "English, German, Scottish, Irish, Americans from north and south." Finally, an ironic note: Weinberg shows that though Northern abolitionists generally disapproved of American escapades in Mexico, some quickly changed position when they heard that the land was not suited to slavery. The previously anti-expansionist *National Era* decided that by bringing Mexico into the Union, the United States would be "its greatest benefactor."[37]

Also to be considered is the supposed Southern superiority in riding and shooting. Regarding the cavalry, it has been noted that Southerners had more than their share of trained officers. In 1855, for example, when two new regiments were formed, a very large portion of the officers chosen were of Southern origin. This may have given the South some real advantage in that arm during the Civil War, though it will appear later that the Northern cavalry suffered as much from short-sightedness on the part of army commanders as from any lack of trained cavalry leaders.[38]

On the general question of horsemanship, it has often been averred that Northerners were not good riders. Fairfax Downey, in his *Clash of Cavalry,* says that because of the railroad and improved roads, which made carriage transport possible, horseback riding had nearly died out in the North, save for those areas that were still in a frontier stage of development. Perhaps there is a degree of truth in the argument: some cavalry recruits seem to have been particularly inept. One officer, explaining his failure to overtake rebel cavalry during an operation early in the war, said that "they leap the fences and walls like deer; neither our men nor our horses are so trained." However, until more positive statistical evidence is brought forward, the general thesis must be regarded with skepticism. The 1860 census returns gave the Northern states a horse population of some 4,688,878, or roughly one for every fifth inhabitant. If only one in twenty-five or thirty of these horses was actually ridden, this would still have given the North a solid body of mounts and riders with which to begin the war.[39]

The argument regarding guns rested on two ideas: that Southerners hunted more than Northerners and that they were more violent in their social relations, shooting each other with frequency. With regard to hunting, it is true that the South had more unfarmed lands where men might shoot game. But it is hard to conceive that many inhabitants of the rural North, who formed the bulk of the population, would not have kept a musket with which to supplement their staple diet. It should also be remembered that it is difficult to determine how much the reputation of the Southern backwoodsmen owed to real prowess with a rifle and how much was simply folk legend, built up from the exploits of a few outstanding figures such as Daniel Boone and David Crockett. In at least one famous episode, the credit given to Southern riflemen does not seem to have been deserved. A recent, outstanding scholar has argued convincingly that at the Battle of New Orleans it was not the backwoodsmen but the regular artillerymen who won the battle.[40]

As for violence within society, it is impossible to deal with so vast and relatively uncharted a field within the few pages available here. But it is hoped to suggest through a few instances that the disparity in the amount of violence between North and South was grossly exaggerated. To begin with, much of the picture of the South as a savage land was built by people antagonistic to slavery who arrived in the region already convinced that the peculiar institution had a brutalizing effect on whites as well as blacks. Hence, they were extremely sensitive to manifestations of violence. This is not to say that they did not witness the shootings, stabbings, and so forth which they described. But similar instances could be found in the North. Crime among urban dwellers, for instance, was high in the nineteenth century as some cases relating to New Yorkers will show.

The Polish immigrant, Count Adam Gurowski, was whipped with a cowhide by the wealthy New York merchant, James E. Van Alen, on account of derogatory words spoken in debate. In 1830, Colonel James Watson Webb of the New York *Courier and Enquirer* caned Duff Green of the *Washington Telegraph* and publicly beat up James Gordon Bennett of the New York *Herald;* William Leggett of the *Evening Post* assaulted Webb. Bennett was again whipped, this time by the lawyer John Graham, in 1854. Much the same was true in politics as in journalism. During the 1835 legislative session, Vice President Martin Van Buren of New York felt it necessary to wear a brace of pistols in the Senate. In 1854, F. B. Cutting of New York challenged J. C. Breckenridge of Kentucky, following a heated debate over Kansas.[41]

The cases go on. While traveling to Washington for the inauguration of President Buchanan in 1854, Samuel Butterworth, a Tammany politician and superintendent of the New York Assay Office, was wounded when the pistol of his traveling companion, Isaac W. Fowler, the New York postmaster, accidentally discharged. In 1857, J. McLeon Murphy, civil engineer at the Brooklyn Navy Yard, challenged the New York politician Daniel Sickles. When Sickles declined to accept, Murphy resorted to a horsewhip. In 1854, Sickles challenged the Tammany politician John Van Buren and a banker by the name of Peabody. Some five years later, Sickles shot his wife's lover dead in the street. At the trial the defense maintained a plea of insanity but also added that Sickles was justified by the "unwritten law" in killing "the defiler of his marriage bed." Sickles was acquitted. The only fault the *Brooklyn Times* could find with him was that he had not challenged first. He could not be "a man of gentlemanly feeling" said the paper. *Harper's Weekly,* a journal of the respectable classes, while disapproving of dueling in most cases, thought there might be some justification for killing those who seduced one's relatives. For, said the paper, women in cities were open to many dangers. Perhaps the threat of a speedy death to "gay young men" who gave vent to their passions might eliminate some of the hazard.[42]

All these examples relate to relatively well-placed persons; a book might be devoted to the common crimes of burglary, larceny, and so on, and the numbers of New York poor who died in fights would certainly equal those in a Southern city. It could be argued, however, that those who spoke of the South as a savage society did not deny that there was bloodshed in the North: they simply suggested that because of the dehumanizing presence of slavery, violence formed a more essential part of the fabric of life and that a case study of New York does not invalidate this. Two points may be made here.

First, it is certainly true that slavery was a disgusting system, which led to gross inhumanities, physical and moral. But was not the contempt for the quality of human life as great among the industrial employers of New York, Philadelphia, Manchester, or London? Theodore Weld filled a book with examples of cruelty to slaves but by culling the reports of the British Sanitary Commission he might have published another hefty volume. On the American scene, the point was made by the New York lawyer, George Templeton Strong, who noted in his diary on January 11, 1860:

> News today of a fearful tragedy at Lawrence, Massachusetts, one of the wholesale murders commonly known in newspaper literature as accident or catastrophe. A huge factory, long notoriously insecure and ill-built, requiring to be patched and bandaged up with iron plates and braces to stand the introduction of its machinery, suddenly collapsed into a heap of ruins yesterday afternoon without the slightest provocation. Some five or six hundred operatives went down with it—young girls and women mostly.

While Strong was no lover of the peculiar institution he concluded: "It becomes us to prate about the horrors of slavery! What Southern capitalist trifles with the lives of his operatives as do our philanthropes of the North?" Stated another way, callous cruelty has been the monopoly of no particular age or place.[43]

A second, more concrete though more narrow, argument can be made regarding slavery and violence. This relates to the mob spirit. Some people who visited the South asserted that it was dangerous to say anything critical of slavery. Buckingham claimed that to attack the peculiar institution placed a man in "imminent personal danger," and an Englishman working in the South told Olmsted that "if one happened to say anything that gave offence, they thought no more of drawing a pistol or knife upon him, than they would of kicking a dog that was in their way." It was true that Southerners did close ranks on the slavery issue in response to outside criticism. But, according to Clement Eaton, who made a close study of the failure to retain freedom of thought in the South, repression of ideas was by no means restricted to the slaveholding states and there was no crime against free speech so great as the murder of Elijah Lovejoy by a mob in Illinois.[44]

There is every indication that mob violence in the North posed a great danger to genuine freedom of speech. There were sufficient anti-abolition mobs during the 1830s alone for a book to be written about them. William Lloyd Garrison, Wendell Phillips, and others less prominent were in constant danger of attack. Abolitionists themselves organized vigilance committees to resist the Fugitive Slave Acts and one of Boston's upper crust, Thomas Wentworth Higginson, led an attack on a jail house to rescue the fugitive slave Anthony Burns. In Wisconsin, during 1860, a man who had been arrested for helping a runaway was forcibly released from the hands of Federal officials. Mobs were raised for other causes also. The Mormons suffered greatly, one recent student concluding that the murder of Joseph Smith was no isolated incident but fitted a fairly common pattern of violent intolerance in the northwest. Other seemingly radical groups included workers for women's rights. In 1853, hoodlums closed one of their conventions and, interestingly enough, only two newspapers condemned the action. Reactionaries too sometimes had cause to fear the people. In 1822, incendiaries burned the house of Federalist Solomon Van Rensselaer, in Albany. In 1842, there was nearly civil war in Rhode Island over the adoption of a more liberal constitution. Small wonder that when Charles Eliot Norton published his attack on popular government, he did it anonymously.[45]

A final point is that much of what was described as Southern violence was properly frontier violence. In all of the raw western states including Indiana, Illinois, and Ohio, as well as Alabama, Mississippi, and Texas, society tended to be wild and disorderly. Lew Wallace, who became a Union general, recalled in his memoirs that the people who lived in Indiana during the 1850s were "primitive in habits, large-hearted, Western in spirit. Instead of taking their quarrels into court, they settled them on the spot, resorting to their fists. Giving the lie and getting ready for instant resentment were simultaneous acts; while, if the party affronted hung back, or quailed, no allowance was made for him; he must fight."[46]

The overall conclusion must be that if the North was not quite as violent as the South, it had a substantial record of bloodshed and intolerance. Northerners served in their fair share of army positions, they fought for expansion on the borders of Canada and in Mexico. They resorted to personal combat over disputes and must have had some prowess with the rifle. For at Bull Run, one of the first major clashes of the war and therefore one in which native skill would have been at a premium, they scored a significantly higher kill rate than the rebels.[47]

Most of the qualities labeled as peculiarly Southern were either exaggerated or could be described more accurately as common American traits. Why then did they come to be associated specifically with the South? The answer seems to be that people saw in the South what they wanted to see or what they had been told they would see. Many Southerners liked to picture themselves as chivalric, ready to fight for honor or country. Even those who disliked the image of violence in their society rarely possessed enough concrete data to deny the popular picture. Many Northerners simply accepted Southern claims to a superior martial feeling at face value, while abolitionists were convinced that a slave society was inevitably riddled with violence. Like most stereotypes, those about the

North and South were compounded of half-truth and ignorance built upon a small grain of truth. But this does not lower their significance for the historian. As a force in human affairs, what is believed to be true may be more instrumental than the truth itself. Whether a view is right or wrong may be less relevant than the fact that a man acts upon it. In the Civil War, the belief that Southerners made better soldiers posed grave problems of confidence for some Northerners. These problems were most acute in Virginia, where fought a majority of soldiers from the so-called heartland of Yankeedom.[48]

3

Prelude

The Secession Crisis and Fort Sumter

Beat! beat! drums—blow! bugles, blow!
Through the windows—through doors—burst like
    a ruthless force,
Into the solemn church, and scatter the
    congregation,
Into the school where the scholar is studying;
Leave not the bridegroom quiet—no happiness
    must he have now with his bride,
Nor the peaceful farmer any peace, ploughing his
    field or gathering his grain,
So fierce you whirr and pound you drums—so
    shrill you bugles blow.

> —WALT WHITMAN,
> "Beat! Beat! Drums!"

The noble sire fallen on evil days
I saw with hand uplifted, menacing, brandishing,
(Memories of old in abeyance, love and faith in
    abeyance,)
The insane knife toward the Mother of All.

> —WALT WHITMAN,
> "Virginia—The West"

In analyzing the Northern mood between South Carolina's secession in December of 1860 and the Battle of Bull Run in July of the following year historians usually make a break at the fall of Fort Sumter in April 1861. During the first period, the Secession Crisis, the Northern mood was one of uncertainty about how to proceed in the emergency. Could the major issues be resolved within the Union? How much could the North afford to concede in achieving this? If compromise failed, should the disaffected be allowed to depart in peace? What was the expedient course with regard to national properties in the seceded states?[1]

This atmosphere of questioning was dissipated by the action at Fort Sumter. The majority of Northerners no longer felt doubt about the right course of action: the flag had been fired upon and the insult had to be avenged. On April 15 President Lincoln issued a proclamation calling for 75,000 men to put down "combinations too powerful to be suppressed by the ordinary course of judicial proceedings." By the end of the month volunteers were pouring into Washington and soon the overworked War Department was asking state governors to curtail the flood of recruits. The rebels, people said, would not be able to withstand the onrush of these eager soldiers. The cry was "On to Richmond" and the prediction was that the war would be over in thirty days.[2]

This division of the months before Bull Run into two parts is obviously a valid one when recreating the major trends of the time. However, this is not our interest here. We know, with hindsight, that the war was not to be over in thirty days, that the premature optimism was to be swept away, and that years of disappointment were to follow. What we are looking for are themes in Northern thought that would become central in the discouraging times to come after Bull Run. Neither the limited issues of the Secession Crisis, such as the problem of government properties, which became academic after Sumter, nor the heady optimism of the post-Sumter days are critical. I shall attempt to trace certain threads that run throughout the period and that were ultimately to produce disunity and lack of confidence. In particular, I shall note a lack of deep faith on the part of certain people in the government and institutions they were about

49

to defend and some feeling that the secessionists had material advantages in the military confrontation. These were not majority opinions, at least in the months after Sumter. They were whispers beneath the whirr of Whitman's proud drums. But they would grow in the days of defeat.

Major Robert Anderson's gallant defense of Fort Sumter excited great admiration in the North. Then the rallying of the people following Lincoln's call produced more general astonishment and an intoxicating joy. Only days before it had seemed that the North would stand idly by and see the nation fall apart. Henry Villard, a young journalist in Washington during the first weeks of Lincoln's administration, said that there had seemed to be an inertia about the capital. Many "were under the impression that the Government was afraid of decisive steps and was simply drifting with the current of events." Officers were allowed to desert to the enemy with impunity; government officials were left free to resign their posts and leave for the South at their leisure. Worst of all, it appeared that even if the government did take action "it would not have the support of the majority of the Northern people," for the Republicans were divided and the Democrats loud in clamors for peace at any price.[3]

Hotheaded Southern secessionists sneered that they would drink every drop of blood spilled in a war to preserve the Union. The Confederate peace commissioners in Washington told William Howard Russell of the London *Times* that trade, the pursuit of gain, and the base mechanical arts had so degraded the whole Yankee race that they would not attempt to strike a blow for the Union. In proof they cited the cases of Northern politicians who had allowed themselves to be insulted without challenging the offending parties. New Englanders, they added, were the worst of all.[4]

To those who wished to coerce the seceded states, such attacks on Northern manhood contained a bitter truth. The New York *Times* admitted that "the best among us began to despair of a country which seemed incompetent to understand its dangers, and indifferent to its own destruction." But Sumter had changed all this, for "American loyalty leaped into instant life and stood ready and radiant for the fierce encounter." The unity of sentiment in favor of war amazed the Boston merchant George Ticknor. "I never knew before what a popular excitement can be," he wrote. "Holiday enthusiasm I have seen often enough, and anxious crowds I remember during the war of 1812–15, but never anything like this."[5]

It now seemed safe to laugh at the Southern fire-eaters who had scorned Northern manhood. Cartoonists had a field day depicting the national government—usually symbolized by Columbia—coming down heavily on the secessionists. Newspapers also ran anecdotes that suggested the Southerner was a paper tiger. One such piece, in the New York *Tribune*, related to Roger A. Pryor of Virginia, an ex-member of Congress, who had accompanied a Confederate captain sent to solicit the surrender of Fort Sumter. The paper described Pryor as "the very embodiment of Southern chivalry. Literally dressed to kill, bristling with bowie-knives and revolvers, like a walking arsenal . . ." Once in the fort, he thought himself "monarch of all he surveyed" and in line with this pretension casually drank what appeared to be a glass of brandy. The liquid was, in fact, potassium iodide, a poison that might have killed Pryor had not a Federal surgeon pumped his stomach. "Mr. Pryor left Fort Sumter 'a wiser if not a better man.'" The story was no doubt spurious but this is immaterial. The point is in the mocking attitude to Southern "chivalry." The swashbuckler is really a stupid fellow who is better off not to meddle and whose pretensions are easily exploded.[6]

The unity of Northern sentiment that observers felt they saw and that underpinned their new optimism was certainly there. Sumter had provoked some remarkable conversions to a war policy. Among these were a group of abolitionists whose position was typified by that of the Brahmin radical Wendell Phillips. The Secession Crisis had forced people like Phillips into a difficult dilemma. Should they advocate coercion? It was possible that in a civil war the slave oligarchy might be destroyed or at least might lose control of the social situation. If this happened then slavery would die, but this resolution was by no means guaranteed. There was a strong possibility that the North would lose a war against the South and would be forced into a humiliating peace, yielding the slaveholders even more power in the national government and guaranteeing slavery in perpetuity. Better perhaps to let the seceded states go to the devil their own way than risk a complete Southern victory.

This was the position taken by Phillips. He feared that if a war came the South would win it because, for one thing, Southerners were more used to fighting than Northerners. Like other abolitionists he saw the South as a land weltering in blood, a place where there was awful cruelty to slaves and interminable violence between whites. As early as 1855, when slave and free state men were embroiled in Kansas, he had pre-

dicted that the more peaceable Northerners would be no match for the
ferocious Southerners.[7]

Not only were Northerners peaceable, in Phillips' eyes they lacked
moral spine. He had long hated slavery and attacked slaveholders but he
was not devoid of respect for the best of them. Whatever else they were,
they held to principle and would not sacrifice their cause for expediency.
The same had not been true for Northern politicians and capitalists, who
for decades had temporized with slavery to protect their selfish interests.
John Brown's raid had given Phillips a brief confidence in the growing
moral purpose of the North. "Why, this is a decent country to live in now,"
he cried to an audience in New York. Events during the Secession Crisis
conspired to make this confidence ebb. Talk of a compromise peace based
on stronger constitutional protection of slavery convinced Phillips anew
that conscience was stifled in the North. He therefore rejected the possibility of coercion, saying that the appeasers had no grit for a fight "and
the first result of a military demonstration would be the complete surrender
of the North, and the concession of everything that might be demanded
at their hands."[8]

Phillips' conclusion that it would be best to dissolve the Union in
hopes that Southern moral sickness could be quarantined at the Northern
border was shattered by the popular reaction to Sumter. In the face of
overwhelming war feeling it would be madness to hold out for separation.
So Phillips, with those like him, was brought into support for the war.
He publicly repudiated his recent attacks on Northern character, saying
that he had been mistaken in believing Massachusetts too "choked with
cotton dust and cankered with gold" to fight. From now on the war would
have his "hearty and hot" approval.[9]

To the right of Phillips stood conservatives, who had also tended to
be lukewarm about coercion. Some of these were motivated, as their opponents charged, by self-interest. Merchants and bankers feared the loss
of lucrative Southern trade, Democratic politicians hoped to preserve their
Southern political alliance through conciliation. But there was also a
genuine sympathy for the slaveholders—a feeling that secession had been
more or less forced on them by abolitionist pressure. Viewed in this light,
coercion might be morally wrong. Some said that if there were a war it
should be waged against the black Republicans who had caused all the
upset. Moreover, State Rights philosophy was by no means dead in the
North by 1860; numerous conservatives saw a constitutional difficulty in
the way of using force against the South. And had not the nation been
born in the belief that a people that objected to the form of government
might break away and establish its own system?[10]

Most of these arguments were blown away with the smoke from Sumter's guns and the majority of conservatives fell into line behind the Federal government. As with the radicals, the change partly represented nothing more than a sober realization that it would be futile to oppose the war fever any longer. But there was more to it than that. Conservatives felt genuine outrage at the Southerners who had deserted their friends by firing on the national flag. The slaveholder was no longer the aggrieved but the aggressor. This sentiment was made possible by a peculiar quirk of logic, common to Northerners of different political persuasions. They pictured Major Anderson and his garrison at Fort Sumter as being in a passive, inoffensive pose. In the immediate context, this was correct: it was the South Carolinians who had fired first. But viewed from a broader perspective, the Federal soldiers were the aggressors. When in March Lincoln told the South that he would hold government properties he was in effect declaring war on South Carolina. The state was given only two choices—it could tolerate an armed Federal fort in the harbor of its major city, which would make a mockery of its claim to sovereignty or it could fight for possession of the post. Much conservative anger after Sumter would have been dulled had it been seen that holding the forts, even in a defensive posture, was in and of itself coercion. But the point was not seen.[11]

Among those who had been reluctant to think about war were a number of regular army officers. It is worth pausing to look at their views, both because professional officers would virtually monopolize top army positions where their views would profoundly influence events and because their case forms a nice study of the conservative viewpoint. As the sectional crisis approached, regular officers naturally viewed the situation with concern because they had formed friendships that transcended the Mason–Dixon line. Joseph Pearson Farley, a Northern West Pointer, recalled that "between the men of the several sections of the country there was no bitterness manifest, nothing but expressions of sorrow and disappointment." And from the other side, R. S. Ewell commented that the officers of the army did not want a war as they felt no sectional bias and had friends from all parts of the Union.[12]

However, certain Northern officers not only felt an emotional repugnance for a brothers' war; they positively identified with the Southern position. There was much feeling against the abolitionists. In 1859 John F. Reynolds wrote to his sister regarding the execution of John Brown, "I think if they could hang, along with old Brown, Gerrit Smith, Wendell Phillips, and a few more of the abolition stripe, it would effectually stop this agitation for a time, at least." In November of the following year,

William Tecumseh Sherman wrote to his wife that "the abolitionists have succeeded in bringing on the 'Irresistible Conflict.' " Damn the niggers," he added. And as late as May of 1861 Gouverneur Kemble Warren wrote to his friend Henry L. Abbot, an officer from Massachusetts who was to become a Union general, the revealing comment, "You, perhaps (I know in fact), charge all the trouble to the Abolitionists of the North, and that may or not be so."[13]

Some officers claimed that they knew of Northern colleagues who accepted the State Rights doctrine. James Longstreet, who became a Confederate general, said that he discussed the question with Alfred Gibbs, an officer who was to rise to general rank in the Union army. Longstreet asked Gibbs "what course he would pursue if his State should pass ordinances of secession and call him to its defense. He confessed that he would obey the call." Captain Abner Doubleday, one of the Sumter garrison, said in his memoirs that he was the only officer in Charleston who favored the election of Lincoln. He claimed that Anderson, while determined to preserve his professional honor, "expressed himself as openly opposed to coercion. He was in favor of surrendering all the forts to the States in which they were located. This course would simply be an acknowledgment that the sovereignty did not vest in the United States."[14]

In trying to explain why so many officers were lukewarm toward the Republican administration Doubleday suggested that slavery had long ruled the nation with a "rod of iron." The strength of the South had been so great that "all the pathways to political power, all the avenues of promotion in the army and navy, lay in that direction." In other words, Southerners had made sure that only pro-slavery people could get ahead. The argument was being stated even more boldly, as will be seen later, by others who charged during the Secession Crisis and later that Southerners had deliberately brainwashed West Pointers as part of a long-standing plot to destroy the Union.[15]

What truth was there in all this? It was seen in the last chapter that Marcus Cunliffe has disproven the thesis that Southerners had disproportionate representation at West Point and in the ranks of the officer corps. It may be added that there was no truth in the idea of a Southern conspiracy to subvert West Point. Doubleday was wrong in picturing an iron hand of the South at work. But he was correct in sensing that many of his colleagues were sympathetic to the Southerner. Army officers, like other Northerners, often respected slaveholders as outstanding military material. And they admired them as men. But their admiration came rather from a sense of class distinction and a shared position in society than from indoctrination in pro-slavery principles. The charge that West

Point was a Southern institution was less true than the charge that it was an aristocratic one. As a professional institution with high academic standards the academy stood outside the Jacksonian framework of the age in which the native abilities of the untutored common man were taken as a model. Like other gentlemen of standing, West Pointers often frowned on undisciplined democratic society. In abolitionism and other "isms" they saw the same threat to social order that critics had seen in Jacksonianism. Thus they naturally tended to identify more strongly with the supposedly class-conscious society of the South than with the hurly-burly democracy of the North. As a naval officer put it to Russell of the *Times* on April 12, if it came to force the war would be between "the gentlemen and the Yankee rowdies."[16]

When the tug came with Sumter, most Northern officers decided that they must in fact stay with the flag. Not only did the action at Charleston touch their professional honor, it seemed to them as to other Northerners that the secessionists had perpetrated an unjustified act of aggression. We seem therefore to have a Northern consensus—the great uprising of the Union which occasioned so much joy. Radicals, conservatives, all appeared to be in accord. Yet, if we take a long-term perspective, the unity was shallow indeed. It would be enough to take the North up to Bull Run but what of the time after? All that the various groups had agreed on was that the insult to the flag must be avenged. They had been swept along by the tide of popular emotion. When passions cooled and men got down to the sober job of defining what the ultimate aims of the war should be and how they were to be attained, deep differences would surface. Rallying to the flag was essentially a defensive action and all groups agreed that the Northern states must be defended. But marching into the South was offensive and Union men would disagree violently as to what they were doing there. For radicals, some of whom had been pacifists, the blood expended in conquering the South would only be well spent if slavery were extinguished. To conservatives, the war would be immoral if it went beyond re-establishing the old arrangements. Some army officers who had gone to war to preserve the national honor would come to feel that their main enemies were in fact in the rear.

Even in the period after Sumter symptoms of malaise were discernible. Acute observers noted that some army officers, although apparently aware of the course dictated by duty, had an odd lack of enthusiasm about the Union cause. Jacob Dolson Cox, a volunteer officer, wrote later that typical of this type was a certain Colonel Crook, who had "no deep sympathy with the National cause, and had no personal objection to the success of the Rebellion."[17]

Before Bull Run the deep division between radical and conservative over war aims was becoming apparent. When a general advanced into slave territory he came up against a difficult problem of definition, for which there was no clear solution. Were the troops engaged in taking alien soil or liberating a friendly population from the grip of secessionist terrorists? (One justification for coercion had been that the bulk of people did not wish to leave the Union: they had been forced out by evil leaders.) If the people were loyal, then were their possessions to be protected? In particular, were their slaves to be treated as property or greeted as allies in the Union cause? In answering these questions, both regular and volunteer officers got into trouble. When Benjamin F. Butler, a volunteer, offered Maryland authorities the use of Massachusetts troops to put down a possible slave revolt, he ran afoul of Massachusetts Governor Andrew. Prefigured here was a struggle between the "gentlemen and rowdies" for control of the war.[18]

Before Sumter there had been a certain uneasiness about Southern military strength. Some people questioned whether, even given that coercion was legitimate, it was feasible. Some regular officers, who, as has been said, tended to think highly of the Southerner, predicted that the South would fight a hard war. Joseph W. Revere, a military man, gave as "the prevailing sentiment among the old officers of the army and navy" the views of Philip Kearny, who was to become a Union general. Kearny maintained that the Northern people were "ignorant of the art of war in all its varied aspects" and that Southerners "are the best soldiers." However, he saw hope for the Union in the fact that Southerners had shunned business and hence lacked practical experience in administration. Thus their armies might be wasted through sheer inability to master the problems of logistics and supply.[19]

To other Northerners business sense did not appear as an asset. Social critics had complained for years that pursuit of wealth had deformed character; material comfort had emasculated Northern manhood. Charles Eliot Norton, a Brahmin, announced that the North was strong enough to win but that she would achieve nothing until purged of commercialism and the rottenness induced by long prosperity. George T. Strong, also a gentleman of the old school, was even less optimistic. Disgusted by Northern cries for appeasement of the slaveholders he asked if any Southern aggression could "stiffen up the spiritless, money-worshipping North? Strange the South can't kick us into manliness and a little moderate wrath. Southerners rule us through our slaves of Fifth Avenue and Wall Street."[20]

The wrath came after Sumter and with it a great deal of optimism about the North's military chances. It was not that people now denied the physical prowess of the Southerner, they simply no longer saw it as the deciding factor. The New York *Tribune* was content to allow that most Southerners were brought up to consider bravery the first requisite of manhood and skill in arms the first necessity of a gentleman. But the *Tribune* also led the cry of "On to Richmond." The point was that a united North fighting in the transcendent cause of preserving Old Glory would overcome the mere physical skill of the Southerner. Martha Perry Lowe told the rebels, "Arms are your pastime, and 'fight' is your word," while "we love the plow and the loom, and the pen." But, she boasted, "We'll tear down *your* flag at the Capitol's gate!"[21]

The upsurge of patriotism was so unexpected that people spoke of it as the dawn of a new era. "A nation hath been born again,/Regenerate by a second birth!" wrote W. W. Howe. And the *Madison State Journal* (Wisconsin) ran a poem telling of "A people long grown servile-necked/ With bowing under Mammon's yoke," which suddenly broke its bonds and "to-day stands haughtily erect." Northerners felt they could now look the slaveholders in the face, for the democratic people had shown they were willing to fight. "Though we may not be all 'gentlemen born,'/ Don't upon that account laugh us to scorn," said a writer for *Vanity Fair*. "Though we've no serfs to turn pale at our nod,/Yet we can fight for home, Freedom, and God."[22]

It no longer seemed a mean thing to be a Yankee trader or mechanic. When a Southern newspaper ran an anecdote about a rebel backwoodsman who said he would win a fight with any Yankee he met simply by buying his gun from him, a Northern paper replied that the Yankee would certainly sell the gun but he would deliver its contents first. This casual ability to turn back the joke about Yankee sharp practice was a new thing and a good indication of increasing pride.[23]

New Englanders were especially relieved by the turn of events, for they had been taunted most frequently as cowards. Two incidents occurred to Massachusetts troops in the weeks after Sumter that, in different ways, appeared to augur well for the future. First, while en route to the defense of the capital, the Massachusetts 6th was attacked by secessionist sympathizers in Baltimore. The scuffle took place on April 19, anniversary of the skirmish at Lexington in 1775, and people were quick to note the coincidence. "We've been told of our degeneracy for years and years," wrote Henry Lee Higginson, son of a wealthy Boston merchant. Yet the troops were "the same men who fought in '76, a thousand times better than any soldiers living." The second incident involved the 8th regiment, which contained a fair sprinkling of engineers and other skilled industrial workers. When a railway engine needed to carry them through Maryland was damaged by secessionists, these men repaired it and continued on their way. The North thrilled to the little affair: the Yankee mechanic was coming into his own.[24]

Now that Northern industrial and financial might did not have to be listed in the debit column of the national ledger, people began to talk positively about the Union's material advantage over the rebels. The *Watchman and Reflector* of Boston pointed out that though "The South is full of enthusiasm, and its people are chivalrous and impetuous . . . it must yield at length to superior force." *Harper's Weekly* deduced from the 1860 census returns that the North had over twice as many men as the South and was in an incomparably better financial position. Also, noted the paper, the rebels possessed little mechanical skill and so might run short of weapons and other materials.[25]

It seems at this point that Northerners had left behind any major anxieties they might have had about Southern military strength. But note that in all this exuberant comment there was little actual denial of rebel martial qualities; they were simply pushed out of center stage by the spotlight on rejuvenated Northern character. This was fine now, but how would Northern character look after Bull Run? What would the spectacle of routed Union troops do for faith in the sovereign people? Faced by the apparent inadequacy of half-trained volunteers, it would no longer be possible to say that Southern military aptitude did not matter. It would seem central to Northern defeat.

In other words, Northern confidence in the period between Sumter and Bull Run was of the most unstable, wrong-headed kind. Instead of being based on a sensible realization that Southern volunteers would be just as green and naively eager as themselves, people posed an artificial difference between Northern spiritual strength and Southern mechanical expertise. This led them to misinterpret the meaning of the Bull Run defeat: instead of seeing that the raw Southern army had simply been more lucky than their own, they assumed that Southern skill in arms had been key.

That Northern confidence was not strong enough to withstand the strain of defeat was evidenced before Bull Run. Despite the boastful trumpet blasts Northerners were quick to spot signs of unredeemed corruption in every adverse circumstance. Thus, when *Harper's Weekly* heard rumors that city merchants were concerned that the war would ruin them, the paper commented sharply that too many people still put duty second to profit. Such types might take a lesson from the rebels, for "people talk and think much more about honor at the South than about dollars."[26]

Moreover, not everyone had been transported into boundless optimism by the uprising of the people. George Strong, a conservative gentleman not likely to be carried away by faith in the spiritual power of hastily assembled democratic levies, warned that the North should avoid a battle for as long as possible because each day gained meant more time to train the men. In a premature clash the Union volunteers might lose, "for they have been mostly men of peace, unlike the Southern sepoy . . . who habitually carries his knife or revolver."[27]

Conservative army officers also tended to be less enthusiastic about the military potential of the democratic masses. One volunteer observed that numbers of regular officers entered the conflict "with little hopefulness or zeal. There were still others who did not hesitate to predict defeat." One reason for pessimism was that numerous Southern officers had left the service to go with their states. To army men, who believed that planters made particularly good military material, this could not be anything but troubling, especially as some of those who left were considered to be among the most promising in the service. This loss to the North was gleefully recognized by Southerners, who passed around a little anecdote about the despised Blair family, which was close to Lincoln. The Blairs, so the tale went, needing "a good officer to do some of their dirty work," sent for Robert E. Lee, then John B. Magruder, Joseph E. Johnston, and finally Smith Lee. All had resigned. "Good God!" said a Blair, "Have all our good officers left us?"[28]

The story was probably false but it was true that in the house of Montgomery Blair, on April 18, field command of the army facing Virginia had been offered to Lee. He refused the offer and did so again in a later interview with General-in-Chief Winfield Scott. The general was deeply disturbed by the loss of Southern officers, whom he sometimes spoke of as the best in the army. When asked by Secretary of State Seward what the North was to do for generals, Scott was only able to reply that there were some captains and lieutenants who could eventually do good service but that "unfortunately for us, the South has taken most of those holding the higher grades."[29]

The officers who were troubled by the South's military reputation were in a minority of the population. But they would have an importance out of proportion to their numbers, for they would occupy high positions which would make them the brains of the army, supplying its essential character. Defeat would seem to confirm their pessimism and make it increasingly intelligible to the society at large.

Even during the days of optimism a thread of ideas was growing *within the mainstream* that would prove damaging to Union military performance. This was the so-called "conspiracy thesis." Briefly, the thesis was that secession was not a spontaneous reaction to Lincoln's election, but the consummation of a long-laid plan to destroy the Union. To ensure success, Southerners had made secret military preparations and had insinuated themselves into high Federal positions where they could emasculate the national forces. The first accusations of Southern preparation appear to have come from Northerners resident in the South. As early as January of 1860, they began to warn of substantial military activity in that region.[30]

Then, in December of 1860, rumors erupted that the Buchanan administration was giving military aid to the secessionists. Most serious was the charge that Secretary of War Floyd had been robbing Northern arsenals to arm the South. An investigation by a House Committee, set up on December 31, failed to reveal evidence of treasonable activities by Floyd and most historians have held him to be innocent. Kenneth M. Stampp has argued very persuasively that Buchanan was neither a coward nor a traitor; that his attitude to rebellion was parallel to Lincoln's. Both men were determined to hold Federal property, by force if necessary.[31]

Despite the facts, Northerners remained convinced that the cabinet had sold them out. This is not surprising as the popular mind is often impervious to fact, especially in a time of emotional crisis. Some people saw sufficient evidence in the fact that Buchanan was a pro-Southern Democrat who had tried to hold Kansas for slavery. The special circumstances of Washington, the nerve center of the nation and the place where many plot stories originated, must also be remembered. The meeting point of North and South, the city was well situated to generate the tensions and anxieties upon which rumor thrives. Throughout the Secession Crisis, Southern politicians, ex-government employees and their families could be seen leaving for the Southern states, unhindered by an administration that seemed shamefully unwilling to exert its authority. Southerners who remained often spoke openly of their secessionist sympathies. So did many permanent residents of the city, for Washington was Southern in many ways with Southern ties and affiliations. By December of 1860 it was even possible to buy secessionist cockades in stores located only a short distance from the capitol.[32]

Unionists, uncertain of their own strength in the country and acutely conscious of the disloyalty around them, were soon ready to credit any rumor of intrigue. A flood of plot stories poured out from the city. Daily reports told of secessionist plans to capture Washington and kill Lincoln before he could assume office. So seriously were these taken that the President-elect was persuaded by his advisers to enter the capital in secrecy.[33]

Fertile soil for the growth of plot stories in the country at large had been prepared over many years by abolitionist charges that the slaveocracy was involved in a gigantic conspiracy to fasten slavery on the national life. The Mexican War had been charged to Southern desire for new cotton lands. In 1857, only four years before the Civil War, Hinton Rowan Helper, a Southern abolitionist whose work was widely read in the North, brought forward powerful documentary evidence to support the charge that slaveholders dominated most branches of the Federal government. He also argued that the planters kept the bulk of their own people trapped in poverty and ignorance so that they could not interfere with their selfish schemes. Helper ended by arguing that if the Union ceased to serve its special interests, the oligarchy would secede. In 1860 this thesis was a popular one with Northerners, for they wished to believe that most Southerners did not hate the Union, that secession was not a popular movement but the work of a few evil leaders.[34]

Belief in a conspiracy continued to grow after Sumter. This was due in large part to the defections of army officers, which began before April but increased in pace thereafter as the inevitability of armed conflict became certain. Angry Northerners charged that secessionist principles had been inculcated at West Point. In fact, a disproportionate number of officers did not leave the army: of 1,108 in the service, only 313 departed. Most of these were Southerners, who naturally might be expected to go with their states. But many Northerners did not see the matter this way. They had assumed that regular army men, bred to national allegiance, educated and advanced by the Federal government, would stand by the flag.[35]

Suspicion of treason was increased by the boasts of ex-army men in the Southern service that their Northern colleagues would not fight against the Confederacy. Though the majority of officers did rally to the national cause, the fact that some of them were evidently empty of enthusiasm did not help their standing. The politician John Sherman told his soldier brother William, "The old army is a manifest discredit." In the atmosphere of mistrust, innocent actions of army officers became subject to suspicion. The reluctance of Irvin McDowell, field commander of the Union army at Washington, to advance before his men were properly trained, was seen as strange by a North that thought raw enthusiasm was enough to bring victory. It was whispered that he was avoiding action to give the rebels more time to prepare and it was even reported that "our soldiers have been requested to fire blank cartridges in all engagements with Southern forces." When McDowell attempted to stop the pillage of property held by loyal Southerners he was immediately called a traitor.[36]

The charge that Southerners had deliberately subverted the army was difficult to substantiate in terms of concrete documentation. But Northerners did come up with one piece of "evidence." In 1836 the Southern political philosopher Nathaniel Beverley Tucker had published a novel called *The Partisan Leader*. The book was published primarily as a campaign document during the presidential race of 1836. Its main thrust is an attack on the Democratic leadership, which had opposed state sovereignty in the Nullification Crisis. Van Buren is pictured as having made himself king. He is supported by the bayonets of the Federal army. The lead in resisting the tyrant is taken by John C. Calhoun, who spearheads a Southern independence movement. Calhoun convinces a young Southern West Pointer to become the leader of the Southern forces and he defeats the regular army in battle. The book is a novel and in no sense can it be taken as an official Southern memorandum regarding secession. But the fact that it did predict the coming of civil war at some future time through the agency of Southern leadership meant that it was well suited to back up the charge of a Southern conspiracy involving the military. Seven thousand copies of the work were printed in New York and distributed during May of 1861.[37]

Northern West Pointers even came to believe the charges against the army and the War Department. Some had retired from the service before the war and had no way of knowing what developments had taken place after they left; hence acceptance of the plot stories was not difficult. Even serving officers, dotted in small units around the country, often knew little about happenings outside their immediate vicinity. It was hard for them not to believe the accusations against Floyd and Buchanan when men high in government circles, like Secretary of State Seward, continued to endorse them. The desertions by Southerners, the obvious distaste for war shown by some Northern colleagues, made certain officers ponder anew on what exactly had been taught at the Point. John F. Reynolds, commandant of cadets, became convinced that Jefferson Davis, while secretary of war, had carefully planted in the soldiers' minds "the poisonous weed of secession, . . . the depth of his treachery has not been plumbed yet," he concluded darkly.[38]

In one sense the notion of a conspiracy was healthy, for it made people hate the secessionists and want to punish them. But in the long run it was more dangerous, for the assumption that Southerners had been making military preparations over an extended period of time led to the conclusion that their forces must be better trained and equipped than the Union troops. General Philip H. Sheridan, recalling after the war his feelings in the period before Bull Run, said that though he had expected ultimate victory, he had been made uneasy by "the thoroughly crystallized organization" of the rebels. The belief that the rebels had a mighty war machine, long in the building, would lead some Union generals to constantly exaggerate the numbers and resources of their opponents with the result that their generalship became overcautious.[39]

The conspiracy stories throw light on the extraordinary psychological stance taken by some Northerners when dealing with the South even during a period of so-called confidence such as that which followed Sumter. On July 4, John Jay made a speech that sought to expose the "secret history" of the rebellion. Jay argued that without the knowledge of the American people, Southern leaders had been planning rebellion for over 30 years. This idea that Southerners could conspire for decades without their design becoming transparent assumed for the secessionists an incredible skill in organization and powers of subterfuge. Similarly, it was impossible for Jefferson Davis to have sown treason in the army without his scheme having been found out. Equivalent situations may be found at other periods of history. For example, there is the American habit of grossly overestimating Communist ability to infiltrate their political structure or the inclination of some British people in World War II to attribute superhuman powers to the Germans. Fabulous rumors are generated: the Communists are fluoridating the water, the Germans have produced an amazing cardboard tank or, in the case of the North, the bizarre idea of the "masked batteries."[40]

The business of these batteries caused a great deal of unease in the

North during the summer. It all started when Union General Robert C. Schenck, patrolling toward Vienna, Virginia, with no advance guard and having no clue as to what lay ahead, blundered into a Confederate ambush. In his report Schenck stated, either because of genuine ignorance or a desire to make his defeat seem less criminal, that he had been fired upon by "raking masked battteries." In fact, the rebels had used two field cannon supported by infantry and that was all. But from this time on masked batteries were, in the words of one historian, "anathema to all commanders of advancing columns." McDowell's cautious advance on Bull Run was partly due to the memory of Vienna. The password on his march, revealing enough, was "caution." In picturing the Virginia countryside honeycombed with subterranean fortifications and masked batteries Northerners unwittingly showed that the rebel was becoming a larger-than-life figure; he was mastering the imagination.[41]

How can this be explained? The simple answer would be that we have here an unconscious exhibition of awe for Southern military ability. This is obviously true but the complete picture requires a little more detail. There was a well-established theory among political philosophers that an aristocracy would necessarily be stronger in war than a democracy. In the former state, so the argument ran, the clique of rulers was free to bend all the national energies to efficient prosecution of the war unhindered by the vagaries of legislative assemblies. In a democracy, where the public had to be consulted on major issues and where parties might differ as to the best method of conducting hostilities, war measures would necessarily be slow in materializing and often fumbling in execution.[42]

The South had long been seen as an aristocracy where the bulk of people were excluded from participation in public affairs. During 1861 it became widely believed that Jefferson Davis had assumed dictatorial powers, which he wielded with draconian efficiency. This assumption that the South had dispensed with the democratic process partly explains why Northerners credited it with superhuman organizational powers. But how is this to be reconciled with the evident Northern faith in the power of a democratic people fighting in the cause of popular government? Take, for example, the comments made by the Reverend S. H. Weston to the 6th New York Regiment prior to its departure for Washington. "You are engaged in a righteous quarrel; never was there a juster, a holier cause," said the minister. Above the troops would stream the banner of constitutional liberty borne at "canonized Lexington, Bunker Hill, Saratoga, and Yorktown." The 14th Regiment was told by Charles P. Kirkland that it went "to certain victory" in a war whose "only object is to maintain and transmit to future generations the great boon of civil and religious liberty purchased for them by the blood of our fathers. It is, indeed, a glorious cause."[43]

The victory was apparently guaranteed to the side fighting for constitutional liberty. But certain points need to be made here. First, a man's belief in his cause may be accompanied by an unrealized fear of the enemy; witness the terror created by Hitler's troops in the hearts of people who knew their cause was just. Second, there is a difference between a devotion to abstract principle and respect for the actual functionaries who run the government. In this case, respect for the democratic people often stopped short of the politicians in Washington, whose profiles were sometimes conspicuously absent from laudatory sermons on democracy. Particularly was there a tendency to take a skeptical view of government among professional army men frustrated by undisciplined democratic politics and among conservative civilians, who felt that too many party hacks and vulgar demagogues held power in Washington.

One or two anecdotes may point up the lightness with which government was taken by certain groups. Erasmus Darwin Keyes was a regular army officer who spent a number of years in the capital as aide to Winfield Scott. His service did not apparently breed deep reverence. He recalled "how often I was lured to the brink of the precipice" of secession simply by the enticements of attractive Southern belles. Yet Keyes had a reputation among his brother officers as a man of unusually firm Northern principles.[44]

Another hint of the lightness with which the business of politics could be taken was given by two incidents that occurred while troops were quartered in the Capitol building during the first weeks of the war. The aristocratic New York 7th Regiment, billeted in the Hall of Representatives, proceeded to improvise a speaker and hold a mock session "in which the speech-making and business proceedings are said to have been of the richest order." When the 7th moved out to make way for the 11th New York, the celebrated Fire Zouaves, the new residents repeated the farce. And, as befitted firemen, they indulged in new tricks such as hanging like monkeys from the Capitol dome, until stopped by General Scott in person.[45]

All this might be dismissed as insignificant horse play but for an article written by Major Theodore Winthrop of the 7th, in which some deeper feelings were articulated. Winthrop, a young Boston aristocrat alienated like many of his peers by what he saw as the low tone of political life, castigated the recent civilian occupants of the Capitol for their "bosh," "cowardice," and "imbecility" in failing to sort out the sectional issue. The presence of troops in "our palace" was made necessary, he said, by the men "who had here cooperated to corrupt and blind the minds of the people."

The soldiers would sort out the tangle made by the politicians but, warned Winthrop, if the men in Washington let such a thing happen again the soldiers might sweep them out of power.[46]

Winthrop was not the first to threaten a military dictatorship. During the seemingly treacherous administration of Buchanan men as diverse as the conservative Edward Everett and the radical Republican Salmon P. Chase had suggested that Winfield Scott should be made temporary dictator. At least as early as May of 1861 talk of a coup against Lincoln was in the air. Francis Barlow, a young Harvard graduate, heard about the danger of an overthrow "from the President himself." The amount of adverse comment on Lincoln's administration during this period brings out clearly the existence of contempt for the actual workings of popular government both on the part of elitists and people holding an abstract devotion to democracy who would have been astonished had they realized the implications of their own feelings.[47]

Lincoln was not popular during his first weeks of office, as it appeared that he was going to follow the same supine policy as his predecessor. Edwin M. Stanton, late attorney general under Buchanan, wrote from the city on April 11, "No one speaks of Lincoln or any member of his Cabinet with respect or regard." Lincoln's call for troops after Sumter increased his public esteem but before long he was again being accused of lacking energy. Oliver Otis Howard, a West Pointer who was colonel of the 3d Maine at this time, said that his impression of Washington during June and July was that "no one seemed to know what was to be done or what could be done." Dissatisfaction even infiltrated the Cabinet. Edward Bates, the new attorney general, wrote in his diary that the rebels were safe in defying the government "because we hurt nobody; we frighten nobody; and do our utmost to offend nobody." Moreover, people tended to assume that, in the words of Adam Gurowski, "they do it differently on the other side of the Potomac." In contrast to "this senile administration" of the North, "the Southern leaders do not lose one minute's time; they spread the fire, arm, and attack with all the fury of traitors and criminals."[48]

In fact, the rebels had shown little if any more energy or ability than their Northern counterparts. People scorned Lincoln for backing his generals in their attempt to avoid a premature advance on Richmond. Yet the Confederates gave no sign of making their much-feared attack on the capital. They did capture some Federal arsenals and navy yards but these were in Southern territory and could not have been held with the men available. Moreover, the administration had some solid achievements behind it. Lincoln had played a sophisticated political game, waiting for the South to fire the first shot so that it would appear the aggressor and thus unite the North on the fundamental issue of coercion. Also, Union troops had made some gains, notably in western Virginia where the rebels were beaten at the Philippi Races (so-called because the rebels ran after the battle) on June 3. Finally, the government was doing a more or less successful job of feeding and arming the thousands of new soldiers pouring into Washington.[49]

If people were not looking at the reality of Lincoln's administration, then they must have been looking at an image instead; they were making basic assumptions about the quality of government. I have stressed the fear in America during this period that because of the popularization of politics national office had fallen into the hands of professional politicians whose claim to prominence was based solely on party rather than on attainments in statesmanship. The people, it seemed, were not always capable of making choices based on an appreciation of quality.

Lincoln appeared to fit squarely within this framework. The personality and background of the President encouraged neither confidence nor respect in the character of his judgments. Called upon to be the leader of a nation at war, Lincoln could claim only negligible military experience and he had held no cabinet office in a previous administration. His secret entry into Washington (some said he was disguised as a woman) appeared symbolic of the man's fitness to be a war leader.[50]

The new President gave people the impression that he little appreciated the gravity of the situation. During his first months in office he spent much time dealing with position seekers who expected a share in the spoils of Republican victory. The image created was of a backwoods Nero playing his party fiddle while the Republic burned—an image reinforced by Lincoln's habit of being flippant on serious occasions. A humble birth and western upbringing had left Lincoln with a certain lack of polish that irritated the polite society of Washington. They could not think that there was much of value in a man who told coarse jokes and had even stopped on his way to Washington to measure height with a coal heaver.

By comparison, Jefferson Davis must have appeared to be the ideal war president. A cultured man and a West Pointer who had gained distinction in the Mexican War, he also had experience of both the legislative and executive branches of government. The contrast, then, appeared to be between a government of the elite led by an aristocrat and a popular government headed by a plebeian. The interesting thing is that despite all the talk about the North's holy cause people showed a remarkable willingness to downgrade the efforts of their own leaders and exaggerate those of their opponents. Lincoln's critics were almost certainly not in a majority; we have here a sub-theme to set against the mainstream faith. But the important point is not the quantity of adverse feeling—it is the fact that it existed. The strain was particularly virulent among high army men whose relation with Lincoln would affect the conduct of the war. Of course, the great irony in all this is that people had become so used to stereotyping democratic politicians that they could not look under the surface of Lincoln's actions to see the deep capacity below; to see that while he spent time office filling he was also studiously applying himself to the task ahead.[51]

Before going on to the Bull Run battle a word must be said about Southern feeling in the period of the Secession Crisis and Fort Sumter. It would be wrong to see the South before Sumter as full of people all eager to rush into battle and manhandle the Yankees. For one thing, though the bulk of Southerners accepted the legality of secession, many were not sure that Lincoln's election had provided sufficient provocation for the actual act. Also, there were those who felt that if war did come it would be long and wasting. This feeling was particularly strong in the border states, which could expect to be the battleground between North and South, and among regular army officers, who saw bitter nonsense in the boast of extreme secessionists that the Yankees would not fight. So there was in the South the same kind of troubled questioning and weighing of issues there was in the North. But Southerners did have some solid ground in that there was a rough consensus on two points. First, while secession might have been precipitous, the Federal government did not have the right to coerce a sovereign state. Second, if the Yankees did invade and war came, the South could exact a heavy toll on the battlefield and quite possibly win the struggle.

Confidence in Southern fighting ability was most pronounced among extreme sectionalists, who believed that Northerners belonged to a different and inferior race. Thus the *Southern Literary Messenger* proudly asserted that every slaveholder was a feudal soldier and every plantation his garrison of defense. Should the North not leave the South in peace these planter-soldiers would make it read the error of its ways by the light of burning Northern cities. After all, the paper reminded its readers, Southerners were descendants of the Norman race, a breed that had virtually monopolized the chivalry and military glory of the modern world. The *Mobile Advertiser* also thought that Southerners were by nature a more martial people. On February 12, 1861, the paper likened the Southern states to a collection of modern Spartas which together could defy the armies of the world.[52]

The uprising of the North after Sumter surprised hot-headed secessionists, who had claimed that the Yankees were too corrupt to fight, and troubled more thoughtful men, who saw the South's great material disadvantage. Of particular concern was the fact that the northwest had risen in support of the government, for Southerners tended to have more respect for the fighting qualities of western farmers than they did for those of Yankee mechanics. Before Sumter the strong prejudice of many westerners against eastern capitalists and New England abolitionists had given Southerners some grounds for believing that the west might side with them or at least remain neutral.[53]

The unexpected display of patriotism by the capitalists and industrial workers of the northeast was also disconcerting. Newspaper editors who had sneered at Yankee manhood were hard put to explain the fact that troops from the commercial centers of New York and New England were gathering in Washington. Some said that Northern enthusiasm for the war was simply a new fad of the vulgar masses. The shallow craze would soon pass away and "Yankees will be Yankees again." A popular suggestion was that the North was raising an army by closing its factories, thus "forcing the operatives into the ranks of the volunteer soldiery" to avoid starvation. The most absurd story in circulation was that Massachusetts could only get blacks for its military and that their commander, Benjamin F. Butler, was the son of "Old Ben," a black barber from New Orleans. The fact that Butler was a politician well-known by Southerners who had served with him in Congress made it hard to believe, even in the Confederacy. But that it was ever put into circulation shows that Southerners had been rattled by developments in the North and were making but a poor attempt at laughing them away.[54]

Despite this, the basic feeling in the South was probably still one of confidence. To begin with, it seemed reasonable to suppose that though the North had been able to raise an army, its raw troops would still be inferior in quality to those of the South. One newspaper reasoned that "the people of the North can neither shoot a rifle nor ride a horse, unless trained." There were still those who argued that one Southerner was equal to at least two Yankees. Moreover, if the North was now united, so was the South. Opposition to secession was dissipated by Lincoln's call for troops. Even stout Unionists were prepared to defend the Southern "home and fireside." In their determination to resist invasion Confederates had a war aim at least as inspiring as that of Union. So thought P. G. T. Beauregard, the Southern hero of Sumter, who told the people of Charleston that "whatever happens at first we are certain to triumph at last, . . . the history of nations proves that a gallant and free people, fighting for their independence and firesides, are invincible."[55]

Not least among the factors contributing to Confederate feelings of invincibility was Virginia's secession from the Union on April 17. Virginia was the most venerated of Southern states, its people seemingly the closest in character to the cavalier ideal. And if its secession gave a boost to the rebels, then it was also a blow to the Union. By and large, Northerners respected the state because it was, as one of them said, "The oldest, noblest, proudest one, / Of all our household band." Virginia had spawned many of the nation's revered patriots including Washington, Jefferson, and Patrick Henry, so that when it left the Union there was a sense that a part of the national soul went with it. Even Walt Whitman felt constrained to write a note on its passing to place beside his pulse-beating national poems.[56]

Just how much the North felt the loss of this state would become clear later in the conflict when it was shown that not all the victories in the west could compensate some Northerners for the fact that Virginia still stood firm.

4

The Penalties of Defeat

Northern Reaction to the Battle of Bull Run

*Victories gained . . . early in a war engender
that feeling of self-confidence which is, in fact, the
twin brother of success.*

> —GENERAL VISCOUNT
> WOLSELEY, *United
> Services Magazine*

*One of our returning colonels expressed in public
that night, amid a swarm of officers and gentlemen
in a crowded room, the opinion that it was useless
to fight, that the Southerners had made their title
clear, and that the best course for the national
government to pursue was to desist from any
further attempt at stopping them, and admit them
again to the lead, on the best terms they were
willing to grant.   Not a voice was raised against
this judgment, amid that large crowd of officers and
gentlemen.*

> —WALT WHITMAN,
> *Specimen Days,* "Battle of
> Bull Run, July, 1861"

On July 21, 1861, the Union army under Brigadier General Irvin Mc-Dowell was defeated at Bull Run, the first major encounter of the war. Most historians have argued that this defeat was ultimately beneficial to the North: it ended the vain talk of a short war and brought a more sober realization of the price of victory. For the first time, it is argued, many people saw that enthusiasm alone was not enough; it must be coupled with superior numbers, preparation, and organization. The South, which had been equally overconfident before the battle, failed to learn this lesson and therefore slacked off effort at a time when renewed activity was imperative.

This thesis is valid in so far as it goes. In the period before the battle, some Northerners had seriously underrated the magnitude of their task. The North did not have the overwhelming military preponderance to end the war quickly. Its assets in men and materials were largely offset by the offensive role it was forced to play, against an enemy occupying a million odd square miles of land space. The South enjoyed all the benefits of the defensive, including interior lines of communication, familiar terrain (in 1861 the U.S. War Department did not even have detailed maps of the South), and a friendly civilian population willing to supply information and encouragement.

Moreover, struggles involving the basic values of whole peoples are rarely decided by a single encounter. Rather, the enemy must be ground down until he loses the will to fight. In the case of the Confederacy, Lincoln's call for troops had united the South in defense. Thus the Union armies faced a resolute foe in a reasonably strong military position. Some people needed to learn this and Bull Run helped teach them.[1]

Yet it is also true that men can be made overcautious by defeat. They can become so aware of their difficulties that they lose sight of their assets. It will be argued here that some Northerners overreacted to Bull Run, reading into it an unwarranted significance. The South had been as little prepared for battle as the North. Yet Northerners took their defeat as proof that the old fears of Southern military skill and preparation were justified. Such fears had never died out entirely, even during the period of confidence after Sumter, but now they had far greater force. Moreover, if victory made some rebels overconfident, it gave others a deep and abiding faith in the strength of Southern arms. This moral advantage would be exploited during the war. In this sense Bull Run was prejudicial to the North.

The first reports to filter north from the Bull Run battlefield told of a great Union victory. And, indeed, for much of the day it looked as though the Union troops might well achieve a victory. By 3 P.M. they had taken the key position around the Henry and Robinson Houses and were putting such pressure on the Confederate lines that the whole rebel position was endangered. But then Southern reinforcements arrived and turned the tide. The Union troops retreated, most of the men falling back in good order. But some panicked and could not be stopped until they reached the capital, some 25 miles away.[2]

In his diary, Adam Gurowski hinted that the defeat was at least partly the responsibility of generals who scared the volunteers "by stories of the masked batteries of Manassas, with its several tiers of fortifications, the terrible superiority of the Southerners, etc., etc." Such stories there certainly were but it is doubtful that they seriously marred the performance of the troops during the critical hours of heavy fighting. By all accounts the majority of the soldiers fought as well as any men under fire for the first time. If anyone was troubled by the rumors of masked batteries, it was the generals themselves, whose approach to the battlefield was possibly cautious.[3]

However, fear of the seemingly terrible Southerners did contribute to the panic that gripped some of the troops during the retreat. Their discipline gone, they gave way to terror. William Howard Russell of the *Times*, who was in the rear, met people leaving the field who babbled about masked batteries, while the whole mass of fleeing men seemed to believe that they were about to be cut to pieces by cavalry. Yet, said Russell, not a single horseman was to be seen. On reaching Washington, the demoralized soldiers communicated their panic to the civilians. Walt Whitman heard "terrible yarns, bugaboo, masked batteries, our regiment all cut up, etc." And "among the great persons and their entourage, a mixture of awful consternation, uncertainty, rage, shame, helplessness, and stupefying disappointment." The rebels were hourly expected and people talked openly of surrender. "Resolution, manliness, seem to have abandoned Washington," said the poet.[4]

The rosy enthusiasm of the past months had departed as dramatically as it had appeared. There was little talk now of the magnificence of Yankee mechanics who had gone to make war: the invincibility of landed society seemed apparent. Richard S. Fay, Jr., a correspondent of Benjamin F. Butler, wrote that it had been a mistake to suppose that the "offscourings" of New York could just walk over the Southern gentry and farmers. He added that "the hopelessness of the attempt to conquer 'Dixie' is commonly spoken of." There was little laughter about the claims of Southern gentlemen to better breeding and chivalrous sentiment. Charles Russell Lowell, nephew of the poet James and a captain of cavalry, spoke bitterly of the officers who had deserted their men and were now "skulking about Washington." If this were to be typical of the North, said Lowell, it would lose the war, for "I know that my Southern classmates would never have treated their companies of poor white trash so contemptuously."[5]

With their extravagant hopes dashed, many Northerners fell prey to defeatism. Horace Greeley, whose *Tribune* had led the cry of "On to Richmond," wrote a hysterical letter to Lincoln on July 29, in which he suggested that "if our recent disaster is fatal" there should be an armistice with a view towards the permanent division of the Union. Yet this sense of total powerlessness did not last long. The rebels did not come pounding up Pennsylvania Avenue, the army around Washington was pulled back into rough shape, and many people heaved a sigh of relief. From defeat they drew resolution. Under headlines such as "Cast Down, But Not Destroyed," newspapers urged people to make a further sacrifice for the Union. There was a fresh wave of volunteering and soon the soldiers were drilling under a new field commander, George B. McClellan, who replaced the unfortunate McDowell. McClellan came fresh from victory in western Virginia and it was hoped that he would triumph in the east. By September, some newspapers were predicting that the rebels would lose the next fight.[6]

Looking back on Bull Run after the initial scare was over, numbers of people began to feel that the defeat might not have been such a bad thing after all. Their earlier expectations of a quick victory now seemed rather naive. They felt that perhaps they had needed to be humbled before they could see things clearly. Charles Francis Adams, Jr., had written on July 23 that

Bull Run was a disaster which had destroyed Scott's campaign and assured the rebels of independence. But by August 27 he had decided that the battle had in fact been a blessing, for it had shocked the people out of their ruinous pride and arrogance. And George William Curtis, the editor, wrote of the defeat: "We should have suffered more dreadfully in the end had we succeeded now." For the North had tried to make war without knowing how, a mistake which could now be put right.[7]

Later writers were inclined to agree with this argument. John D. Billings, a Union veteran who published his memoirs in 1888, wrote that Bull Run was a disaster as a battle but "a grand success to the North in other respects" because it sobered the "hasty reckless spirits." And from the Southern side, Thomas Cooper DeLeon, a rebel official whose recollections were published in 1890, argued that while Bull Run made the North brace "every muscle for a deadlier gripe," it made the South waste time in a ridiculous lauding of her strength. Much the same has been said by recent writers. Bruce Catton suggested that "Bull Run was what awakened the North to reality" while "it may have had an opposite effect in the South." James A. Rawley, in his *Turning Points of the Civil War,* pointed to the significant mood of iron resolve in the North after Bull Run, and Allan Nevins wrote that the effect of the defeat on the North "was as stimulating as a whiplash. It blew away illusions like rags of fog in a northwest gale."[8]

This theory seems to make two valid points. Bull Run did make some Southerners dangerously smug and it did alter the mood of many on the Union side. The atmosphere was more grim in the North after the battle. Yet it may still be questioned whether the defeat was ultimately a good thing for the North. To begin with, the South gained far more than it lost by victory. For in a war against great physical odds, a primary asset of the rebels was faith in the invincibility of their outnumbered soldiers. Complacency was a small price to pay for the preservation and nourishment of this faith through victory.

It is true that Bull Run sobered many Northern people but this does not necessarily mean, as most historians argue, that it gave them a more realistic outlook. They were simply more stoical in their approach to the war. This point has been missed because it has been assumed that there was only one significant illusion in the North before the battle: that of a quick victory. But we have seen that beneath the surface confidence were other, less hopeful and more dangerous, illusions about the superiority of Confederate military forces. Bull Run destroyed the illusions of the optimists and confirmed those of the pessimists.

The disappearance of the "On to Richmond" mentality was by no means a total blessing. For whatever had been naive or simple-minded about it, it had at least given the North a rare sense of having the upper hand of the warlike South. Perhaps with victory the cocksureness might have developed into a mature sense of strength. The enthusiasms of the period between Sumter and Bull Run were often more healthy than the assumptions made after July. For if Greeley's notion that the Union troops could do anything was typical of the one period, George B. McClellan's belief that they were asked to do the impossible often typified the other.

What are some areas in which Bull Run was unhealthy for the North? Most obviously, there is the business of the cavalry. During the Bull Run rout men kept crying "The Cavalry! cavalry are coming!" The roots of this fear may be traced to the antebellum period when Southerners had been credited with a love of fine horses. The image was of young bloods drinking, fighting, and dashing about on fast horses. Even before serious fighting began, some Northerners appear to have been reluctant to tangle with these fellows of fearsome repute. On June 7, 1861, for example, Union troops bolted from rebel cavalry scouts. The Confederate commander reported that at the head of some 24 Virginia cavalry he had collided with about 31 men of a Massachusetts infantry regiment. The Yankees had thrown down their arms and fled, yelling "Look out, look out for the d——d Virginia horsemen; they are down upon us." The rebels, in hot pursuit, met two further companies of Federals who also rushed away shouting "Virginia horsemen." Southern cavalry had not done anything yet in the war to justify this fear but it was real nevertheless.[9]

Bull Run vastly amplified Northern awe of the rebel horse. Hearing gory tales of what the rebel cavalry had done in the pursuit after the battle, some Union soldiers, for as much as two years after the battle, were thrown into confusion by the words "rebel cavalry." And few in the North cared to question Southern preeminence in the saddle. Thus in November of 1861, *Wilkes' Spirit of the Times,* the leading sporting sheet, ran an article on rebel superiority "in the number and excellence of their cavalry." Two factors explained this, said the paper. First, the North had neglected to prepare for war; in the race for the "almighty dollar" military pursuits had been ignored. Second, the South had better mounts because Southerners had always raced more than in the North. To get a competitive horse, the North must begin racing again, concluded the article.[10]

Was there any real basis for the notion that rebel cavalry showed extraordinary skill? In the context of the first months of the war, the answer must be no. When resolutely met, the rebel horse could be overcome. For example, before Bull Run there was a minor action at Fairfax Court House on May 31, in which a company of U.S. Dragoons drove a detachment of Southern cavalry through the village and took five prisoners. The discipline of the regulars was sufficient to decide the outcome. At Bull Run the rebel cavalry did not play the decisive role in the fight. The much-reported charge by Stuart's troopers through the ranks of the New York Fire Zouaves appears to have taken place after the regiment had already begun to disintegrate. Moreover, the Zouaves turned around and shot several of the rebels, while the remainder were dispersed by regular cavalry. After the battle, Confederate troopers did harass the retreating enemy but the pursuit was not pressed with vigor and the main work of destruction was done by field artillery. The Black Horse Troop of Fauquier County, Va., which fit the description of their pursuers given by the Union soldiers, did not even take part in the chase. The men were pursued by phantoms. Years of talk about the wild men of the South acted upon the usual fear of cavalry experienced by retreating troops to make them believe that hell had opened and poured out savage slaveocrats breathing fire and whiskey fumes.[11]

The irony of this was that, amidst all the nonsense talked about the rebel cavalry, a very real lesson about the value and function of the mounted arm was missed. In the months before Bull Run the Northern command had assumed that cavalry would be of little use in the war. This idea seems to have been based on the fact that the tremendous defensive firepower available to infantry and artillery of the period, together with the broken-up nature of the Virginia countryside, would prevent cavalry dominating the field as it often had in the Napoleonic wars when infantry could be broken by massive mounted attacks across open ground. But this view overlooked the point that cavalry were still crucial for obtaining intelligence, screening, and pursuit. When the German immigrant Carl Schurz offered to raise a regiment of men who had served in European cavalry units, he was bluntly told by General Scott that the war would be over long before volunteer cavalry could be trained and that the surface of Virginia was so broken up by fences, and so on, "as to make operations with large bodies of cavalry impracticable."[12]

The error in this view should have become clear at Bull Run. Not one regiment of volunteer cavalry moved into Virginia with McDowell and the battalion of regular cavalry that accompanied him was too small to carry out the reconnaissance duties assigned to it or to play a full part in the battle. Despite this, Union commanders continued well into the war to underplay the role of cavalry, frittering the troopers away on escorts and on picket duty for the infantry. When in December of 1861, the Joint Committee on the Conduct of the War took evidence on the cavalry needs of the Army of the Potomac, no less than five general officers suggested that the country south of the Potomac was not suitable for mounted operations and that the number of cavalry in the service could be reduced.[13]

In other words, there seems little truth to the legend that Southerners were naturally better cavalrymen. Northern horsemen were handicapped in achieving efficiency by the negligence of their own high command. This combined with a psychological mastery developing before the war but strongly reinforced at Bull Run to give the rebels an edge in mounted operations that talented officers like Stuart could not fail to exploit. Most important of all, because the gun and horse were centrally placed in the collage of characteristics that made up the image of the martial South, the superiority of rebel cavalry had ramifications beyond the limited sphere of mounted operations: because the legend of Southern horsemanship seemed proven, it was natural to assume that all other aspects of the Southern image were also true.

The battle fostered some general notions about the quality of Northern and Southern troops that were damaging to Northern confidence. While many in the North had become more optimistic about prospects by September, some still lacked confidence in the volunteers. On August 22 a soldier called William T. Lusk wrote, after a mutiny in the 79th New York Infantry, that "the South sends its best blood to fight for a phantom, but we, in the North, send our scum and filth to fight for a reality." Lusk was himself a volunteer but distrust of the men was deepest among regular officers. They, as a class, had been least optimistic about the value of an early advance on Richmond, for they could not see the volunteers as serious soldiers.[14]

The roots of this attitude lay in the long-standing animosity between regular and volunteer, which Americans had inherited from the British. We cannot go into the history of the conflict here. Suffice it to say that many volunteers looked on regulars as arrogant martinets and as mercenaries, while the professionals condemned citizen soldiers as ill-disciplined, even worthless rascals. The dislike of volunteers was revealed by both Northern and Southern regulars in the Mexican War. Although the men fought reasonably well when given a modicum of training, some West Pointers missed no chance to criticize them. Ephraim Kirby Smith, brother of Edmund, the future rebel general, wrote on May 5, 1847, that the volunteers were "expensive, unruly, and not to be relied upon in action." And John Sedgwick, a future Union general, said bluntly that one regular was worth three volunteers.[15]

It was with this conviction that many officers entered the Civil War. For example, Winfield Scott's biographer states that the general was reluctant to admit that the war would have to be fought by volunteers, for in the three wars where he had been associated with them they "had proved to be an endless source of trouble and embarrassment." Scott preferred to place his main reliance on a solid nucleus of regulars. McDowell too made no secret of his lack of enthusiasm for leading volunteers, though he thought that all regiments desiring service should be accepted, "to overwhelm and conquer as much *by the show* of force as by the use of it." McDowell was hoping that a bold front would conceal what he saw as essential weakness. Some of the same distaste was felt by regulars in the Confederate service. But the problem was a much greater one for their Northern opponents, many of whom believed that Southern volunteers were much better than their own troops. Bull Run ended part of the anxiety among Southern regulars, though it should be noted that the Confederate commanders did not feel sure enough of their raw troops to risk a dash on Washington after the battle. Friction between volunteer and regular did not cease but Southern officers were brought more into the mainstream of Southern belief that the boys from Dixie were invincible.[16]

The situation in the North was the reverse. Bull Run seemed to confirm the worst suspicions of the professionals about the reliability of their amateurs. Shortly after the battle, Captain James Barnett Fry, a West Pointer who had served in the Mexican War and was now on McDowell's staff, told the journalist Henry Villard that one of the main reasons for the defeat was "the lack of courage and discipline among the troops." The feeling was shared by General George Gordon Meade who told his wife on October 12 that the men in his command were not soldiers "in any sense of the word." Around the same time General John F. Reynolds wrote that if the rebels attacked his brigade he would not be able to hold them. "You cannot make soldiers of volunteers," he said, adding that this had been his thinking in Mexico and only the perilous state of the country had induced him to take a command over them.[17]

What is interesting here is that while Reynolds' strictures seem to cover all volunteers, he is in fact referring only to Northerners. He assumes that someone has managed to make soldiers of the rebels: they approximate the professional standard, they can run right over him. The point was made bluntly by Philip Kearny, an officer who entered the war believing that the South was a more military nation. In a letter of August 29, he referred to the New Yorkers posted near him as little better than beachguards, quite unlike the highly disciplined men of the South. Thus, the fruit of Bull Run for some regulars was a confirmed belief in the inferiority of the men under them. Meade and some others became more optimistic as McClellan brought order to the camps. But the doubts did not disappear. Kearny wrote on January 13, 1862, "that *every* high officer distrusts (& with reason) our volunteer troops." This was only two months before the start of a campaign which the public was told might end the rebellion.[18]

The Bull Run defeat also decreased confidence in the abilities of available Northern officers. General Scott was accused of senility and the old man himself became depressed about the situation. In August he told Lieutenant James Harrison Wilson that the best officers were in the South. "How we shall make head against them, or how it will all end I dare not say, but my heart is full of doubt and sorrow!" he confessed. Heads rolled, including that of McDowell, who was relieved from field command. This was perhaps one of the most unfortunate results of Bull Run for it brought McClellan to the center of the stage.[19]

Was it true that there was a serious disparity between the quality of the two armies? The question is twofold: did the rebels show more native ability, and did they mobilize for war sufficiently ahead of the North that their men were better trained? Let us look first at the question of native ability. The strictures on Northern officers do not seem justified. Some men did perform badly in the campaign. During the battle itself, Colonel Dixon Miles was drunk and rode around the field wearing two hats. He was removed from the head of his division before the day was over. Daniel Tyler, another divisional commander, blundered off on some side expedition of his own. But most of the senior officers performed their functions correctly if not with flair. McDowell's plan of attack was a sound orthodox one, no better but no worse—in fact, almost identical to—that of the rebels. It could have worked, especially if the Confederates had not been reinforced, an error attributable partly to the slowness of Robert Patterson, a superannuated officer who was quickly retired from the service. McDowell had certainly not proven himself unworthy of high command. Indeed, after Bull Run he was the only Union general blessed with the experience of having fought a major engagement with the rebels.[20]

There is little evidence that the Southern volunteers had any advantage in terms of such qualities as courage, aptitude for military routine, or shooting skill. Both sides showed bravery at Bull Run: numbers fled the front but the majority stood and fought until the pressure became extremely intense. General discipline or the ability to adapt to military routine appears to have troubled the contestants about equally. Almost without exception, Confederates who recalled the atmosphere of the army in 1861 said that the men lacked discipline and had to be trained into the military way of thinking. This is what one would expect. The Northern assumption that the majority of Southern privates were poor whites who accepted blindly the orders of the planters was based on a misconception. The average Southerner, like the Northerner, was a farmer or mechanic. And he faced the same problems of adjustment to army life.[21]

On the matter of shooting skill, some concrete figures are available. The defeat at Bull Run gave impetus to the old idea that Southerners were better with a rifle. On August 12 the New York *Tribune,* discussing the relative merits of the two armies, suggested that the rebels excelled in sharpshooting because Yankees were too industrious to idle away their time in hunting. The majority of scholars have accepted this assertion. Benjamin P. Thomas, for instance, wrote that "most Southern boys could ride and shoot; more Northern lads must learn those skills." Yet the available statistics point in the opposite direction. Every 1,000 U.S. soldiers present hit 100 of the enemy, but each 1,000 rebels hit only 80 men, a difference of 20 percent. Such figures are not absolute proof, but they certainly do not support the Southern case.[22]

These same statistics throw doubt on the idea that the rebels had also received more training. The belief in Confederate preparation was popular in the North. In November of 1861 *Harper's Weekly* asserted that "the treacherous leaders of this conspiracy had been maturing their plot and preparing for the contest several years before the idea of a fight entered the minds of loyal citizens." This was an important factor in causing Northern reverses said the magazine.[23]

In fact, this interpretation totally misread the mood of secessionists on the eve of war. Southerners tended to believe that the Yankees would not fight or, if they did, that they would make but poor opponents for Southern men. The forging of a professional military machine hardly seemed necessary. Typical was the report of an officer attempting to train North Carolina volunteers. On April 28 he wrote that the men would not take drilling seriously because they already "think our southern man equal to ten Yankees."[24]

This complacency also inhibited the acquisition of sufficient arms for the newly independent states. After secession, most authorities made some attempt at preparation but the effort was haphazard and casual. Richard Taylor, who became chairman of Louisiana's Military and Defense Committee in March of 1861, claimed after the war that he had been continually thwarted in his attempts to make the state enlist enough men or buy adequate guns for the emergency. And when in May Josiah Gorgas, Chief of Ordnance in the Confederate army, made a list of materials in the Southern arsenals he could only find 159,010 small arms of all descriptions. It has been calculated elsewhere that at about the same time the U.S. government had in its keeping enough muskets and rifles of one kind or another to equip half a million men.[25]

Only one Southern state, the most radical, had a long-range military program. In 1850 South Carolina laid plans for the purchase of ordnance and small arms to protect the state from Northern invasion. Under the provision, thousands of weapons were purchased. But more typical of most states was Virginia, where the lack of preparation was apparent. In May of 1861, Colonel A. S. Taylor, commanding the Potomac Department, was called to account for withdrawing from an advanced position. He explained that some of his men were without arms and that others lacked ammunition. On May 16 two cavalry companies were mustered in which had no arms save for sabers, while there were seven infantry companies with no weapons at all. Small wonder that when the equipment stored at Norfolk was removed to a place of safety, General Lee asked that even the pikes be brought away, explaining that "as there is a deficiency of arms in the cavalry, some pikes might be usefully employed in that service."[26]

Where there had been some sort of prewar preparation for a crisis, for example, by forming volunteer companies, the initiative was usually local and individual rather than sectional or even statewide. In the North, too, perceptive people who realized that war was coming began to read manuals of tactics and to organize small bodies of soldiers. Overall, there appears to have been little difference in ability, training, or equipment between the men of the two armies in the east during the first months of the war.[27]

This does not mean that they would continue to be equal. Northerners would increasingly be better equipped than their opponents. But perhaps counterbalancing this, the rebels had the advantage of confidence gained through victory. This, and later triumphs, would give them an impetus, an élan, which might be lacking among Union soldiers in the Virginia theater. Union soldiers might lack confidence in themselves and their leaders. Abner Small, a volunteer at Bull Run, recalled that in the months after the battle his unit "held on rather miserably, lacking confidence in many of our officers and refusing to take for granted the proficiency of more distant superiors. We had been led to defeat, not victory, and our lack of success rankled."[28]

Perhaps there was implicit in Small's statement a condemnation not only of the North's military but of its political leadership also. Certainly the battle further weakened faith in the strength of democracy at war. At a distance of a hundred years it is easy to see that the North could have won if events had worked out a little more favorably. But immediately after the battle there was a feeling that the defeat was almost inevitable; that Lincoln had sanctioned an advance before the Union army was ready. The President's stock fell drastically. The radical Benjamin Wade remarked that he might desert to Davis "as he has brains." In fact, the Confederate had not materially influenced the military events of the first months. But he was a West Pointer from the South and a planter, which automatically gave him credit in some Northern eyes. *Wilkes' Spirit,* accepting as true a rumor that Davis had died in September, noted that this was a powerful blow to the rebellion because Davis was "a man singularly well qualified to assume the virtual dictatorship to which he was speedily elevated. Daring in character, inflexible in will, and not without some military fame and talents."[29]

The assumption that the South had set up a "virtual dictatorship" was a natural one for many Northerners to make. The South had never been seen as democratic to begin with. Moreover, there was a popular opinion in the North, as *Harper's* put it, that a despotic form of government was best suited to carry on a war. As the South was seen as first in all military improvements, it must surely have adopted this one also. Some Northerners were talking now of following its example, for Bull Run seemed to show that Lincoln did not have the necessary military acumen for the post of war leader. And there was a good case for arguing that he had been partly pushed into ordering the advance on Richmond by the pressure of public opinion. The only way to stop that pressure might be to throttle the avenues of democratic communication by installing a military regime. This talk of dictatorship, growing after Bull Run, was to reach dangerous proportions in 1862. During the process, much intellectual energy that should have gone into winning the military fight was misdirected into an internal political conflict between Northern groups.[30]

One man who did have more faith in Lincoln after Bull Run was William Tecumseh Sherman. In other respects, however, his case illustrates that the first months of the war were not good for morale. It might be interesting to follow his history in a little detail.

A West Pointer from Ohio, Sherman left the army in 1855 to try his hand first at banking and then the law. Achieving no real success in either field he was in danger of drifting when he was rescued by old army friends who secured for him the position of superintendent at a new military academy in Louisiana. Almost immediately upon arrival in the South he became sure that the people of that region were preparing for war. In October 1859 he wrote to his wife that "the Southern states, by military colleges and organizations, were looking to a dissolution of the Union." In February of 1860 he warned his brother John that commissioners were being sent through the Southern states and military establishments were being organized in the expectation of secession.[31]

When disunion overtook Louisiana in January 1861, Sherman resigned his post and traveled north. He was appalled to find that, whereas in the South people seemed "earnest, fiery and angry, and were evidently organizing for action," there was "not the least sign of preparation" in the Northern states through which he journeyed. In an interview with the new president, he attempted to impress upon Lincoln the seriousness of what he had seen. Lincoln, who still hoped to avoid war, gave him something of a snub, saying that he expected to "keep house" without the aid of military men. This in turn brought out an innate contempt of politicians in Sherman, who exploded upon his brother, a prominent Republican. "You have got things in a hell of a fix," he said, "and you may get them out as you best can." True to his word, Sherman left Washington to join his family and it was only after some two months that he could be induced to take a position in the Union army.[32]

The soldier's distaste for the political process went back a long time. Perhaps the conjunction of a relatively high social background and a military education was responsible for a certain elitism in Sherman, a taste for strong government. Broad democracy was not to his liking. For example, he blamed much of the sectional problem on democracy and the egalitarian spirit, which, he said, placed popular opinion above the law. It allowed "the old women and grannies of New England" to defy the Constitution and the South to flout the banner of secession in the face of the central government. The politicians who either encouraged the ferment or, like Buchanan, appeared too timid to enforce the law, he despised. Thus it was perhaps not without a certain pleasure that he repeatedly predicted a civil war "will ruin all politicians, and that military leaders will direct the events."[33]

Sherman's opinion of the way in which democracy handled its affairs did not change after Sumter. Few people, it seemed, understood the volume of the crisis. He was sure that the Confederacy had established a dictatorship that ruthlessly pushed aside individual interests in the pursuit of victory. Such earnestness appeared to be lacking in the North. For example, the rebels, said Sherman, were doing a far better job of silencing the press in the interests of military secrecy. He felt that Lincoln's calls for troops were inadequate, first because they did not call for enough men to beat the well-organized rebels, and second because they called for the wrong kind of soldiers. Sherman, like other professionals, wanted the mainstay to be regulars and not the ill-disciplined democratic masses (the volunteers whom, he noted a few days before Bull Run, "do pretty much as they please"). If he were in command of regulars, he said, he would not doubt the outcome of the fight, "but these volunteers are subject to stampedes."[34]

Inevitably, Bull Run appeared to confirm Sherman's worst fears about the North at war. "Democracy has worked out one result," he wrote, in the disgraceful rout of the volunteers who "brag, but don't perform." While he worked hard to bring the men back into fighting trim and earned himself a promotion from colonel to brigadier general, the months after Bull Run were depressing for Sherman. It is true that his respect for Lincoln was growing but this did not come from some new-found faith in democracy: Lincoln had backed him in disciplining a mutinous officer and it was this imposition of authority that Sherman appreciated. His assessment of the general situation was gloomy. Even after Bull Run it did not seem that the people appreciated the gravity of their position. The soldiers "clamor for discharge on every possible frivolous pretext," "the new enlistments drag," and "our rulers think more of who shall get office, than who can save the country." Few people, Sherman felt, saw that the South was well prepared, energetic, fiercely hostile and that it would take all the resources of the North to win a war that "will, of course, involve the destruction of all able-bodied men of this generation and go pretty deep into the next."[35]

Late in August Sherman was transferred from Virginia to a more important post in Kentucky. The weight of his new responsibilities and the strain of believing that he was almost alone in appreciating the colossal task facing the North began to tell on him. He started to believe that he faced an overwhelming enemy army. At a time when the Union and Confederate forces in Kentucky were about equal, he insisted that he was outnumbered five to one. On September 27 he wrote (sounding much like McClellan), "I am to be sacrificed" to a rebel army under Simon Bolivar Buckner who, said Sherman, was menacing him with 15,000 men. In fact, the Confederate had only 4,500. Later, Sherman stopped George H. Thomas from advancing on Cumberland Gap because he said the rebels under Felix Zollicoffer were coming with overwhelming force. At the same time, Zollicoffer was begging for reinforcements to meet Thomas' army, which was, in actuality, larger than his own. Sherman was becoming overwrought. Finally, a misunderstanding with Secretary of War Cameron led to rumors that the general was insane and in November he was sent home on the verge of collapse.[36]

Few soldiers became as acutely upset as Sherman but the pattern of his thinking was not unusual. First came the notion that the South was making military preparations for secession. This, together with the idea that the South must be under a dictatorship led to the assumption that the rebels must be organizing their war effort with terrible efficiency. At the same time, contempt for the abilities of Northern political leaders and for the character of the democratic man ended in the conviction that the North was militarily weak and inefficient. It appeared militarily essential and politically desirable that the North should follow the South's example in curtailing public freedom. All this seemed to be confirmed by Bull Run and the general became even more gloomy. The idea of Northern military inferiority now took complete hold of him and he started to see imaginary armies.

Sherman's history is thus a paradigm for the argument advanced here that the first months of the war were not necessarily healthy for the Northern mind. The South had not entered the war with better armies. But victory in the opening round of the conflict gave the rebels a real advantage—psychological mastery over some of their opponents. This mastery was to be all too apparent in the case of McClellan.

5

One Man's Role

McClellan: His Military Significance

My own experience, therefore, supports the conclusion . . . that an army's enterprise is measured by its commander's, and, by a necessary law, the army reflects his judgement as to what it can or cannot accomplish.

—Jacob Dolson Cox,
Reminiscences

If we have lost the day we have yet preserved our honor, and no one need blush for the Army of the Potomac. I have lost this battle because my force was too small.

—George B. McClellan
to Secretary Stanton

George B. McClellan, the man chosen to replace McDowell, has never attracted middle-of-the-road opinion. In his own time, he was worshiped by the majority of his soldiers and by much of the public; yet a sizable proportion of Northerners despised him as a coward and traitor. The historians' debate has been equally partisan. McClellan is portrayed either as the savior of the Union who could have ended the war if only he had been given time; or he is seen as a man who could not bring himself to the aggressive state of mind necessary to win complete victory over a tough foe. I hold to the latter view. I do not intend to rehearse the whole argument concerning McClellan's generalship: it has been stated satisfactorily by Kenneth P. Williams and, in a more charitable fashion, by T. Harry Williams.[1]

I intend only two things: first, to suggest a fresh explanation of why McClellan failed, given my basic assumption that *he did* fail; and second, to suggest the significance of that failure for the psychology of the North at war. Briefly, I maintain that McClellan was overcautious because he believed he faced a militarily more efficient people and that his attitude was communicated to those who surrounded and adored him.

McClellan was a timid general and yet he was called to Washington after Bull Run partly because he appeared to be exactly the reverse: cool, efficient, aggressive. The mistake is easy to understand because the general appeared to be all confidence during the early stages of the war. While directing operations in western Virginia during May to July of 1861, he was wont to issue grand proclamations that spoke of sweeping away rebel tyrants and annihilating whole armies. Here it seemed was a fighting general—one who when asked for reinforcements by a subordinate, answered curtly that he wished under him only men of action and determination who would fight and, if necessary, die with the troops they had.[2]

On arrival in Washington late in July, McClellan immediately set about the task of reorganizing and training the defeated army. Everything appeared to be bustle and enthusiasm for action. The new commander liked to picture himself as a steady hand cutting through the bungling and indecision around him. The martial figure of the general, clattering out with his brilliant staff and escort, to inspect the camps, gave the impression that things were on the move. McClellan was optimistic. He was, he told his wife on August 2, going to "carry this thing on *en grand* and crush the rebels in one campaign." He decided that he had been called by God to save the nation, saying "my previous life seems to have been unwittingly directed to this great end." And when, on November 1, after Winfield Scott retired, Lincoln asked him if he felt able to handle the great responsibilities of general in chief, McClellan replied calmly, "I can do it all."[3]

There seems here little room for criticism of McClellan's confidence. Yet the facts make it clear that he was neither so aggressive nor so confident as he sounded. If the campaign in western Virginia is examined carefully, it will be found that McClellan showed little taste for actual fighting. Although he deserves credit for the planning of operations, most of the fighting was done by subordinates. At Rich Mountain, where McClellan planned to catch the rebels in a pincer movement, he failed to carry out his part of the plan, leaving General Rosecrans to bear the brunt of the battle. Again, the tough-sounding lecture to the subordinate who asked for more troops does not stand up to analysis. At that time the unfortunate officer in question, Brigadier General T. A. Morris, had about 4,000 soldiers and his rebel opponents numbered between 4,000 and 5,000. McClellan, on the other hand, was faced by only 1,300 Confederates but had 8,000 men with him.[4]

The same disparity between profession and practice keynotes the period spent by McClellan in the camps around Washington. Despite his boasting that he would smash the rebels in Virginia, he made no major move in 1861. There was a vicious though minor clash at Ball's Bluff in October. But this Union defeat reflected no credit on McClellan, whose vague orders were partly responsible for the debacle and who was quick to shift the whole blame onto the luckless commander of the expedition, Brigadier General Charles P. Stone. When McClellan did finally move on the Confederate works at Manassas, on March 7, 1862, the rebels easily evaded their numerically superior foe by abandoning their fortifications in a tactical retreat they had expected to be forced into much earlier.[5]

McClellan did not pursue the rebels because he was preparing for a descent on Richmond by way of the Yorktown Peninsula, and on March 17 his troops began embarking. The debate over whether the plan of approaching Richmond by the water route was strategically sound will probably never be decided. Defenders of McClellan have argued that his move got him as close to Richmond as Grant was to get in 1864 but without the terrific cost. Critics claim that McClellan's thinking was flawed by his failure to see that the real target was not Richmond but the Confederate army and that by side-stepping an encounter between Manassas and Richmond he merely postponed the inevitable fight. The latter argument seems the more acute, though it should be said in favor of McClellan's plan that if it had been carried out with speed and decision it could have gained for the North a tremendous psychological advantage: a lightning thrust right to the doors of Richmond could have caught the rebels off balance and their demoralized troops defeated in battle.[6]

But the scheme was not carried out with speed. The spring rains turned the dirt roads of Virginia into mud baths and seriously slowed the Union advance. This was not McClellan's fault though it is odd that no one in his confidence guessed at the probable state of the Virginia roads during that season. But even if the weather had not been adverse, McClellan would, as usual, have been too slow to retain the psychological initiative. Indeed, he never had it, for his messages to Washington make it clear that he felt he must act with caution against a superior foe.

As soon as he arrived on the Peninsula in April, the general bogged down before the defenses of Yorktown. Even before a full reconnaissance of the enemy position had been made, McClellan decided that the works were strong enough to necessitate a siege. In fact, the enemy position was a weak one. Not only were the rebels vastly outnumbered but their fortifications were not completed. Yet by such theatrical devices as marching squads of soldiers up and down to give the impression of great force, the Confederate commander, John B. Magruder, was able to convince the Northern general that he must proceed "with my 'slow preparations.'" He was, said McClellan, "quietly preparing the way for great success."[7]

On May 3, shortly after McClellan's batteries opened on the works, Yorktown was evacuated. In the pursuit up the Peninsula which followed, some individual generals including Joseph Hooker and Philip Kearny distinguished themselves by their aggressive fighting but the drive necessary for smashing victory was missing at the top. It is noteworthy that while McClellan was on the offensive, the rebels were the attackers in the key battles that decided the campaign. By mid-May McClellan was approaching Richmond but there was little action until the thirty-first when the rebels hit him while the Union army was divided by the Chicka-hominy River. After heavy fighting the Confederates were driven off, but the Union commander did not take advantage of the situation to counter-attack.[8]

Meanwhile, the Southerners felt confident enough of their ability to hold McClellan at bay that they kept T. J. Jackson raiding through the Shenandoah Valley. After defeating or eluding all the men sent against him Jackson joined the main army and the united force hit Fitz-John Porter at Mechanicsville on June 26. In a series of vicious engagements McClellan was driven back to Malvern Hill on the James River where his army was able to make a stand. The campaign was over. It has been said that McClellan conducted a brilliant retreat, but by the same token it may be argued that he only fought well when on the defensive.[9]

McClellan stayed put until his army was shipped away from him to take part under John Pope in the Second Bull Run campaign. Following Pope's defeat McClellan was called back to his old army and he took it out to face Lee, who had determined on an invasion of the North. It must be said that McClellan's task was not an easy one: many of his troops had been in the recent reverse, others were raw, and the army as a consequence lacked unity and coordination. Yet it is hard to escape the conclusion that the general was as incapable as ever of bold, aggressive action. "I thought an air of indecision hung about him," said one newspaper reporter who saw McClellan at Antietam.[10]

Delay characterized the campaign. During the first six days after he took command in Maryland, from September 7 to 13, he marched only 30 miles. On the afternoon of the thirteenth, McClellan received a copy of Lee's orders revealing that he was dividing his forces, sending part to capture the garrison at Harper's Ferry. The rebel was an easy prey but it was not until the following morning that the Federals began a march to get between the two forces. By this time Lee had been able to put men in a good defensive position at South Mountain where they were able to buy precious time. Even when the rebels were forced to retreat, the Un-ion army was again slow in following up. On the sixteenth Jackson re-joined Lee but the Southern army was still not complete and if McClellan had attacked he would have had a significant advantage. Yet he delayed an attack in force until the following day. At the end of the fighting on the seventeenth, Lee no longer had the strength for anything but defen-sive action. McClellan did: he had not used his reserve and, according to his own estimate, 15,000 fresh troops had joined him during the battle. They were not used. The general made no further attack and on September 18 Lee retreated across the Potomac with no Federal attempt to molest him. Only on the twentieth did Fitz-John Porter move after the enemy and when he was struck by Jackson, McClellan called him off.[11]

The North had been saved but the war to preserve the Union could not be won by defensive battles. McClellan idled after the battle, saying that his army was tired and his equipment worn. In October J. E. B. Stuart for the second time led his cavalry around McClellan's army and got away with it. On November 7 Lincoln removed his slow general.

It is clear that McClellan was chronically overcautious. He may have been a capable administrator, even a sound strategist, but at the point of contact he lacked confidence. The nerve of the successful offensive general was not there. Various explanations of why McClellan was so timid are possible. Perhaps he simply lacked confidence in himself. Some of his contemporaries suggested that he was a friend of the South who wished a compromise on the sectional issue and therefore avoided giving the rebels a death blow. (McClellan's politics will be dealt with later.) Others have argued that the general was constitutionally unfitted to be a warrior: he shrank from the butchery of war and therefore avoided committing his troops in an all-out fight. It is possible, too, that McClellan was made more cautious as a commander by his experience as an official U.S. observer in the Crimean War. (In his report he had written that early allied failures were due to a want of planning—an error that McClellan was never to be accused of.) Finally, there is an argument that McClellan, along with other West Pointers, suffered from too great an adherence to the ideas of Antoine Henri Jomini, a military expert of the Napoleonic period who stressed careful preparation and precisely worked out campaigns involving a minimum of destructive contact between opposing forces.[12]

Most of these theories have something to recommend them. It seems true, for example, that McClellan was a humane man repulsed by the business of killing. McClellan's experience in the Crimea may partially explain his caution at Yorktown: he wrote during the siege that he hoped by proceeding slowly to avoid the mistakes of the allies at the investment of Sebastopol. The Jomini argument has the advantage of seeing McClellan in the perspective of the whole officer corps. It may be suggested, however, that the general also fits a different grouping: that of the men who believed that Southern society was stronger in war.[13]

The evidence for this argument, which helps explain McClellan's excessive timidity, has long been available and, indeed, some writers have glimpsed the idea. But there has been no attempt to fully articulate the point and some aspects have been ignored entirely. Perhaps this is because the evidence from McClellan himself is elusive: the general, who was nothing if not an egotist, never admitted he had been wrong about anything and so he never tried to honestly analyze his own failings. But it is possible to piece together enough of a pattern in his thinking to allow for serious speculation. A clue is provided by a characteristic which has long interested historians—McClellan's continual overestimation of Confederate numerical strength.

From the very beginning of his service in Virginia the general was convinced that he faced a vast rebel war machine. On August 16, 1861, he made the absurd statement that "the enemy have from three to four times my force." By November he had narrowed the margin but he still gave the rebels double their actual numbers. In March of the following year he accepted as accurate a report from his intelligence service which placed the rebel army at 80,000, whereas they probably had between 42,000 and 60,000 men. The same thing was apparent on the Peninsula. Magruder was able to hold the Union army of 100,000 men at bay with only 23,000 because McClellan was sure that the enemy was appallingly powerful. He believed this to the end of the campaign, writing on June 22, 1862, "The rascals are very strong, and outnumber me very considerably." A fair estimate of the relative strengths at this time might give Lee about 85,000 effectives and McClellan 91,000. And at Antietam McClellan was again certain that he was outnumbered though it is now known that he had over 30,000 more men than the rebels.[14]

Some attempt has been made to clear McClellan of blame for these miscalculations by placing the responsibility on the general's intelligence service, and particularly on its head, Allen Pinkerton. William Starr Myers paints a sympathetic portrait of a conscientious and responsible commander accepting the reports of his incompetent subordinate. However, it has been suggested with equal plausibility that Pinkerton simply followed the cautious lead of his superior and fed him the kind of data he wished to read. Anyway, whatever the case, the ultimate responsibility was the general's. Also, he accepted such reports when others did not. Take, for example, the fall of 1861 when McClellan was picturing the capital as threatened by a vast rebel horde. Both Lincoln and Winfield Scott rejected the idea that Washington was in danger of assault. There was plenty of evidence available to justify their skepticism. At the end of October, for instance, McClellan put the enemy strength at 150,000. Around the same time, *Harper's Weekly* carried an estimate made by Prince Napoleon, an unofficial member of McClellan's staff who had visited the rebel camps. He said there were only 60,000 "ragged, dirty, and half starved" rebels. A Confederate deserter drew a similar sketch of the soldiers living on "sea biscuits and poor bacon," while "Buxton," an army agent, reported on October 6 that the rebels looked shabby, were badly paid, and did not think they could cope with the Union forces. Hardly the magnificent army conjured up by McClellan.[15]

On the face of it, the general's habitual preference for the higher estimates makes no sense at all. It took no genius to realize that the South had fewer men, less resources than the North, and that it had neither the transportation system nor the reserves of food and equipment to keep overwhelming forces in the field. Hence, it has been assumed usually that McClellan was either a poor mathematician or was using the inflated estimates as an excuse to avoid action. But if popular notions about the martial superiority of the South are brought into the equation, the choice of the larger figures begins to make sense.

It will be recalled that there was a rumor in the North, begun before Sumter, that the South had been making deliberate preparation for war. The belief was current throughout the war and for years afterwards. Thus, Alonzo H. Quint, in a volume of army notes published in 1864, claimed that the South had begun to arm after the 1859 John Brown raid so that "when the war began, the South was ready, while the unconscious North, which had disapproved the raid, and supposed it had thereby satisfied the slave power, was totally unprepared." McClellan himself, in his autobiography, subscribed to this conspiracy thesis, saying that "at least from the beginning of Jan., 1861, and probably in many cases yet earlier, the work of organizing, arming, and instructing troops began throughout the seceded States," while as late as the attack on Sumter "the general government and the Northern States were utterly unprepared for war." And W. C. Prime, who edited McClellan's work, wrote, "No one but McClellan had observed that the able and educated soldiers of the South had long been organizing that vast machine," which became the Army of Northern Virginia.[16]

It is only by assuming that McClellan believed the rebels had been organizing a "vast machine" that we can credit his overestimations of enemy numbers. Admittedly, the evidence from McClellan's own mouth was given after the war and therefore may not be reliable. The argument must rest on speculation but then so must any explanation, as McClellan during the war never gave a clear reason for his errors on Southern strength. Anyway, mine is the only argument that allows McClellan any intelligence or integrity: other explanations must pose that he lied to avoid action or that he was the simple-minded dupe of his intelligence service. McClellan was no fool in the common sense of the word: he did, after all, graduate second from the top in his West Point class. But he was extremely impressionable and could easily have fallen prey to the common talk of a Southern plot. He was not alone in exaggerating enemy numbers and writers have been wrong in viewing McClellan in isolation. Fremont, Rosecrans, Buell, Sherman, and later Hooker, all overplayed rebel strength. Although it is likely that some of these used false statistics as a shield to avoid action that might reveal incompetence, it is doubtful that all did. Rather, poor intelligence work fitted their preconception of a forewarned and armed South. McClellan was part of a larger pattern.[17]

Of course, rationally speaking, even McClellan should have realized, at the latest by Antietam, that whatever advantage the South had won by preparation was now lost as the greater productive capacity of the North came into play. But thinking on the South was not rational, if by the latter word we mean a process by which conclusions are drawn from observed and verifiable fact. The concept of a martial South, while it contained some truth, involved stereotyping the South and North: the one as warlike, the other as lacking in many virtues. This simplification of reality presumably allowed McClellan to go on thinking that he faced a gigantic enemy army. McClellan's background must not be forgotten here. Son of a professional man—a distinguished surgeon—he was of the old Northern upper class: a product of wealth and culture. Along with a taste for fine china went a certain social snobbery. McClellan was the kind of man who might believe in the military superiority of a supposedly aristocratic South.[18]

Some clues as to McClellan's view of the South are again provided by his autobiographical narrative, *McClellan's Own Story*, which contains some remarks on the peculiar adaptability of slaveholding societies to the conditions of war. Thus, in partial explanation of why he felt the rebels had more good junior officers at the beginning of the war and why Southern troops were better disciplined, the general argued that the slaveholders formed an aristocracy "to whom the poor whites were, as a rule, accustomed to defer." Hence, the two classes experienced little trouble in slotting into their wartime roles as officers and privates. "Discipline was thus very easily established among them." In the North, on the other hand, the officers were not always "intelligent gentlemen; . . . and in these cases the establishment of discipline presented far greater difficulties." The assumption here is that gentlemen are necessary for the molding of an army and that the South has more of them.[19]

There is also some contemporary evidence that McClellan distrusted the reliability of his own men. Such was the opinion of Adam Gurowski who met McClellan in October of 1861. Gurowski was perhaps not the best judge of men but his opinion was supported by such officers as Philip Kearny and General Thomas W. Hyde, whose considered assessment of McClellan was that he "never appreciated until too late what manner of people he had with him."[20]

In McClellan's own writings there is revealed the typical distaste of the professional for the capacity of the volunteer soldier. He wrote during a Mexican War campaign, "I have seen enough on this march to convince me that Volunteers and Volunteer Generals won't do." Apparently, his opinion had not entirely changed by the time he took over command of the troops around Washington in July of 1861. He set about building an army which would be as near as possible to the professional pattern. And occasionally he divulged that lack of confidence in his men which Gurowski remarked upon. On August 16, 1861, for example, he said that if the rebels attacked him he could probably drive them off if, he added in qualification, "my men will only fight."[21]

To some extent, McClellan's fears about the reliability of his troops were justified. He was correct in saying that among some regiments good material was spoiled by poor junior officers. It was also, as he said later, true that when he came to Washington part of the army was demoralized and lacking in discipline. Yet it never seems to have occurred to the general that the enemy might suffer from the same problems. When McClellan spoke of the deficiencies of volunteer troops he meant not all volunteers but Northern volunteers. The enemy were always "well drilled and equipped." The reason is clear: to a man of McClellan's class and background, the South, defined as an aristocracy, would naturally have a better disciplined and more effective army than the democratic North where individual rights were allowed to get in the way of military priorities.[22]

But, for McClellan, the military weakness of a democracy at war was demonstrated most critically not at the level of the private soldier but at the highest rank: the civilian leadership. It is well known that McClellan had unbounded contempt for his civilian superior, President Lincoln, and for the secretary of war, Edwin M. Stanton. Partly, this lack of respect must have been an outgrowth of the general's belief in rebel preparation. Lincoln did not share this belief and McClellan, like Sherman, must have felt intensely frustrated by his inability to convey to his

chief his own vision of mighty rebel power and the need for colossal con-
centrations of men and material to destroy that power. On a day when he
claimed that the enemy had three to four times his strength, McClellan
also wrote that the "incapables" around him could not grasp the position.
"They sit on the verge of the precipice, and cannot realize what they see.
Their reply to everything is 'Impossible!' They think nothing possible
which is against their wishes."[23]

McClellan's view of the administration as incompetent was helped
by Stanton's blunder in stopping recruiting just as McClellan was embarking on his Peninsula campaign. But even without this mistake, Mc-
Clellan would not have listened to the civilians. Lincoln's pleas that he
had given the general more than enough resources to do the job fell on
deaf ears. For Lincoln was the social inferior and McClellan made it
plain he did not respect those who were not gentlemen. The famous
snub of the President, when McClellan went to bed knowing that Lincoln
was waiting to see him, is only one graphic example of the general's attitude. We now know that Lincoln gave McClellan a tremendous material
advantage over the Confederates but to the general it remained incon-
ceivable that an uncouth fellow like Lincoln could field a better team than
the gentlemen of the South. This is why McClellan never explained his
error on numbers: he remained sure until the end that the administration
could not possibly have done what they did. They were not intelligent
gentlemen.[24]

McClellan consistently underrated the resources of his own side. This
can best be explained by speculating that McClellan believed the South
had been better prepared for war and, beyond that, the South was more
capable of waging war because the rebels were governed by gentlemen
and their armies led by them. The North, governed by a common man
and, in McClellan's view, holding to democratic tenets that interfered
with strictly military considerations must, he felt, be weaker. There was
much inaccuracy in all this. Lincoln is now seen as a great war leader.
The South never managed the efficiency postulated by McClellan: one of
Lee's constant problems was to supply his men, who were always outnumbered by McClellan's. And the South may have suffered from democracy more than the North, for junior officers continued to be elected by
the ranks—a procedure that did not make for good discipline—after the
North had given up the practice.[25]

McClellan saw in the South what he would have liked the North to
be: it was an image of the ideal. In so stereotyping the two sides he gave
his opponents the psychological advantage. They used this against him.
For example, for some time in 1861 the rebels maintained an advanced

post at Munson's Hill, which overlooked the Union lines. McClellan was convinced the fortifications were too strong to assault with safety. When the rebels withdrew it was found that their supposedly formidable works were armed with Quaker guns, logs painted black to resemble cannon. The Confederate generals had taken the measure of the man they contemptuously referred to as "George" and the "redoubtable McC." Knowing they had the mastery of him, they foisted Quaker guns on him again at Manassas. These are minor examples. The main point is that McClellan never won a significant offensive victory.[26]

McClellan enjoyed military command during a period that was critical for Northern self-esteem. The first battle of Bull Run had greatly encouraged the martial reputation of the South. On the man who took over from McDowell rested the awesome responsibility of preventing this reputation from growing any further; he must destroy it if possible. McClellan failed. When he left his command the Army of Northern Virginia and its generals had assumed legendary proportions in Northern eyes. In the month that McClellan was fired, the *Cincinnati Gazette* noted that he "has given the rebel Confederacy the prestige of military success, and has subjected the national Government, and the section which stands by it, to the appearance of military impotence." This was the real damage done by McClellan: the soldiers and the people would feel inferior long after he was gone.[27]

The justice of the *Gazette's* indictment can be gauged from the tenor of some newspaper articles which appeared around this time. One was the report of an address delivered during October by the Reverend Henry W. Bellows at a Unitarian conference in New York. Bellows was President of the Sanitary Commission and a conservative gentleman of good connections. He was the kind of man for whom the defeats of 1862 would have solemn significance. Southerners, he was reported as saying, were a charming breed with "a chivalric spirit and manners." They were an aristocratic people who possessed "a certain in-bred habit of command; a contempt for life in defense of honor or class; a talent for political life, and an easy control of inferiors." The very real heroism they had shown in the war "must have increased the respect felt by the North for the South. Its miraculous resources, the bravery of its troops, their patience under hardships, . . . and the courage they have shown in threatening again and again our capital, and even our interior, cannot fail to extort an unwilling admiration and respect."[28]

Bellows said later that he made the address to impress on the public mind the magnitude of the North's task and the need to enlist all energies in the cause. His aristocratic friend, George Strong, agreed that "He said much that was good, valuable, and new (to the public, at least)," but he was skeptical as to the wisdom of Bellows' timing. And for good reason. The address brought down a storm of abuse on the minister's head. The Washington *National Republican* commented that Bellows had fallen into the common error of conceding that Southerners belonged to a superior race. The large preponderance of them, said the paper, were in fact blustering, bragging, brutal, and barbarous. Yet the *Republican*, interestingly, felt obliged to accept that the rebels did have courage, "a sort of commendable desperation in fight," and ended by saying that Northerners could take pride in the fact that their enemies were Americans.[29]

Despite the avowed purpose of scolding Bellows, a reluctant respect for the Southern soldier came out. About a month later the paper further compromised its position by an article lauding the "courage and constancy" of Virginia in the war. "No people, with so few numbers, ever put into the field, and kept there so long, troops more numerous, brave, or more efficient, or produced generals of more merit, in all the kinds and grades of military talent," said the article.[30]

McClellan's contribution to Southern prestige in the North is easily stated. He was given a huge and splendidly equipped army, which he handled so clumsily as to make the military machine look impotent. His March move on Manassas gave the army nothing but a set of Quaker guns. McClellan looked foolish. Secretary Bates wrote mockingly that it was uncivil of the rebels to leave without warning McClellan, for they left the general to advance " 'with fainting steps and slow' from one deserted entrenchment to another."[31]

More serious was the failure of the Peninsula campaign. McClellan had acted so haltingly that he made his enemies look brilliant, even when they often were not. At times Jackson had lacked his usual energy, rebel coordination had been poor, and Lee made a number of questionable moves, including the assault at Malvern Hill. But he had achieved something, his opponent had not. Defeat appeared to be becoming the norm in Virginia. "The energy and military science of the South have proved superior to ours now as generally heretofore," wrote Willoughby Babcock, the military governor of Pensacola, Florida. And General Philip Kearny wrote, in a letter which was to be much quoted in the North, that people deceived themselves who thought such failures isolated episodes. The Southerners were a Spartan race and the North must reckon with the fact.[32]

The Antietam campaign again redounded to the credit of the rebels. Lee split his force in what should have been a fatal gamble but McClellan's failure to capitalize on the situation made foolhardiness look like genius. Jackson's swift march from Harper's Ferry to rejoin Lee so contrasted with the dull movements of the Union soldiers that the fundamental virility of Northern manhood was brought into question. How was it, the *New York Daily Tribune* had asked at the beginning of the campaign, that the poorly armed, clad, and fed rebels marched 25 miles a day and fought desperately while Northern regiments did not march at all until fully equipped? The real reason was that McClellan dawdled until every detail was taken care of. But this was not entirely clear to a Northern public, which saw only the difference in performance. These Northern soldiers, concluded the *Tribune,* "will hardly be a match, whether at fighting or running, for Stonewall Jackson's gaunt and ragged levies."[33]

McClellan's slowness had some positive consequence in bringing on emancipation. But it also made Union men cease to believe in their soldiers. Perhaps worst of all was the business of the cavalry. Twice during the McClellan period J. E. B. Stuart rode around the Union army and got away with it. The raids damaged the pride of the soldiers, especially the cavalry. Equally important, they drove home to Northerners the idea that the South was a society of chivalric gentleman soldiers, the successors of the Cavaliers who fought under dashing Prince Rupert, men born not to work but to ride and fight. "Thus far in the contest," said E. H. Derby in the *Atlantic Monthly* for October, the month of Stuart's second raid, "the South has possessed one great advantage. The planter's son, reared to no profession, in a region where the pursuits of trade and the mechanic arts have little honor, has been accustomed from childhood to the use of the horse and rifle."[34]

In fact, there was a reason for rebel superiority in the saddle which was closer to home than the Southern plantation. Stuart's soldiers formed one corps and were used to working with each other. McClellan's cavalry were not. Regiments were broken up to form details for use as orderlies and infantry pickets. So that many of the men who tried to catch Stuart were not used to riding together and lacked the rebel esprit. Because of this error in structure Fairfax Downey, a student of the cavalry war, calls McClellan "the evil genius" of the mounted arm.[35]

Of course, McClellan was not alone responsible for the growth of rebel prestige in 1862. If he had been it would have been easier for Northerners to dismiss his failures as the isolated errors of one man. But the other generals in Virginia had been equally unlucky. It was not McClellan but the generals in the Valley who in May fought a campaign which helped make Jackson into a legend. Secretary Bates noted then, "It is shamefully true that the enemy's officers are vastly superior to ours in boldness, enterprise and skill."[36]

A glimpse of the damage done to morale by the Valley fighting is provided in the diary of David Hunter Strother, a Union officer from Virginia. He entered 1862 on an optimistic note. In March he wrote that the Virginians were "a decadent race. They have certainly gone down in manners, morals, and mental capacity." Riding over captured rebel works at Winchester he felt humiliated as a Virginian "to see such wretched exhibitions of engineering from my own people." But by May his emotion had turned to disgust at Union efforts in the Shenandoah. He noted a bad feeling among the men, "discouragement and a sense of inferiority which will tell unfavorably if they get into action."[37]

Jackson improved his reputation during July and August against Pope so that Adam Gurowski felt justified in saying, "Jackson is already the legendary hero, and deserves to be." Much the same was true of Lee. "I am lost in wonder, too, at the generalship, the daring and endurance of the Southern army," wrote one woman after Pope's defeat. "We have no generals with heads on their shoulders, and God alone can save the Republic" said James Fowler Rusling, an officer in the 5th New Jersey Volunteers.[38]

The fact that Pope, whom the government brought in to replace McClellan, got thrashed worse than his rival ever did was ultimately unfortunate for the Army of the Potomac. For it gave credence to a belief in that army that McClellan was the best general the Union had. As their hero only fought defensively, this was tantamount to saying that outright victory over Lee was impossible. This was to be the legacy of McClellan: long after he was gone his army would fight to survive, not to win.

That McClellan had tremendous charisma cannot be disputed. He cared sincerely for the welfare of his men and they adored him for it. Unhappily, this adulation included acceptance of McClellan's belief that the army faced a much stronger foe. That the army agreed with the commander's view of things was apparent as early as the Manassas fiasco in March of 1862. There was a clear difference in tone between the disgusted comments of civilians about the results of the expedition and the complacent remarks made by soldiers. Major Thomas W. Hyde of the 7th Maine wrote, "We expect to be in Richmond in a fortnight." And

Colonel Alexander Hays of the 63d Pennsylvania wrote somewhat later that the army looked "grand and sublimely so . . . I never was so proud of my country and countrymen."[39]

Even when the Peninsula campaign ended in defeat the soldiers did not feel that the army had failed. Had they not fought a more powerful foe and escaped annihilation, as the general said? It was only when the army was ordered north to join Pope that morale began to drop. After Second Bull Run "some, for the first time, began to regard our cause as a losing one," recalled Warren Lee Goss, a private soldier. "Most of the soldiers believed the Confederate armies were more ably commanded than our own." The troops were desperate to have McClellan back. "Could the reader have seen," said General Oliver Otis Howard in defense of Lincoln's recalling of McClellan, "the Union army with broken ranks and haggard looks come straggling and discouraged to the protection of the encircling forts of Washington, he would have realized the crisis." The Antietam campaign did not shake the army's faith in "little Mac."[40]

The most dangerous feature of the implicit belief in McClellan was that it profoundly influenced the senior officers, who were the nervous system of the army, giving it life and tone. With few exceptions, like Hooker and Kearny, the officers accepted McClellan at his own estimate, swallowing whole the idea that the rebels outnumbered them. General Jacob Dolson Cox, who became after the war one of McClellan's most bitter critics, confessed that at the time, "I shared, more or less fully, the opinions of those among whom I was. I accepted McClellan as the best authority in regard to the enemy's numbers" and hence saw the general's slowness as reasonable prudence.[41]

A good idea of the views held by officers close to McClellan can be gained from the work of a Frenchman. The Prince de Joinville joined the Union army in September of 1861. He and his nephews, who served on McClellan's staff, were part of the intimate circle at headquarters. The relationship must have shaped Joinville's view of the war. In a book on his experiences published in 1863 Joinville developed an argument of Southern advantage which parallels the view we have reconstructed from McClellan's writings. The argument, we may assume, was the popular one at headquarters.

The rebels, said Joinville, had been ready for war while the Union had not. Southerners "had created a permanent militia, ready to march at the first signal" and "special schools . . . to form a race of soldiers." West Point had been packed with Southern men while martial pursuits had been neglected in the North where "the career of arms was looked upon as that of an idler." As a result the North had entered the war upon an unequal footing and had lost at Bull Run because "the South has the warriors, the arms, the organization, the will and the passion."[42]

After Bull Run, the Union went to work to create an army but because Northerners did not esteem professional soldiers they created a force of volunteers, "an ephemeral army, comparatively inefficient, and above all, ruinously expensive." The volunteers were ignorant of the military art and they had no discipline. This was the unpromising material McClellan had to work with. The unreliability of the volunteers, thought Joinville, went far toward explaining the army's apparent slowness. Commanders could not trust their men to obey them and "hence, hesitation, and with it conditions unfavorable to any dashing enterprise."[43]

But did not the South have the same problem? As usual with such apologies for Northern slowness, the rebels were seen as experiencing far fewer difficulties. To help him create an army, said Joinville, Jefferson Davis had the cream of the national army's staff. Also, the South could call upon its planters, who were used to enforcing discipline, to fill the junior officer positions. And Davis, noted Joinville, had abandoned the volunteer system in favor of conscription. Thus Joinville removed responsibility for failure from the shoulders of Union generals at the expense of arguing that Northern soldiers were inferior. The argument was a familiar one around McClellan.[44]

McClellan cannot be held entirely responsible for the views of his subordinates. To some degree his preconceptions simply coincided with theirs. But a commander is ultimately responsible for his army's estimate of itself. By arguing that he always faced huge odds McClellan retained his popularity with the troops: failures were not attributed directly to him; there was always some other force too powerful to have been overcome. But in understating the strength of his army, McClellan gave it an unworthy definition of success: avoiding outright defeat became an accomplishment. Perhaps the shrewdest comment on McClellan's moral failure as a leader was made by General Cox who wrote of McClellan, "The general who indoctrinates his army with the belief that it is required by its government to do the impossible, may preserve his popularity with the troops and be received with cheers as he rides down the line, but he has put any great military success far beyond his reach."[45]

6

Desperate Measures
The Politics of War in 1862

More than thirty years later I heard a retired
officer of the regular army who, in 1862, occupied
a staff position in the Army of the Potomac, assert
positively that he knew of a conspiracy then on
foot in that army, the object of which was to resist
and balk the policy of the government.

> —CARL SCHURZ, *The*
> *Reminiscences of Carl*
> *Schurz, 1853–63*

The order depriving me of the command
created an immense deal of deep feeling in the
army—so much so that many were in favor of my
refusing to obey the order, and of marching upon
Washington to take possession of the government.

> —GEORGE B. MCCLELLAN,
> *McClellan's Own Story*

By the summer of 1862 there was a great deal of desperation in the North. The "great experiment" it seemed, was about to fail. Thus, on July 3, John Beatty, a Northern volunteer serving in Alabama, asked, "Shall we hail the Fourth as the birthday of a great nation, or weep over it as the beginning of a political enterprise that resulted in dissolution, anarchy, and ruin." Some eleven weeks later, Lincoln issued the Preliminary Emancipation Proclamation. It was, as a recent scholar puts it, "a rather frantic measure, an act of last resort." Shortly thereafter, he took another grave step by removing McClellan from command of the Army of the Potomac.[1]

Partly responsible for this crisis mentality was the military situation. Perhaps people exaggerated the extent of their troubles here, for in the west Union troops had made notable advances. Federal forces attempting to drive a wedge through the Confederacy had control of the Mississippi above Vicksburg by June. Earlier, in April, a Union fleet had forced the surrender of New Orleans at the mouth of the river and two months later it steamed north to join Grant at Vicksburg. The capture of this citadel was still a year away but at least there was the possibility of victory.

But in Virginia things had gone badly and it was this that Northerners could not bear. For many of them, Virginia was always central in their view of the war for it seemed to most truly represent the Cavalier ideal. They felt it was here that they must ultimately prove that they could whip the gentlemen of the South and, so long as it held out, the South seemed to have a good chance of winning the war. The failure of McClellan's Peninsula campaign had been greeted with disappointment, which turned to despair after the humiliating defeat of Pope. McClellan had saved the North at Antietam, but it was not enough. In a year of slow generals he was the slowest and he let Lee get away.

Thus, while the situation was, realistically, by no means beyond salvage, it seemed desperate to many watching Virginia. This military crisis brought on another, a crisis of conscience. As military tensions rose, the deep philosophical divisions over the proper nature of the American republic, which had been simmering for decades, came to a head. That part of the struggle between the radical anti-slavery camp on the one hand,

105

and the conservative-republic men on the other will be examined here. Both groups felt America had taken a wrong turn but their answers to the problem were diametrically opposed. To radicals, slow generals and beaten troops were symptomatic of the deep moral rot in the North: of the triumph of pro-slavery principles in the hearts of men. To combat the apparently greater conviction of the rebels, they pleaded for emancipation to give the North a dynamic moral incentive. To conservatives, emancipation was horrifying—it might cause race war, it could drive the South into undying resistance and, perhaps worst of all, it was a revolutionary attack on the status quo. Conservative anger was intensified by a belief that the Lincoln administration was siding with the radicals and was trying to ruin McClellan, the conservative hero. Faced by these seeming challenges, conservatives talked of counterrevolution. Most serious were the threats issued by officers close to McClellan. Usually, these have been dismissed as camp-fire bitching typical of soldiers, a view that involves two errors. First, the soldiers' anger was deeply felt and should not be taken lightly. Second, they spoke not only as military men but as conservatives; as such, their ideas have much wider significance.

When the dust of conflict finally settled after the removal of Mc-Clellan, the conservatives had not resorted to force to impose their view of America. This does not mean that there might not have been an attempt to make McCellan a dictator had the general sanctioned the attempt. Anyway, the real significance does not lie in the question of whether a coup was possible, but in the attitudes revealed by both sides in the political war. Conservatives showed a deep alienation from the political process and a remarkable willingness to contemplate destruction of the supposedly sacrosanct republican structure. Radicals revealed a similar lack of attachment to the American fabric through their contempt for the idea of Union as a war aim. Finally, there is some significance in the fact that from a military point of view both sides wasted much energy in a struggle that proved barren of real results. Radical faith in the military potency of emancipation was misplaced. While the Proclamation was a moral advance, it did not give the expected punch to Union armies.

The originality of Alexis de Tocqueville's *Democracy in America* has often been overstated. The famous comments on the tyranny of a majority and the threat to liberty posed by equality were reiterations of sentiments in common currency among gentlemen of property and standing throughout America. For this was the age of Jackson and of deep concern among the better people over the rumblings of great social change. Undoubtedly, Tocqueville gained the idea of majority tyranny from these people and then documented it with personal experience. His relationship with the rich and well born was an intimate one. To a stranger and a Frenchman, they were willing to concede their secret dislike for the ignorance of a democratic people. Tocqueville warned, from his knowledge of them, "that the rich have a hearty dislike of the democratic institutions of their country. The people form a power which they at once fear and despise. If the maladministration of the democracy ever brings about a revolutionary crisis, and monarchical institutions ever become practicable in the United States, the truth of what I advance will become obvious."[2]

The crisis came with civil war and the conservative coup envisioned by Tocqueville appeared to be a strong possibility by the fall of 1861. Conservatives were beginning to talk of a military dictatorship. Why should this have been? Behind the general dislike of democratic doings stood some more concrete reasons for conservative dissatisfaction. It will be recalled that the firing on Fort Sumter had united men of widely differing political philosophies behind the government. But this alliance was fragile: welded in emotional heat it could not stand the strain of defeat and the disappointing months of inactivity in the autumn of the year.

Much conservative concern focused on the Lincoln administration. Gentlemen had been able to put behind them Lincoln's humble origins, his uncouthness, and his apparent status as a hack party politician for a short while after Sumter. The President's manly and patriotic call for troops inspired admiration. But as the year wore on contempt grew for a man who appeared to spend more time filling places than planning victories. Typical was a comment in the *North American Review* that the North suffered because "there remain to us few or no men of the first rank, whether in political or military life." The corruption that people had long felt was eating at the roots of American life appeared to be at work in the cabinet. By late 1861 it was clear that Simon Cameron, Lincoln's first secretary of war, had allowed men close to him to practice graft in awarding government contracts. More revelations of venality came early in 1862. The administration, it seemed, might be a stumbling block to Union success. "The most dangerous symptom in our condition now, as for many years past, is the want of a high moral tone," said *Harper's Weekly*.[3]

As if this were not enough to make gentlemen of extreme views consider whether Lincoln could be allowed to remain in the White House, there was some suspicion that Lincoln was moving toward the radical position on slavery. (There is some irony here in that, while Lincoln's ability to appear all things to all men helped him manoeuver politically, it made him extremely unpopular with both left and right. The radicals thought he was soft on slavery.) The idea of attacking slavery troubled conservatives for a number of reasons. To soldiers like General Meade it had practical drawbacks, for it "will forbid any hope of the Southerners yielding so long as there is any power of resistance left in them." The loss of ground for a compromise peace also troubled ex-President Buchanan, who even objected to the renaming of Fort Calhoun as Fort Wool because it would "exasperate the people of the Cotton States."[4]

In addition to alienation of the South, emancipation posed the problem of constitutionality. And, in a less tangible sense, it threatened what was left of rank and social discipline in America. If the slaves were declared free, they might rise up in rebellion, raping and killing. Even if they did not, they would ultimately demand civil rights, perhaps even social equality. And, of course, the planters would lose the investment in their chattel. Thus emancipation would assault the very cornerstones of conservative faith: property rights and social position.

The radicals had the better part of the moral argument, but their opponents were right in sensing that they placed a low priority on social stability. They rejected the established institutions that did not work for their ends. By the fall of 1861 some were admitting openly that they would not long support a war fought only for the Union and for the status quo on slavery. Congressman Sedgwick of New York allegedly told the rebel agent, Mrs. Rose O'Neal Greenhow, "that he did not care a rush for the flag" and that if "he thought that by this war the old Union could be restored, with its constitutional guarantees for slavery, that he would not vote a dollar or a man." The strain of supporting a war fought only for the Union was perhaps worst on those who were not only anti-slavery but who had been pacifists before the conflict. Such were Horace Greeley and Charles Sumner. As the casualty lists increased, so did the pull of conscience. These men had to have a higher purpose for the war than the preservation of the slaveholders' status quo.[5]

In finding the means to their own salvation, it appeared to the opponents of slavery that they had also discovered the key to putting life in the slow-moving Union war machine. One problem seemed to be a lack of spirit. This was suggested by Generals Meigs and McDowell when they testified in December before the radical-dominated Committee on the Conduct of the War. Perhaps the North was losing because of a spiritual deficit: it lacked inspiration. To defeat the rebels, said Charles Sumner, "something more is needed than men or money. Our battalions must be reinforced by ideas." The North must define what the South was fighting for and oppose it "by a force superior to its own." Slavery, thought Sumner, "is the ruling idea of this rebellion. It is slavery that marshals these hosts and breathes into their embattled ranks its own barbarous fire." A blow must therefore be struck at this "mainspring." The North should proclaim freedom.[6]

There were some strong points in favor of emancipation. Morally, it would pay off a debt owed the blacks since the birth of the nation. It might also have importance as a diplomatic tool in keeping Britain and France out of the war. And radicals were right in contending that by no means everyone was inspired by the war aim of Union. Nathaniel Hawthorne, for example, had confessed in May of 1861, "I don't quite understand what we are fighting for, or what definite result can be expected." General Buell admitted that he was not sure what the war was about. The problem was a particularly vexing one for soldiers like Buell, who had to deal with such unclear issues as the status of runaway slaves. Perhaps by declaring that the war was fought for freedom some might see a more clear and pure purpose in the fight. On the other hand, the radicals ran the danger of alienating as many people as they might draw into full support of the war effort.[7]

In fact, as a direct aid to the troops in the field, emancipation was not that potent for it ignored some practical realities of the rebellion. For example, it cannot be doubted that back of some emancipation talk was the belief that on hearing of their freedom many slaves would revolt or would at least throw down tools, hamstringing the rebel economy. This was an assumption based on an unrealistic view of the black, who was rarefied into a self-sacrificing being who would accept certain destruction to aid his white saviors. The real slaves, having the normal amount of courage and common sense, knowing that they were without arms or organized leadership, waited for a sensible opportunity such as the arrival of Union soldiers before deserting the rebel cause. Then they left with or without Northern permission.[8]

The limitation of radical assumptions was also demonstrated in their approach to the selection of generals. Concentrating on the war as one almost entirely of ideas, they distrusted the loyalty and competence of any officer who was not anti-slavery. Unable to forget the soldiers of the pre-war period who had fought in Mexico and returned fugitive slaves, they insisted on moral rectitude as a military qualification. In doing this they made some tragic mistakes but they were often right in hounding conserva-tive generals who were a liability to the Union cause, timid soldiers who doubted the rightness of the Union cause or who put more faith in the rebel army than in their own.

But it did not follow from this that all radical officers would make good generals. Fremont, Butler, and Burnside are cases in point. The essential flaw here was in placing all the emphasis on moral fervor. For, in this single-minded approach, the possibility of other significant factors in the makeup of a winning general was lost sight of. For example, Grant was not fervently anti-slavery but he won battles. In his case, as in Lincoln's, the key point could be that he saw no especial merit in being born a gentleman and hence did not stand in awe of people like Lee. In any case, the quality of fervent moral fire was missing.[9]

To understand this narrowness of view, we must recall the direction of much antebellum reform. Some people had gone into reform because, like their conservative opponents, they rejected participation in rowdy democratic politics. They turned from the active running of affairs to moral persuasion as a medium for change. Their achievement reflected the choice: they were good propagandists but poor group workers. This stress on moral change was a legacy that dogged them in the war and made them back officers with high morals but poor plans.[10]

In their own way, the radicals were as trapped by inferiority feelings as were their conservative opponents. Men like Wendell Phillips had al-ways believed that Southerners showed greater attachment to principle than did Northerners. Now, by again holding up the public spirit of the rebels as an example, they were arguing that the North must copy the South to win. This was a psychological error. The winning general would be one who felt that the North could win as she was and on her own terms—not after some hypothetical moral revolution.

Conservatives who contemplated a coup most frequently cast George B. McClellan in the role of leader to replace Lincoln. He was the obvious choice. Known to be a conservative, he wished a war for "the Constitution as it is, the Union as it was." He was a gentleman of good background who patently was not afraid to snub the commoner Lincoln. Finally, and of great importance, he was a charismatic soldier whose popularity with the troops might be sufficient to win their support for the new regime and guarantee its stability. Thus, from the time he arrived in Washington, McClellan received intimations that he should make himself dictator.[11]

Word that a dictatorship was in the air quickly got around. A writer for the *North American Review*, undoubtedly troubled by the close proximity of McClellan's vast army to Washington, pleaded against "man-worship," which "was the ruin of ancient republics, and has brought our own to the brink of dissolution." Inevitably, those hottest on the trail of dictatorship rumors were radicals. When McClellan first came to Washington, they were charmed by the confident young general. But his prolonged inactivity came to look increasingly evil. Was he dragging his heels to avoid inflicting a total defeat on the South? Did he want a compromise peace to save slavery? Was he trying to discredit Lincoln and force him out? It was whispered that McClellan was a traitor; that he had been offered a military command by the Confederates; and that he was a Knight of the Golden Circle (a largely fictitious secret organization thought to be working for Southern independence). The accusations got as far as Lincoln, who on March 8, 1862, confronted McClellan with the rumors about his "traitorous intent."[12]

A vicious spiral of fear and suspicion between conservative and radical was initiated. The more radicals hounded McClellan, the more convinced were his supporters that here were evil men bent on destroying the American fabric. Were they not hamstringing the North's best general, just because he was not anti-slavery and might win a victory before emancipation? And the more conservatives rallied around McClellan, the more frightened of a conservative revolution did radicals become. The only person who could have lowered the passion was McClellan who, taking a nonpartisan stand, could have flatly rejected the idea of dictatorship. But he did not.

McClellan was fascinated by the idea of himself as man on horseback. On August 9, 1861, he wrote to his wife, "I have letter after letter, have conversation after conversation, calling on me to save the nation, alluding to the presidency, dictatorship, etc." The general went on to say, "I have no such aspiration," but in the next sentence admitted, "I would cheerfully take the dictatorship and lay down my life when the country is saved." A reliable source reported that in the same period McClellan was riding with General McCall and said to him, "I understand there is a good deal of talk of making a dictatorship," adding, "It's me they're talking of."[13]

It was possible that things would quiet down once McClellan left the capital early in 1862. Away from Washington's atmosphere of intrigue, the general might have been expected to think less about political schemes. For their part, the radicals might be less suspicious of McClellan now that he was finally on the road to Richmond. However, developments did not follow this pattern. Critics did leave McClellan alone for a while at the beginning of the Peninsula campaign, waiting to see how he would perform. But as his chronic slowness became apparent, the suspicions about his motives were revived. Was he not dragging his feet to ruin the government, or worse, the nation?

There was some real justification for attacking McClellan's competence and his faith in democratic values. But as is usual with the charges made by fear-ridden men, the valid concern voiced by radicals degenerated at times into hysterical absurdity. Some people were convinced that anything McClellan did must have sinister intention. Thus, when the general, out of "respect for the memory of the greatest man our country has produced," stopped soldiers occupying and possibly damaging a house that had been the "residence of Mrs. Custis when she was married to Washington," he was accused of deliberately sheltering the property of Robert E. Lee, whose family owned the estate.[14]

McClellan was not the man to shrug off such attacks as the inevitable burden of high office. He lived in a state of bitter indignation. He was sure that the radicals were bent on undermining his position to prevent a military victory before emancipation. And he believed that the administration was involved in the attempt. It was said in the last chapter that McClellan always believed he faced an overwhelmingly superior foe. He was not able to convince his civilian superiors of this. Indeed, Stanton actually stopped recruiting at the beginning of McClellan's campaign. The general was left to conclude that the top men were either immensely stupid or evil. He increasingly favored the latter interpretation. Thus, on June 22, 1862, he wrote to his wife that though he was outnumbered he would still succeed, "notwithstanding all they do and leave undone in Washington to prevent it. I would not have on my conscience what those men have for all the world."[15]

What is interesting about this business is McClellan's behavior in the circumstances. Given his impression that enemies in the rear awaited only the opportunity to ruin him, the logical course was to act with absolute correctness in all public affairs. Yet he showed a cavalier disregard for proper form and conduct. For example, though he claimed to "have the proof that the secretary [Stanton] reads all my private telegrams" and probably also his letters home, he did not modify his very abusive private statements, referring in one message to the people in the capital as "a mighty trifling set." At another time, letters from a prominent Democrat advising McClellan to ignore the administration were withheld until they could be delivered by an officer who was trusted to discreetly point out the gravity of their content. After talking with the officer, McClellan thanked him for his good sense, adding that if he had received the letters promptly "he would have felt compelled to make some reply that would probably have placed him in a false position."[16]

That McClellan needed coaching in the responsibilities of his position is significant. For much of the time he wrote and sometimes acted as though he were above the usual restrictions of high office. He spoke contemptuously of his superiors and others who opposed him, he smiled on those who spoke treason. It would be foolish to see these things simply as personal failings, for others around McClellan acted in the same way. What we see in his case is an outcropping of that contempt for the democratic structure and the people who manned it which was central to conservative alienation from American life. This is not to say that all the old elite would have endorsed his attitudes. Some would not have lowered their dignity to attack Lincoln and his colleagues; many were too responsible to play with treason. McClellan's was an extreme case, the result of natural arrogance and high military position. But the differences were of degree rather than of kind. In his anger at the radicals, the bringers of change, and in his contempt for the democracy and its right to make demands upon him, McClellan typified gentlemen of the old school. It should not be forgotten that he was a hero to many of them.

McClellan's feelings affected those around him. A charismatic man, he had the trust of the soldiers. When he cast himself as the disinterested patriot hounded by evil men, they naturally believed him. Men who did not share his philosophy or dreams of personal glory were still angered by the more ridiculous charges leveled against the commander. In April 1862, General John Sedgwick wrote, "The vile slanders that are daily promulgated in Washington against our best officers are enough to disgust all decent persons and take away all the zeal we have in the cause."[17]

The identification with McClellan was strongest among those who were physically and spiritually closest to him. The general's arrogance was shared by them: within his charmed circle they talked and acted irresponsibly. On McClellan's staff was George Armstrong Custer, a young West Pointer and admirer of the general. Custer was one of those people who saw much of value in Southern culture. As a cadet he had read novels that romanticized Southern plantation life. His friends had been Southern and he had detested the Republicans as fanatics endangering the Union. He stayed with the flag in 1861, but he did not forget his Southern friends. When the Army of the Potomac captured James Washington, a rebel officer and an old acquaintance, Custer posed with him for a photograph that included Washington's slave boy, sitting at their feet. On another occasion, Custer spent a convivial evening singing around the piano with a party of avowed rebel women. The actions seem innocent enough. Many regulars had formed attachments across the lines that survived into the war. At about the same time as the photograph incident, George Edward Pickett was writing from the rebel camp, "You cannot understand the *entente cordiale* between us 'old fellows.'" But the point is that as aide-de-camp to McClellan, Custer was in a delicate position. His actions would adversely affect his chief, who was already thought to be overly sympathetic to the South. In acting as he did, Custer showed a supercilious disregard for Northern public opinion.[18]

Equally rash was an older man and another friend of McClellan, General Fitz-John Porter. From a celebrated military family, Porter was something of a snob, like his chief. Deeply attached to McClellan, Porter shared his view that Lincoln and the radicals were trying to ruin him in order to prolong the war until slavery was destroyed. He made no secret of his reaction, saying, "We are tired of this war," and that he wished "this army was in Washington to rid us of incumbents ruining our country." Porter would shortly pay for his disloyalty, for he would be cashiered in the fall. Though probably not guilty of the specific charges laid against him, he had said enough to compromise his credibility.[19]

The simmering discontent McClellan allowed to develop in his army as it did in no other came to a head in the months between the end of the Peninsula campaign and the general's removal in November. In these months the Northern war effort came as close as it ever did to an internal breakdown that might have cost the Union victory. And Tocqueville's prophecy came as close as it ever did to being fulfilled.

On June 26, Lee hit Porter at Mechanicsville and a day later McClellan began to retreat down the Peninsula. By July 2 he was safely entrenched at Harrison's Landing but the campaign was over. The failure cast a deep pall over the North: it appeared that the finest army ever mustered in the country had been outfought. But the soldiers did not see it this way. Many of the generals accepted McClellan's estimate of enemy numbers and, like him, they felt they had achieved a miracle in keeping the army intact. If they blamed anyone for the defeat it was the people in Washington who, through their blunderings and machinations, had failed to give McClellan the men he wanted. Porter declared that the administration lacked "decision, energy, determination" and suggested that they might take "many lessons in military matters" from the enemy. Feeling that theirs was not the blame, many of the officers and men were not cast down by defeat. What hurt was the order to leave the Peninsula, which implied that the government was trying to hang the responsibility for failure on them; McClellan's strategy was to be abandoned.[20]

To add insult to injury, Lincoln took the further step of bringing in a western general, John Pope, to do the job in Virginia. The move seemed designed to humiliate the army and destroy McClellan because he was a conservative general. There were already strong suspicions of a radical plot. General Gouverneur Kemble Warren had written that the government deliberately failed to promote officers who believed in a "Union that leaves both North and South as they were and dishonors neither." Now Pope made two moves that seemed to offer incontrovertible evidence that his appointment was for political rather than military reasons.[21]

First, Pope issued a proclamation that appeared to reflect on the courage of the Potomac army. He scolded the army for its concern with "probable lines of retreat." He came from the west, he said, "where we have always seen the backs of our enemies; from an army whose business it has been to seek the adversary and beat him when he was found; whose policy has been attack and not defense." The piece has been derided by historians on the grounds that, as T. Harry Williams puts it, "there was a lot of military nonsense in the address" and it was "crammed with purple passages and bad rhetoric." Yet it said much that was accurate about the performance so far in Virginia. The problem was that the officers and men could not see this. They resented this boastful new man. It was said among the generals that he was a mouthpiece for the anti-slavery people who wanted to ruin McClellan's reputation as part of their plan to prevent victory on conservative terms.[22]

That Pope was being used to drive the war into a tougher, more radical phase, seemed evident from a string of orders he issued in July to his new Army of Virginia, warning that he intended to live off the Southern countryside and that he would severely punish rebellious citizens. The orders were heartily disliked by soldiers opposed to emancipation and a hard war, for they felt that such actions would lead to a contest of extermination between the two sides. General Marsena Rudolph Patrick wrote angrily that Pope's order "gives a general license to pillage, rob & plunder—It has completely demoralized my Brigade. . . . I am afraid of God's Justice, for our Rulers & Commanders deserve his wrath & curse."[23]

There was a good deal of bad feeling against Pope and the government among some of the officers shipped northward to take part in the Second Bull Run campaign. As usual, Porter expressed the total distaste of the McClellan men for the job in hand. On August 27, for example, he wrote that the enemy "have a contempt for the Army of Virginia." He intimated that he was inclined to agree with them, saying, "I wish myself away from it, with all our old Army of the Potomac, and so do our companions." On August 29 he wrote, "I hope Mac's at work and we shall soon be ordered out of this."[24]

Disaffection was now more openly expressed than in earlier months. It was as though bitter men were willing a confrontation with the Lincoln administration. An instance was recorded by General Herman Haupt, the chief of railroad transportation, who played an important part in the campaign by trying to rush troops up to the front lines as soon as they arrived from McClellan. Haupt recalled that he had a great deal of trouble with General S. Sturgis of Franklin's Corps, who tried to arrest Haupt and commandeer the railroad. When asked to cooperate for the good of the cause, he "declared 'I don't care for John Pope a pinch of owl dung!'" When cars were given Sturgis for his troops, he failed to load them and the transport was finally put to other use. Sturgis arrived too late to be of aid to Pope.[25]

If there was a lack of enthusiasm before the battle, there was a muted satisfaction after it. After the defeat Carl Schurz, a German officer, "happened to fall into the company of some brigadiers, who expressed their pleasure at Pope's discomfiture without the slightest concealment, and spoke of our government in Washington with an affectation of supercilious contempt." The feeling must have been shared by McClellan, who, on July 22, had written with evident pleasure that "the Pope bubble is likely to be suddenly collapsed. Stonewall Jackson is after him, and the young man who wanted to teach me the art of war will in less than a week either be in full retreat or badly whipped." And at one point in the campaign he suggested to Lincoln two courses of action, one of which was to "leave Pope to get out of his scrape" while all available troops were concentrated for the defense of Washington.[26]

McClellan's return to command was greeted with great joy by his veteran soldiers but the satisfaction was short-lived for some. Soon after the army fought Lee to a stop at Antietam, Lincoln issued the much feared Emancipation Proclamation. From this point to the final removal of McClellan, talk of the military taking command of the government was rife. One reporter, after speaking to army officers, warned that they might "startle the Country and give us a military Dictator." McClellan was urged to come out against the Proclamation "by politicians not only, but by army officers who were near to him." John W. Garrett, president of the Baltimore and Ohio Railroad, told General Jacob Dolson Cox, "You military men have the matter in your own hands, you have but to tell the administration what they must do, and they will not dare to disregard it."[27]

When news that McClellan was fired reached the army, some officers used equally plain language about what should be done. Colonel Charles S. Wainwright noted in his diary that when McClellan wished farewell to his officers there was great emotion, "some using expressions with regard to his removal which they had no right to use, and a few even going so far as to beg him to resist the order, and saying that the army would support him." John Gibson noted that one general called out to McClellan as he rode down the lines, "Lead us to Washington, General. We will follow you there." One of McClellan's staff claimed later that during the fall of 1862 his colleagues discussed "a plan to countermarch to Washington and intimidate the President" and there were also expressions of mutinous sentiment among common soldiers.[28]

But McClellan decided not to rest his future on the bayonets of his soldiers. He left quietly and only once more entered the arena of politics during the war—this time in the legitimate role of Democratic candidate for the presidency in 1864.

A question remains as to whether there was ever a serious possibility of some military demonstration—a mutiny or a move toward a dictatorship—against the ruling political group. Numerous comtemporaries thought there was a grave danger, especially between July and November. There was a good suspicion in Lincoln's Cabinet that McClellan was not to be trusted as early as the fall of 1861. It became a conviction during the Second Bull Run campaign, when it seemed that McClellan was inexcusably tardy in getting troops to Pope. On August 11 Lincoln became "very outspoken in regard to McC_____'s conduct. He said that it really seemed to him McC_____ wanted P_____ defeated." And on September 8 he told Gideon Welles, secretary of the navy, "We had the enemy in the hollow of our hands . . . if our generals, who are vexed with Pope, had done their duty." Welles himself had remarked on September 2 that there was a general conviction that Pope was not supported as he should have been and on the same day Secretary Chase wrote that McClellan's "omission to urge troops forward to the battles of Friday and Saturday, evinced a spirit which rendered him unworthy of trust."[29]

Lincoln was also worried that emancipation might provoke some damaging military reaction. On August 5 he told Senator Charles Sumner that he would free the slaves "if I were not afraid that half the officers would fling down their arms and three more States would rise!" The same apprehension was abroad outside the government. General Benjamin Butler's wife wrote that if the Potomac generals disapproved of the Proclamation "those who desire it are in doubt it may prove but a dead letter." When Lincoln restored McClellan to command after Pope's defeat there was naturally great consternation. *Wilkes' Spirit* warned that at the general's return "the civil liberties of this poor country passed beneath the sword, and a chaos was inaugurated, of which no mind is clear enough to see the end."[30]

Historians, viewing things with more detachment, have not seen much threat of military intervention. Their skepticism is grounded on the fact that no hard evidence exists to show that the soldiers ever got beyond talk to the stage of concrete planning. They would agree with Carl Schurz that "the foundation of all this was probably little more than mere headquarters bluster." S. E. Finer, a British student of the military in politics, notes that American officers, like the civilians around them, habitually speak out on leading issues and that this garrulousness should not be mistaken for a real desire to usurp power.[31]

In evaluating the officers' threats, the Victorian taste for dramatic posture must also be held in mind. The Byronic gesture was much in vogue. This was also a period of great French influence on taste. Women wore the latest Paris fashions. Soldiers dressed in uniforms patterned on those of the Second Empire, for the French army, not yet humiliated by Prussia, was considered the best in Europe. Napoleon I was admired by many officers: they wrote like him, tried to fight like him, and stuck their hands in their coats in imitation of him. It was perhaps natural that they should ape the man who more than any other in the modern world had made the professional soldier a prestigious figure. Thus when McClellan's friends labeled him the "young Napoleon" they may have recalled the soldier more than the political dictator. As a reviewer of a new book on the emperor put it in January of 1861, time had healed the misdeeds of which Napoleon was guilty and only the glory remained.[32]

But it is hard to believe that the soldiers were entirely mindless of Napoleon's political career: part of the man could not be divorced from the rest of him. Assuming that a man's heroes say something about him, why did not "McNapoleon," as his enemies dubbed McClellan, take as his model Washington, the solid soldier who rejected monarchical trappings, rather than the man who used the sword to gain the crown?

It would be wise not to dismiss the threat of internal upheaval entirely. We should not assume that because American democracy has survived it has never been in danger. Respect for orderly process and freedom of speech developed haltingly. Violence against the rights and persons of groups and individuals characterized the decades before the war. In politics, the right to petition Congress, to use the Federal mails, even to speak on the legislative floor, were challenged. Andrew Jackson, Abraham Lincoln, and Andrew Johnson, were all targets for assassins. Jackson, for his part, used Federal power arbitrarily: he threatened force against South Carolina but would not use it to support the treaty rights of the Indians. Lincoln moved swiftly to curtail civil rights when he deemed it necessary. And according to one recent study, many Northern intellectuals supported him in this. In Kentucky, Federal provost marshals arrested unfriendly politicians on dubious grounds: sometimes their only crime was in being Democrats. Clement L. Vallandigham of Ohio was taken into custody and finally put beyond the lines for voicing apparently legitimate opposition to the Republicans.[33]

There were also soldiers who were conservative or Copperhead. Why should they not have seriously considered dealing out the same kind of arbitrary treatment to their opponents? Moreover, we should not draw a romantic picture of the private soldier as a homely but stalwart republican who would necessarily have resisted an illegal act by his officers. In the ranks were the same manner of persons as those who lynched Mormons and abolitionists, broke up womens' rights meetings, and brawled on the streets of Northern cities for control of the local political machines. Legitimacy was not always their primary concern. One young professional officer wrote on November 12 that "If General McClellan had chosen to do so, I believe that he could have taken two-thirds of the army with him. Everyone appears to be discouraged and I believe that there are some that prefer to see this army whipped than to see it victorious with another general." This is certainly an overstatement. But it is worth bearing in mind that many of the soldiers did adore McClellan and numbers of their officers were disaffected from the government.[34]

Irrespective of desire for personal political power, some officers had, from their perspective, good reason to question whether the North could win the war under the existing political arrangements. It will be recalled that as early as 1860 an opinion became fixed in the North that the Confederates had instituted an authoritarian regime. It was thought that by this arrangement they had solved the problem of political interference in military affairs: they envisioned Jefferson Davis, a trained soldier, having dictatorial powers to decide issues strictly on their relation to the military situation without having to consider the political ramifications. In the North, on the other hand, politics seemed to intrude on every phase of the war effort. On September 4, 1862, General Sedgwick wrote, "On our part it has been a war of politicians; on theirs it has been one conducted by a despot and carried out by able Generals. I look upon a division as certain; the only question is where the line is to run."[35]

The democratic structure seemed to hinder the North in a number of ways. First, while it was assumed that the Confederate President was able to appoint generals on the strength of their military credentials alone, it was well known that Lincoln sometimes had to give army positions to civilians whose political support he needed. After Union defeats regulars often lumped much of the blame on these civilian appointees. For example, after Jackson ran roughshod over Union forces in the Shenandoah Valley during May of 1862, regulars were very bitter against nonprofessional generals like Banks. Captain William D. Wilkins, a West Pointer serving on the staff of volunteer General Alpheus S. Williams, was reported as saying that he was "disgusted at the mismanagement and mistakes of the civilians . . . who could only lead their armies to disgrace and defeat."[36]

A further problem was that Lincoln was constitutionally commander-in-chief of the armies but his professional military training, compared to that of Jefferson Davis, was insignificant. Few soldiers at this stage of the war recognized that the President had a fair grasp of military concepts. More often, they saw him as a windy civilian. Jackson's Valley campaign is a good example. To meet the rebel threat Lincoln called back some troops intended for McClellan. It appears that Lincoln wanted the men to try to trap Jackson and annihilate him. But some soldiers interpreted his action as that of a coward putting as many men as possible between Jackson and himself. General McDowell, whose corps was stopped from joining McClellan, remarked testily to General Wadsworth that Washington must "try and get over the flutter into which this body seems to have thrown everyone" or the rebels would succeed "in disconcerting all our plans." McClellan, who had been told he might have to leave the Peninsula to defend Washington could only say, "Heaven save a country governed by such counsels!"[37]

Perhaps the greatest source of concern to conservative-minded officers was the apparent effect of democratic institutions on army discipline: equality promoted insubordination. The feeling was not restricted to the Army of the Potomac: William Tecumseh Sherman, who had little feeling for free institutions, told his brother John, "You doubtless, like most Americans, attribute our want of success to bad generals. I do not. With us you insist the boys, the soldiers, govern. They must have this or that or will cry down their leaders in the newspapers, so no general can achieve much."[38]

An instance of the conflict Sherman was talking about happened in the Antietam campaign when, at the request of the governor of Pennsylvania, General John F. Reynolds was detached from McClellan's army to help organize the state defenses. Reynolds' efforts to shape up the state militia seemed overly rigorous to some newspapermen, one terming his conduct "outrageous." "When will the officers of the regular army learn that the people are their masters," said the paper. This was precisely the problem, for the officers did not believe that the people should run the war. Joseph Hooker, Reynolds' corps commander, had been outraged by the governor for even requesting the general's services, for he did not believe they could be spared. "It is only in the United States that atrocities like this are entertained," he wrote to McClellan. Resentment of civilian interference may have spurred Hooker into calling for a dictatorship several months later.[39]

Although the problem of discipline in a free society might never be completely surmountable, it was felt that more could be done if it were not for Lincoln. Whether the President entirely deserved his reputation for leniency toward deserters and other military offenders or not, it was widely believed that he did not support army efforts to improve discipline. Colonel Wainwright, a conservative volunteer officer from a good family in the Hudson Valley, wrote that insubordinate officers, "dismissed by sentence of court martial are immediately reinstated by the President . . . As to shooting deserters and cowards, whether men or officers, by court martial, that is out of the question, as all such cases have to go to Washington and Mr. Lincoln always pardons them."[40]

That Lincoln was not hard enough to be a war leader seemed obvious too from his failure to resist the pressure in favor of emancipation. To military men certain that abolition would drive the South into undying resistance the Emancipation Proclamation was monstrously irresponsible. Lincoln's action, said Wainwright, would do nothing but "estrange the whole population of the Southern states" and had only been "issued to please the radicals." He asked, "What is to become of us with such a weak man at the head of our government?"[41]

There would have been some consolation in knowing that the South had its share of problems: that Jefferson Davis did not wield dictatorial power, that the rebels were generally lenient to deserters, that their armies suffered from democratic practices such as the popular election of junior officers. But people did not realize this. They were sure that the lordly planters would allow no humane concerns to interfere with military demands. General Philip Kearny wrote to his wife after the failure of the Peninsula campaign that "in the South *every* gentleman is out—and they discipline their men highly—and they despise the North, nearly as *bitterly* as I do."[42]

To some it was incontrovertible that in order to beat the militarily more efficient South the North would have to interrupt democratic procedure. So thought David Hunter Strother, a volunteer officer from Virginia who had the misfortune to serve under Banks before joining McClellan's staff for the Antietam campaign. The people, he felt, needed a strong man to lead them. To beat the rebels, who "are the better soldiers," the North must "cast aside politicians and fanaticisms." Lincoln was not the man to be dictator, for "he has neither sense nor principle." McClellan, too, he doubted, for "he has no capacity to take political lead." Yet Strother was sure there would be a "Napoleon of this revolution," a "king in Israel."[43]

Others saw McClellan as the man. How many would have followed if he had taken some subversive action is hard to say. Indeed, it is difficult to find names never mind numbers, for treasonous subjects rarely oblige the historian by jotting down opinions that may get them shot. But it must be conceded that some, often those of high rank, would have thrown in their lot with him, believing that the cause demanded it. Ultimately, of course, Strother was right: McClellan did not take the lead. Perhaps he was play-acting all along and stopped when he saw a real drama about to begin. Possibly he was not sure enough of support to make a demonstration. Or maybe he was caught on the horns of a dilemma central to the conservative plight. Committed to social discipline, the preservation of order and rank, how were they to maintain these by taking illegal action that could precipitate internal strife and anarchy?

What may be most interesting about the whole business is not the question of whether there could have been a mutiny but simply the kind of attitude revealed during the crisis. These were men who in peacetime were able to hide their sentiments but in war felt obliged to speak up for the good of the country as they saw it. It would be wrong to see their unrest as simply a West Point phenomenon: there is little accuracy in the popular view that soldiers somehow stand apart from society, divorced from social class. Background and association were key: the regular, McClellan, had less in common with the professional Grant than with the volunteer Wainwright, a man of high breeding, who thought Lincoln a gawk and said disdainfully, "Discipline of any kind, save that of public opinion, is unknown in the country, and contrary to the whole education and general habit of our people." In their concern for the discipline of the masses, their rejection of the Jacksonian axiom that the common man could do any job including commanding a regiment, and, most important, in their belief that only real gentlemen were fitted by background to guide the nation, they exemplified the genteel conservatism of the first decades of the republic. It had been forced underground in the twenties but it was not dead and it was not forgotten. Shortly after Antietam, one of the Beecher family who was chaplain of a New York regiment, in explaining Northern failures, commented that "the Democratic party forced into our governmental policy in 1832–33 an element that overcame in man all reverence for law, human or divine, all reverence for obedience as a principle of life."[44]

What happened to the conservative elements after McClellan was gone? As the hate generated by war increased, some, like Custer, turned from purifying the North to punishing the South. Others took consolation in the hope that the gradual tonic of army life might still bring the masses to accept a passive role in society. They were to be disappointed in the Gilded Age when their leadership and sense of restraint were rejected anew. Finally, some fought on only for pride. They were increasingly without real hope, sensing that their world was fast disappearing. "The Genls. he had met with," said General Oglesby, "did not seem to have any feeling about the war, or to care how long it lasted, but seemed only desirous to acquit themselves honorably."[45]

Lincoln's decision to reinstate McClellan following Pope's defeat astonished numbers of people, including members of the Cabinet. The general's loyalty was seriously doubted. Historians have better understood that McClellan was the only officer with the personal prestige to rally the broken troops. What is more puzzling is why Lincoln issued the Emancipation Proclamation while McClellan was still with the army, for he was well aware of the mutinous talk there and of the possibility that there might be violent resentment. One important explanation of Lincoln's action is that emancipation was considered essential to stopping European intervention in the war. But to give the measure moral force—to avoid the appearance of expediency—the Proclamation had to be issued after a victory. And Antietam was the nearest thing the North had to a victory. The argument has much force; the diplomatic motive was plainly there. However, if we change the angle of vision so that we are no longer looking at Europe but at the internal state of the rebellion and we are thinking of the Proclamation in a context not of victory but of defeat and desperation, a further motive for emancipation emerges.

The months between McClellan's failure on the Peninsula and the battle at Antietam were ones of deep gloom. While the Army of the Potomac was not cast down by the retreat to the James, to civilians the failure of so large an army was catastrophic. Benjamin F. Butler's wife wrote on July 3, "If the news we got today of McClellan's defeat should be true I shall despair on every side." Pope's disaster quickly followed. And while McClellan was able to stop Lee in Maryland, the fact that the rebels had been able to invade Union territory and escape without being annihilated brought a powerful sense of Northern impotence. One woman confessed that she "turned rather cold and sick and said 'It is enough!' " and that her sister "went about declaiming out of Isaiah, 'To what purpose is the multitude of your sacrifices; your country is desolate, strangers devour it in your presence.' " Ulysses S. Grant recalled in his memoirs that many despaired of saving the Union in the fall of 1862.[46]

What accounted for Union failures? It was a fixed opinion with many people that because of background and training Southerners were simply better soldiers. Not much could be done to change this. But there did seem to be one area in which Northern improvement might be possible. One large advantage the rebels appeared to have was that they marched faster and fought with greater zeal. Northern generals and men were slow. This gave the enemy the initiative and often the victory. McClellan had been so chronically cautious in his advance up the Peninsula that *Wilkes' Spirit* suggested he had a case of "mud on the brain" for he got stuck in it so much. He was again slow in getting troops to the assistance of John Pope. Lee was more successful in rushing men north and then underlined the point by thrashing some comparatively fresh units under Pope. During the Maryland campaign the Confederates seemed to move faster and with more purpose. When the Union army failed to pursue Lee vigorously after Antietam, even cautious soldiers like Halleck became "sick, tired, and disgusted." He continued, "There is an immobility here that exceeds all that any man can conceive of." The failure did not surprise some. On September 14, a friend of Benjamin Butler had predicted that while the enemy "ought never to get back into Virginia . . . their dash and celerity may be too much for us again."[47]

The slowness was particularly disturbing to a people used to being characterized as more energetic, more go-getting, than the leisurely, even indolent, Southerners. The problem, it seemed, had to be psychological or spiritual. Northern generals and their men must lack inspired feeling for the cause. That the army labored under a spiritual deficit appeared certain to George Alfred Townsend, a reporter with McClellan. After the defeat on the Peninsula, he said, "my own mind was full of grief and bitterness. It seemed that our flag had descended to a degenerate people." Returning to Washington, he was shocked by the mood there. It was "but little better than Sodom," with gangs of soldiers brawling in the streets and brothels everywhere catering to the needs of all ranks. The root cause of Northern failure, he concluded, was an "inherent and almost universal corruption."[48]

That morale was poor, that some inspiration was missing, certain soldiers were willing to admit. "We have got whipped again" said General George W. Cullum after hearing news of a fight in Virginia on September 13. "The trouble is that our men won't fight." General George H. Gordon said in his memoirs that by the Maryland campaign enthusiasm had left the army. At Antietam, he said, "we went to battle to protect our homes. For another advance into Virginia the army needed, I thought, a new inspiration."[49]

Since the fall of the preceding year, radicals had been arguing that only emancipation could give the needed impetus. To those who believed slavery was a mortal sin it seemed clear that the spiritual bankruptcy of the Northern cause resulted from a failure to live by God's precepts. "I have no question," said one woman, "that this and all other defeats are intended to drive us, as a nation, to a higher moral ground in the conduct and purpose of this war." Once declare emancipation, she wrote, and "perhaps we shall begin to have victory, if we haven't already sinned away our day of grace."[50]

Wendell Phillips put the argument for emancipation as a military measure on more earthly grounds. He noted in a speech delivered on August 1 that "there is more danger to-day that Washington will be taken than Richmond." The reason was that the soldiers lacked an invigorating aim; they were fighting a "wasteful and murderous" war without purpose. Slavery had caused the war and given power to the oligarchy that guided the rebellion. Southerners were fighting to preserve the institution and yet Northerners would not fight against it. How could the North perform well when the mainstay of rebellion was held inviolable? The North could have neither self-respect nor victory while "servile in purpose; our soldiers the servants of rebels." Not only this but Northern policy gave rebels added courage because they saw their enemies were too weak to take severe measures. "Every Southern traitor," said Phillips, "can say of Mc-

Clellan's cannon-ball, if he ever fires one, 'We know it is not meant for us.'" To win the war, the Northern people must cry out "for an idea, at the head of our armies."[51]

The basic thesis was that the North was failing because her policy involved a dispiriting contradiction: she was pulling punches in a fight for survival. As Hans Christian Heg, militant colonel of the 15th Wisconsin put it, "When the Government learn to put in generals that are true and loyal, and men that are not afraid to hurt slavery or the Rebels, then we will begin to see the end of this war." By the summer of 1862 the argument had appeal even for some moderates. The editors of *Harper's Weekly* asked why the rebels were able to sustain a war against overwhelming numbers, amazing power and resources. The answer was that they faced "doubtful, hesitating, quarreling opponents." To sharpen the issue Lincoln must strike at slavery.[52]

It was in this mood that Lincoln issued the Proclamation. He had become convinced by the late spring that "we had about played our last card, and must change our tactics, or lose the game!" Nothing that happened in the summer led him to change the opinion. Viewed from this perspective, emancipation was primarily a military measure, as the President said it was. It was aimed at giving fresh impetus to apparently jaded soldiers afflicted with a chronic slowness.[53]

Unfortunately, as a military measure aimed at quickening the pace of war, the Proclamation was largely ineffective, at least so far as the Virginia theater was concerned. There was a flaw in the thinking of the men who had for so long urged anti-slavery views. To the radicals, McClellan was the prime example of a general without the "right idea." He was pro-slavery. They were right in sensing that there was a connection between McClellan's social views and his poor performance. But their understanding of it was too limited. McClellan's main problem was his contempt for the efforts of a democracy compared to those of an aristocracy. He was sure that the Southern armies must be stronger. Thus the root of his failure was dislike for democracy, not support for slavery. The latter was incidental to the former.

The distinction is an essential one, for their concern with the moral rather than the social factor distracted the radicals from finding a real solution to the problem of a winning general. If one had been looking for such a man, one might have been advised to pick someone who was common by background and who did not sneer at the masses. (Of the famous men of the period only three, Lincoln, Grant, and Walt Whitman, never seem to have lost faith in the triumph of the Northern cause. They were all commoners and none of them celebrated the aristocratic way.) The radicals looked for a moral general, an anti-slavery man. And they became so obsessed by this that they forgot a commander must also have military sense. Wendell Phillips was led into the foolish position of arguing that only radical generals like Fremont had "the earnest belief, the single-hearted, intense devotion to victory, the entire belief in justice, which can cope with Stonewall Jackson." That Jackson had a great deal more of pure military talent escaped him. This limitation in thinking led radicals to support such military mediocrities as Fremont, Pope, Butler, and Burnside, while they were often late in coming to see the value of Grant.[54]

Anti-slavery people were right in saying McClellan had to go but, unfortunately, by the time their advice was heard his imprint was too deep on the army to be erased. Many soldiers were convinced that the rebel army was stronger than their own and they were ceasing to believe in victory. Giving them a new idea at the head of the army could not change this very much. No doubt emancipation encouraged some soldiers to realize that the North would have to fight a hard, ruthless war to win. But it probably alienated as many as it enlightened. This too was militarily important. Assuming that the radicals could not get rid of all the conservative soldiers who hated abolition and "fanaticisms," they ought to have calculated on not achieving any miraculous change in the spirit of the army through emancipation.

To conclude, the radicals were not valueless as military critics, especially in their hounding of McClellan, which helped Lincoln see his shortcomings. But they had for too long been exiles in their own land. Fighting for years in a seemingly hopeless cause, they became obsessed with the one point and assumed that once it was won all problems would cease. But Northern inferiority feelings were much too complex to be diagnosed as springing simply from pro-slavery sentiments. A poem published in the *Atlantic Monthly* of November 1862 illustrates the moral grandeur and military naiveté of the abolitionists. The continual use of the word magic unintentionally reveals the impossible hopes held out for emancipation. The poet told the legend of Cassim, who discovered a cave filled with gold but in his excitement forgot the magic words which opened the door and so was trapped within. The Northern people, said the author, had been trapped in by "thick walls of gloom and doubt" but Lincoln could lead them out. He could "Open a vista to celestial light,/Lead us to peace through eternal Right." All he need do was say the magic words "BE FREE!"[55]

Lincoln said the magic words, but the war went on. And less than a month after the poem was published the Army of the Potomac, fighting without hope, met bloody defeat at Fredericksburg.

7

Fighting for Defeat
Fredericksburg to Gettysburg

*The small means of observation I have are enough,
however, to convince me that the Army of the
Potomac is thoroughly demoralized. They will
fight yet, but they fight for defeat, just as a brave,
bad rider will face a fence, but yet rides for a fall.*

> —Letter of CHARLES
> FRANCIS ADAMS, JR.,
> January 30, 1863

*We are the boys of Potomac's ranks,
            Hurrah! Hurrah!
We are the boys of Potomac's ranks,
We ran with McDowell, retreated with Banks,
            And we'll all drink stone blind—
                    Johnny, fill up the bowl.*

> —Lyrics popular in the
> Army of the Potomac
> during late 1863

The army McClellan left in October 1862 possessed a stubborn sort of courage and more of such qualities as discipline than was realized at the time. But some of the soldiers, at least in the higher ranks, were ceasing to hope for offensive victory. They fought only to preserve the army and protect the soil of the North from invasion. This unhappy fatalism was remarked upon by Darius N. Couch, a divisional commander who was startled and refreshed by a conversation with Lincoln because, unlike the officers, the President "had an idea that the war would sometime end." Even some of those who felt that the North could win based their argument solely on Northern superiority in numbers; skill they did not feel was with them. James Harrison Wilson, who served as a volunteer A.D.C. to McClellan at Antietam, predicted afterwards that the Union victory "would not be due to superior generalship and discipline, but rather to superior resources in men, money, and determination—in short, 'to main strength and awkwardness.'" Men believing this are likely to lack the spirit that produces brilliant results.[1]

Much of the defeatist mentality was inspired by the figures of Lee and Jackson, two soldiers of large talent with the confidence to make use of it to the full. Both were accorded an almost superstitious awe in the North as the most prominent and successful defenders of the rebel cause. There were even books published on them in the North during 1863. Jackson seems to have provoked a straightforward, unalloyed fear. He was the deadly professional who had played cat and mouse with Federals in the Valley and who stalked John Pope to defeat. There appeared to be something sinister about this austere Presbyterian, the avenging angel enlisted in an evil cause. In Whittier's "Barbara Frietchie," for example, he appears in a guise reminiscent of Milton's Satan—a brooding, threatening yet magnetizing figure in a dark slouch hat whose former nature shows through in an act of respect for an old lady but who at the same time threatens to shoot his own men like dogs. Respect for Jackson was based primarily on fear.[2]

There was also great fear of Lee among Union men. The value of his military talents had been grasped in the North before it became clear to the Confederates. He was offered field command of the Union army in April of 1861 but it was not until May of the following year that he obtained a commensurate position in the rebel service. By the end of 1862, many Northerners would have agreed with the estimate of John Chipman Gray, a young Union officer, that Lee came as near to being a master mind as the war had yet produced.[3]

Yet there was more to it than this: Lee excited admiration not only as a soldier but as a man. General Hancock's wife, who had known Lee before the war, described him as "the beau ideal of a soldier and a gentleman." And General John Schofield recalled that when he was a West Point cadet "Colonel Robert E. Lee was superintendent of the academy; he was the personification of dignity, justice, and kindness, and was respected and admired as the ideal of a commanding officer." Such noble qualities as these, suggests Edmund Wilson, account for Lee's lasting prestige in North and South. His dignity reminded men of the Founding Fathers. He belongs, says Wilson, "as does no other public figure of his generation, to the Roman phase of the Republic." A similar point was made much earlier by John Esten Cooke, a Confederate soldier who compared Lee to George Washington. Neither man, he said, excelled in every particular of learning or statecraft but both were good soldiers who did their best with the resources available and both were men who sought justice and fairness all their lives.[4]

The Roman virtues, the tradition of Washington . . . In our context the point might be restated thus: in its final struggle the Old South was fortunate in finding a man who seemed to prove in detail its claim to have preserved intact the virtues of the early Republic. He was a gentleman. As a soldier this meant that he wished the war to be settled by armies with a minimum of interference to the civilian population. In politics he was conservative and as a man he followed principle as he saw it. These qualities had meaning for Northerners as well as Southerners. More than any man on their own side, Lee seemed to represent a part of the national heritage which they deeply honored and wished to preserve. This was not a happy position for soldiers at war: it was hard to fight the son of a Revolutionary soldier on the soil of a revered state.[5]

The three battles of Fredericksburg, Chancellorsville, and Gettysburg can be treated as reflections of the awe in which Union men held the Army of Northern Virginia. It will be argued here that respect for the Virginians, and for Lee in particular, made it inevitable that the traits that had spoiled McClellan's generalship would continue to operate. There would be the same overestimation of enemy strength and ability, leading to the failure of nerve and the loss of opportunities. Hooker would fumble his opening at Chancellorsville. And less than a year after McClellan allowed Lee to escape from Maryland, the Army of the Potomac again failed to follow up a defensive victory on Northern soil, this time at Gettysburg. To the Potomac generals, avoiding defeat was a criterion of achievement.

It is worth noting, for the sake of perspective, that by the time of Gettysburg the war in the west was taking a different turn. While the Army of the Potomac was in Pennsylvania, Grant took Vicksburg and the Mississippi was entirely in Union hands. The psychological balance would steadily shift to the North (though Northern fears would not be stilled, as will be seen in the case of Sherman). Perhaps awe of the rebels had never been quite such a problem in the west as in the east. Westerners had long been more respected by Southerners than were the "Yankees" of the northeast and the men of the northwest had less misgivings about their manhood than did the citizens of Boston and New York. They were, after all, closer to the frontier stage of development and the robust state of society advocated by men like Parkman. Moreover, the Union men in the west had three advantages in the war. They had the substantial help of the Federal navy, which vastly outweighed its opponents; they did not have to face Lee on the soil of Virginia; and though they had labored under slow generals (witness Halleck's cautious advance on Corinth in April of 1862) they also had Grant. This unusually realistic and level-headed general had made errors and had tasted failure, but he based his successful strangling of Vicksburg on a shrewd assessment of rebel inability to break his grip. In Virginia, there was little such appreciation of the fact that the Confederacy was wearing down. In fact, it is remarkable that some veteran officers did not see Gettysburg as a turning point and did not feel that they could now inaugurate a new or better act in the war drama.

The choice of Ambrose E. Burnside to replace McClellan failed to satisfy many people. To some radicals he quickly came to appear as a watered-down version of "McNapoleon"; to the soldiers he was a poor substitute for their beloved leader. By the end of the year whatever confidence there had been in Burnside was gone, for he was defeated in an awfully wrong-headed campaign.[6]

When McClellan was relieved, he was slowly pursuing the rebels south along the line of the Orange and Alexandria railroad. Burnside altered this plan, moving the army southeast to a point on the Rappahannock River opposite Fredericksburg. His argument for this change was that it would shorten his lines of communication and afford better protection to Washington. He then planned to quickly bridge the river and march on Richmond, hoping to get into the city before Lee caught up with him. As Lincoln pointed out, to succeed at all, such a scheme required great speed. This was achieved on the march to the Rappahannock. However, when Burnside arrived he found that pontoons which he considered essential to a safe crossing had not arrived. From this point on, he became indecisive. Even after the bridging materials arrived, he allowed some two weeks to elapse before making a move. By this time, Lee's whole army had arrived and was strongly entrenched on the heights commanding Fredericksburg. On December 13, Burnside initiated a series of costly frontal assaults.[7]

Certain peculiarities of the campaign have always puzzled students. It seems unreasonable that Burnside should have delayed the crossing of the Rappahannock until the attempt became suicidal. Burnside's own explanation of his failures was "I did not feel . . . that I was competent to command such a large army as this." Many historians have accepted the view that the general was simply not qualified for the job. But there must have been more to it than that. Burnside's mistakes were not simply the bad judgments of a poor commander; they were elementary blunders that should have been avoided by any man with military training. For example, it was clear to most of Burnside's officers and to a great number of privates that the attack on December 13 could not possibly work. This suggests that Burnside was bordering on the irrational.[8]

Taking up the question of Burnside's mental state, Martin Schenck has suggested that Burnside was badly rattled by his experience at Antietam. In this battle he had been given the important task of taking the Lower Bridge over Antietam Creek. His men began to assault the bridge shortly after 9 A.M. but were quickly repulsed. Unwilling to expose his men further, Burnside delayed and it was not until 3 P.M. that a crossing was forced. McClellan severely censured his friend for this failure, which helped save the Confederates from outright defeat. According to Schenck, Burnside was determined not to repeat the error of allowing concern for lives to rob him of victory. This is why he ordered repeated attacks at Fredericksburg. The explanation for the battle, says Schenck, is to be found "in the field of psychology—or perhaps phychiatry."[9]

The argument is interesting. Yet the real lesson of the Lower Bridge was the need for greater speed and initiative. If Burnside had learned from Antietam, he would have crossed the Rappahannock much sooner than he did. The value of Schenck's argument is that it points to the psychological dimension of the problem even though it is not convincing in its immediate application. A more comprehensive view of Burnside, using the psychological approach, is possible.

To begin with, Burnside had not shown any great incompetence before he joined the Army of the Potomac. Indeed, he had successfully shouldered an independent command, carrying out operations against the North Carolina coast early in 1862. His first fumble was in fact at Antietam where he made the elementary mistake of not looking for fords across the river which would provide an alternative to the Lower Bridge. The same mistake was made on the Rappahannock where Burnside assumed without making a full survey that the river could not be crossed in force without pontoons. This suggests that there was a direct relation between Burnside's transfer to the Virginia theater and the beginnings of incompetence. Facing the Army of Northern Virginia, he began to show the same lack of initiative, the paralysis of the aggressive instinct which defeated McClellan.[10]

When he took over the top command, Burnside was already psychologically defeated. He believed that McClellan was the one man who might whip the rebels and he knew that many officers agreed, a fact which cannot have helped him. From the beginning he tried to avoid a showdown with Lee. This, it may be suggested, was a primary reason for the change of base to the Rappahannock. Commenting in his post-battle report on why he chose the Fredericksburg route, Burnside said that this was the shortest route to Richmond, the capture of which "would tend more to cripple the Rebel cause than almost any other military event, except the absolute breaking up of their army." Burnside was inadvertently admitting that he had chosen the lesser objective because he saw no chance of destroying Lee's army.[11]

When the army arrived at the Rappahannock and found rebels on the other side, Burnside revealed his awe of Lee by assuming that the Southerner had guessed his game and was there with strong forces. In fact, Lee was still not certain about what the Federals intended and had allowed Jackson to remain in the Shenandoah. As late as November 19, when Burnside was writing that he faced "a vigilant and formidable foe," Jackson was still 40 miles from the scene. It is feasible that Burnside could have placed himself between Jackson and Lee and beaten them in detail. But at Fredericksburg, as usual, the Federals overestimated the strength and acumen of their opponents.[12]

Burnside's campaign was ruined by his conviction that Lee would certainly know how to counter his moves—that he was waiting to devour him. It was not the failure of the pontoons to arrive that accounts for Burnside's indecision but his mistaken belief that Lee had caught up with him. Knowing that he must fight, and believing that he would lose, his intelligence went into eclipse. Finally, like a mad bull in the arena, he lashed out simply to end the torment. He was defeated not so much by Lee as by the idea of Lee.

Fredericksburg had a deeply depressing effect on the North. Never had the failings of Union generalship been so apparent as in Burnside's simplistic plan of attack. Nor could much consolation be taken from the west where toward the end of the month Grant sustained over 30,000 casualties in assaults on Vicksburg. "Is it not strange," wrote ex-President Buchanan, "that among a population so numerous & so intelligent & enterprising as ours, the war has not yet produced one great General?" During the French Revolution, he noted parenthetically, many generals emerged "possessing dash & strategy & capable of conducting a war of invasion in the most efficient manner." To some it seemed that the cost of finding a winning general might be too high. Civil War people were used to long casualty lists but the killing at Fredericksburg had been tragically one-sided.

> Eighteen hundred and sixty-two—
>   That is the number of wounded men
> Who, if the telegraph's tale be true
>   Reached Washington City but yester e'en

So began a poem published in New York during December. Blundering was the cause of the casualties, charged the author, and he warned that the public would not tolerate it much longer. "In their frenzied grief they would end such scenes,/Though that end be—even with traitors—peace." Horace Greeley, the mercurial editor of the New York *Tribune,* who had been saying a few weeks previously that emancipation would bring a quick end to the war, now began to talk again of an armistice as he had after First Bull Run. "If three months of earnest fighting shall not serve to make a serious imperssion on the rebels; . . . let us bow to our destiny, and make the best attainable peace," he suggested.[13]

Bitterness about the generalship was naturally high among the men of the Potomac army. Warren Lee Goss, a private, wrote later that "gloom pervaded every rank. The feeling was deep and universal that it was of but little use to fight, unless the government could find some one to command who would not throw away our lives in useless experiments." Fredericksburg reinforced the fatalistic outlook of the troops. They expected defeat and they found it. Some of the men were nearly mutinous. Yet the Army of the Potomac had not reached the point of disintegration as an effective fighting unit: most of the soldiers were willing to try again. Oliver Wendell Holmes, Jr., for example, wrote that he thought that slavery often triumphed over civilization in war and this gave him a "disbelief in our success by arms," but he was "as ready as ever to do my duty."[14]

This philosophy of stoic courage in the face of a seemingly cruel or irrational fate has been found of value by men in different times: Ernest Hemingway in the aftermath of World War I or Victor Frankl caught in a German concentration camp. In the Civil War the idea was best articulated by the New England Brahmins, perhaps because they were most preoccupied with the question of manhood. Many of them had no great commitment to the issues of the war; nor did they feel that military glory offered any lasting satisfaction. But they kept going by believing that doing one's duty well, no matter how futile it might seem, was meaningful.[15]

In the army as a whole, this idea was taking the shape of shared pride in the ability of the army to fight hard under impossible leaders. It was this pride that animated the hopeless charges at Fredericksburg. After the battle there was the consolation of knowing that great courage had been shown. But Burnside nearly managed to rob the army of this cold comfort when, in January, he undertook an advance on the enemy lines under dreadful weather conditions. The troops were humiliated in front of the rebels, who came out of their trenches to jeer at the Union soldiers stuck in the mud. The morale of the army fell to a point lower than it had been immediately after the battle. General Alexander Hays, who had been willing to give Burnside another chance after Fredericksburg, saying that he "has still the confidence of the army," now wrote mournfully that within six months it would probably be necessary to recognize the Confederacy.[16]

It was obvious that Burnside would have to go. But would this solve the problem? Beyond Burnside were the politicians who had appointed him. What if their next choice were as bad? The North might lose the war it seemed, for even the most patriotic newspapers were saying that the public would not stand for another such massacre. One way to avoid the problem was to take the choice out of the politicians' hands: to set up a military dictator. So there was again talk of a coup in the North. General Hooker remarked after the battle to Swinton of the New York *Times* that the President and government were "played out" and that nothing would go right until a dictator took over. And Benjamin Wade, a radical in Congress, "advocated the creation of a Lieutenant Genl. with absolute and despotic powers."[17]

It might seem that it was at this point, rather than after McClellan was removed, that the possibility of an attempted coup was strongest, for Lincoln was never more hated in the North than in the weeks after Fredericksburg. As a war leader he appeared hopeless. The rebellion seemed stronger than ever. "Lincoln compares to Jeff Davis, as a wheel-barrow to a steam engine!" commented a leading Democrat. The President was despised in the Army of the Potomac especially. The soldiers' faith in McClellan as the only man equal to the rebels seemed confirmed by Burnside's defeat. Charles Francis Adams, Jr., wrote on January 26, 1863, "It is a fact that McClellan alone has the confidence of this army. They would rally and fight under him tomorrow and under him only." There seemed to be diabolical provocation in the government's choice of this month to try McClellan's friend Porter. Small wonder that Lincoln's folksy traits did not appeal to the soldiers. Captain Lusk wrote that though the army had no brains to lead it, "perhaps Old Abe has some funny story to tell appropriate to the occasion." When Lincoln sent a message to the army, thanking it for courageous service, the McClellan camp took it as a poor joke. "Mr. Lincoln is more flattering to this army when defeated than when victorious," said Colonel Wainwright. "He had not a word to say to it after South Mountain and Antietam."[18]

In addition to the personal dislike of Lincoln, Fredericksburg added to the fear that democracy could not beat despotism. It was believed that the newspapers had helped precipitate the disaster by pushing for fast results as they had at Bull Run. In the Confederacy, people said, the ruling clique did not allow the public to make policy in this way. John Beatty, a Union volunteer, wrote, "In the South the army makes public opinion and moves along unaffected by it. In the North the army has little or nothing to do with the creation of public sentiment and yet is its servant. The people of the North, who were clamoring for action, are probably responsible for the fatal repulse at Fredericksburg and the defeat at Bull Run." General Sherman, who was no lover of the public, accused the press of continually revealing critical data about Union troop movements, enabling the rebels to concentrate men at the point of contact. The South, he said, had enforced censorship from the beginning "and the result has been, they move their forces from Virginia to Mississippi and back without a breath spoken or written." To his brother, Sherman remarked that while Northerners had denounced the South's suppression of freedom of speech and her conscription of soldiers as tyrannous, "We must follow their example."[19]

There were even some blunt statements of lack of confidence in democratic methods within the legislative halls. In a speech delivered on February 24, 1863, Congressman Sargent said that the North should have adopted European methods of conscription from the beginning. European military men were correct, he said, when they insisted that the North should not rely on volunteers, for they were incapable of real discipline. The interesting point is not that Sargent was arguing for a draft but that he should have appealed to European precedent for justification. In 1861 such a speech would not have been delivered in Congress for it was part of the democratic faith that America was a haven from the police methods of European despotism. So far had Americans surrendered the democratic creed.[20]

In portraying the South as an efficient despotism, Northerners said more about their own assumptions than about the actual state of the South. It was true that the rebels were more successful in keeping military information out of the newspapers but the general assumption that the Confederate government had complete control of resources was wildly wrong. Yet Northerners did not know this and there was enough talk of following the South into despotism to convince *Harper's Weekly* that "matters are rapidly ripening for a military dictatorship." In fact, such a thing was no longer possible, for the man who could focus dissatisfaction was gone. McClellan had quietly surrendered his power and no other military figure had sufficient support to be a dictator.[21]

The possibility of a coup became even less likely as February turned to March and the gloom of winter was relieved by a hint of spring, bringing a sense of rebirth and fresh hope. More concretely, there was the steady beneficial influence of a small pamphlet published in the latter part of 1862 by Charles J. Stillé and called *How a Free People Conduct a Long War*.[22]

Stillé's work had few of the dramatic appeals, the rhetorical flourishes, that attracted the Victorian reader. It was a rather pedestrian account of the tribulations experienced by the British people in bringing the Peninsular War of 1809–1814 to a successful conclusion. Yet the work sold hundreds of thousands of copies and its success as a propaganda piece led Lincoln to consider the author for headship of a Bureau of Emancipation. Stillé's strength lay in the subtlety of his essentially conservative yet optimistic stance.   An acquaintance of men like George Templeton Strong and Henry W. Bellows, he must have been thoroughly exposed to some of the most stringent criticism of a democratic people at war.   In his pamphlet, he did not try to ignore these criticisms or combat them with patriotic rhetoric: he grafted them onto his argument.   Thus he agreed with the common opinion that "we are not a military nation," pointing out in one instance that "much inconvenience has necessarily resulted in our case from the ignorance of Regimental officers."   And he accepted the argument that public opinion in a democracy could "often prove, as we shall see, more fruitful of embarrassment to the favourable prosecution of a war, than the active operations of the enemy."[23]

Stillé maintained however, that such weaknesses of democracy need never prove fatal if people learned "a stern endurance."   The English, he said, had been taught this by their experience in the Peninsular War.   At the start, "there was the same wild and unreasoning enthusiasm with which we are familiar; the same bitter abuse and denunciation of the government at the first reverses; . . . the same discouragement and despondency at times on the part of the true and loyal."   Eventually, wrote Stillé, after three years of seemingly barren fighting, "So profound was the conviction of the immense superiority of the French, both in numbers, and in the quality of their troops, that the public mind was in a state of feverish anxiety, and many of the stoutest hearts gave way to despair."   Fortunately, the English ministry saw that not only the outcome of the war but the fate of the nation was at stake and so, "although ignorant of the true mode of prosecuting hostilities, had sense enough to perceive that their only true policy was perseverance."   Soon the storm broke and England emerged triumphant.[24]

It was not a very profound thesis but it did fit the situation of the North in the winter of 1862–1863.   It was reassuring to know that another nation, and the mother country at that, had emerged stronger from crisis.   The argument that a people could learn manly endurance despite democratic forms encouraged those who believed the North suffered from lack of social discipline: perhaps something meaningful might come out of the long struggle after all.   Thus, Stillé's pamphlet worked its slow tonic effect on Northern minds.[25]

Incidentally, a point which Stillé managed to gloss over was that while Britain had in Sir Arthur Wellesley an outstanding soldier, the North had found no man capable of thrashing Lee. But by February people were beginning to believe that Lincoln had at last found the right person for the job in Major General Joseph Hooker. The appointment of Hooker to command the Army of the Potomac is another factor of tremendous importance in explaining the revival of Northern spirits.

At first, many of the officers doubted the wisdom of Lincoln's choice. Some disliked Hooker for his wild habits, which were said to include a well-developed taste for liquor; others felt that he had been too critical of his superiors to be a man of great character; and there were still those, like George Armstrong Custer, who did not believe in anyone except McClellan. Nevertheless, Hooker gradually won the respect of the vast majority of the army. After the humiliating Mud March in January, the pride and discipline of the army had begun to disintegrate. General Oliver Otis Howard recalled, "We had suffered desertions by the thousands. I brought two commissioned officers about that time to trial for disloyal language, directed against the President and the general commanding." Yet Hooker, he said, "by his prompt and energetic measures, soon changed the whole tone of the army for the better."[26]

It has often been said that McClellan organized the Army of the Potomac best, but in the short time before Chancellorsville Hooker did much more. First, he revived the pride of the army. Each corps and division was assigned a distinctive badge to be worn on the cap, a device which encouraged *esprit de corps*. Again, Hooker was careful always to speak well of the soldiers. And he gave them a sense of aggressive power which had not been there before. In his order assuming command of the army he stated, "In equipment, intelligence, and valor the enemy is our inferior; let us never hesitate to give him battle wherever we can."[27]

Hooker's treatment of the cavalry is typical of the new air in the army. Understanding the need for identity within an organization, Hooker saw that McClellan had been wrong in breaking up the troops into small details. He reshuffled the men into brigades and divisions of the Cavalry Corps of the Army of the Potomac. Testimony to the effectiveness of this move was given to the Committee on the Conduct of the War by General W. Averell, a divisional commander of cavalry, on February

17, 1863. "I think that we now have in the Army of the Potomac the best organization for cavalry," said Averell. Before, the cavalry had been worn down by such duties as picketing, but now "There will be a better prospect for our cavalry in the spring, I think, than there ever yet has been."[28]

Again following the pattern used in his handling of the whole army, Hooker took pains to stress that his cavalrymen were in no way inferior to the enemy: the business of invincible Southern horsemen he discounted as a myth. When Fitzhugh Lee crossed the Rappahannock and captured 150 men, Hooker stormed at one of his brigadiers that there must be no more such surprises because "I know the South, and I know the North. In point of skill, of intelligence, and of pluck, the rebels will not compare with our men, if they are equally well led. Our soldiers are a better quality of men." The general stressed that the cavalry could and would take the initiative in aggressive action. Giving orders to General Stoneman for an expedition to begin on April 13, Hooker wrote, "Let your watchword be 'fight, fight, fight, fight,' . . . Bear in mind that celerity, audacity, and resolution are everything in war." Bold words for a commander of this army.[29]

The men believed Hooker and responded to his exhortations. The change in tone was demonstrated when, on the evening of April 30, the 6th New York Cavalry, on a scouting mission toward Spotsylvania, tangled with the 5th Virginia. The enemy were, in the words of General Pleasanton, "completely routed," despite the fact that General Stuart and his staff were with them. Stuart began to calmly withdraw his whole cavalry. But the rearguard, in a panic reminiscent of the Northerners at Bull Run, "threw the whole column into confusion by the cry, 'The enemy is upon us.' "[30]

The same confident spirit animated the whole army. Even in an article written by General Couch for the *Century Magazine* some two decades after the war there can still be sensed the feeling of imminent victory which pervaded the army as it entered upon the Chancellorsville campaign. Perhaps for the first time, the soldiers believed that they were going to tear up Lee. Hooker certainly seemed to have the qualifications for the job. He had somewhat the same power to sway men as McClellan but he appeared to have the confidence to make that power work for him as well. His strategic sense was sound, and if he had been able to carry through, the war might have been ended a year or more before it was. Unfortunately, at the critical moment, Hooker failed to believe his own rhetoric.[31]

The plan of the Chancellorsville campaign was a good one. Hooker arranged to leave a substantial force at Fredericksburg under General Sedgwick while he took the rest of the army some 20 miles up the Rappahannock and crossed the river opposite Chancellorsville. By means of rigid security measures, he hoped to keep Lee guessing as to which portion of the army posed the major threat until the bulk of the army was upon his flank and rear. The force under Sedgwick would then press Lee from the front, while the Cavalry Corps under Stoneman cut rebel communications with Richmond. Caught in a pincer movement, the rebels would either have to retreat or fight a losing battle on two fronts. As Hooker put it, "Our enemy must either ingloriously fly or come out from behind his intrenchments and give us battle on our own ground, where certain destruction awaits him."[32]

The movement of the main body began on April 27 and by mid-day on April 30 the leading corps under General Meade was at Chancellorsville. Hooker's plan was working perfectly. One of Lee's generals tried to claim after the war that the rebels knew exactly what Hooker was up to but the weight of evidence suggests that Lee was still not certain about the enemy's intentions and had not begun to dispose the bulk of his men in front of Hooker. The Union generals in the advance sensed that this was so, for they had met no serious opposition. The usually somber Meade was in high spirits, shouting to a fellow officer, "This is splendid, Slocum; hurrah for old Joe! We are on Lee's flank and he doesn't know it." Meade and the others were anxious to press on out of the wooded area around Chancellorsville into the open country beyond, where the army could maneuver more freely and complete its offensive operation.[33]

At this critical point Hooker refused to sanction a further forward movement. To the generals, who believed that Lee had finally met his match, this was a staggering blow. They realized with horror that Hooker seemed to be losing his nerve. General Pleasanton, who rode to headquarters to plead with the general to carry on toward Fredericksburg, recorded that "I was much surprised to find that General Hooker, who up to that time had been all vigor, energy, and activity, received the suggestion as a matter of secondary importance, and that he considered the next morning sufficiently early to move to Fredericksburg." Pleasanton thought that a golden opportunity had been lost.[34]

The situation might still have been retrieved on the following day when the march was renewed. But when the troops ran into some serious opposition, Hooker ordered them back to Chancellorsville. The generals, who were confident that they could drive the enemy, were again unable to reason with Hooker. Darius N. Couch, commander of the Second Corps, was so angry that he became insubordinate on the field of battle. On this day, he wrote later, it became clear "that my commanding general was a whipped man." The analysis was correct. By returning to the wooded area Hooker gravely restricted his field of vision and ability to manoeuver. More important than this physical loss, he surrendered the psychological initiative to the enemy. Lee, realizing that Hooker had adopted a defensive pose, felt confident in assuming the offensive. The campaign was as good as over before the serious fighting had begun.[35]

There have been various attempts to explain why Hooker failed at Chancellorsville. It was rumored that he was drunk during the battle but there is no evidence to support the charge. More plausible is Couch's suggestion that Hooker had given up liquor before the battle and that the loss of alcoholic stimulation accounts for his lack of spirit. But the simplest explanation was that offered by Hooker himself in a remark made after the battle to General Abner Doubleday. "For once," he said, "I lost confidence in Hooker." Or, to put it another way, the nearer he got to contact, the more respect he had for Lee.[36]

The point at which Hooker's nerve failed can be traced exactly to the time when it became clear that Lee was not going to take the option of inglorious flight but was going to stay and fight it out. It was at this point that Hooker had to order the men into the final march on Fredericksburg, and he could not do it. In the end he was as incapable as every other commander of the Army of the Potomac of believing that he might destroy the enemy. There seem to be no special factors in Hooker's make-up or background that account for his awe of Lee. He had simply served too long in an army trained by McClellan and generaled by Burnside. On the other side, it is apparent that Lee quickly took the measure of Hooker after he retreated to Chancellorsville. The risk taken by the rebels in sending Jackson across Hooker's front has perhaps been overplayed. In the face of a vigilant, daring commander it would have been an act of boldness. But commanders of the Army of the Potomac had consistently shown that they were incapable of grasping their advantages. Lee was not so much daring as contemptuous of his foe.[37]

On September 9, 1863, Lincoln's secretary, John Hay, dined with Hooker. During the meal the general remarked that the Army of the Potomac was "the finest on the planet." It was, he said, "far superior to the Southern army in everything but . . . vigor of attack." For this he blamed McClellan who took it when it was new and molded it "into a mass of languid inertness destitute of either dash or cohesion." All this was true but it was not the whole story. Hooker failed to mention, perhaps because he could not face it, that the army had not lacked vigor at Chancellorsville; only the commander had failed. Incredible as it may seem, Hooker had been able in the few months before Chancellorsville to instill in the soldiers an aggressive impulse. At the start of the campaign, the feel of victory was in the air. General Meade, who was known for his steadiness rather than his energy, was straining at the leash in the beginning. The same eagerness was broad among the common soldiers. Couch remembered that as the army went into bivouac around Chancellorsville on April 30 the men "were in exuberant spirits at the success of their general in getting 'on the other side' without fighting for a position. As I rode into Chancellorsville that night the general hilarity was particularly noticeable, the soldiers, while chopping wood and lighting fires, were singing merry songs and indulging in peppery camp jokes."[38]

But all this was dependent on Hooker, who, in the position of responsibility, fell a victim to the ghost of past inferiority feelings. The spirit of victory in the army quickly ebbed as it became apparent that something was wrong at the top. Couch noted that when the troops were pulled back to Chancellorsville on May 1 "the high expectations which had animated them only a few hours ago had given place to disappointment." It was business as usual. By May 6 the army had retreated back across the river to near Fredericksburg. All that Hooker had accomplished in the preceding weeks was lost. "There was a want of *nerve* somewhere," wrote General Gouverneur Warren glumly. "What with killed, wounded, and missing, and discharges of men whose time has expired, we are 30,000 weaker than before we moved." Disappointed men returned to familiar thoughts and there was again talk of bringing back McClellan as the only man who might whip the rebels.[39]

In the eyes of many Northerners, the Army of the Potomac was a disgrace. Hooker's defeat, said John Sherman, "is a terrible event. Experience should have taught us not to hope much from his army, and yet the impression was so strong after his confident assertions and his promising commencement that we all feel the disappointment. It is gloomy." Horace Greeley snorted, "130,000 magnificent soldiers so cut to pieces by less than 60,000 half-starved ragamuffins!" In the west where Grant was winning a series of victories below Vicksburg and Benjamin H. Grierson had completed a cavalry raid deep into enemy territory, the soldiers felt confident enough to take a pitying attitude toward their eastern colleagues. "Hooker appears to have been beaten badly," wrote Captain Alfred Lacy Hough, a soldier with George Thomas. "Who will lead them next? The Army of the Potomac appears to be the grave of would be great men; but I hope it will yet redeem itself."[40]

Laboring under the weight of defeat and condemnation, the army again left Fredericksburg, in mid-June, pursuing the rebels who crossed the Potomac heading north. It has often been said that the low spirits of the men improved on the march. Philip Regis de Trobriand, an officer in the army, stated in his memoirs that, while "Our soldiers, humiliated by defeat, shaken in their confidence in themselves and in their commander," were depressed after Chancellorsville, their spirits quickly improved on the trek north, for they were marching to the defense of home and fireside. Later writers say much the same. Bruce Catton comments that though the soldiers "had no idea where they were going, it seemed to them that at last they were marching to victory."[41]

This view is too colored by hindsight: because the army won a defensive victory at Gettysburg it is assumed that the outlook of the body must have been a happy one. But there is evidence against this. At least among the senior officers there was not a confidence in outright victory; they were still thinking defensively. For one thing, there was some apprehension about fighting a second battle under Hooker. On June 13 General Patrick confided to his diary the opinion that "We are likely to be outgeneralled & for aught I know, whipped out again by Lee, at Manassas." Patrick's faith did not increase on the march. Significantly, Hooker had fallen into the common habit of grossly overestimating rebel numbers. As provost marshal general, Patrick interviewed many Confederate prisoners and knew from them that his chief was wrong. Hooker was using the numbers business, thought Patrick, to avoid giving battle—"He knows that Lee is his master." Patrick was probably right, though the extent to which Hooker was aware of his own motivation is debatable.[42]

Some generals, such as John Gibbon, were considerably relieved when Meade took command of the army on June 28. But a certain uneasiness stayed. The new commander was feeling rather like the leader of a lost hope as the North was apparently failing to unite behind the army. On June 23 he read that Pennsylvania troops refused to be mustered into the service for fear that they might be kept six months. "I give up in despair," he wrote. Perhaps the soldiers overdramatized their isolation as defenders of the Northern soil. This was partly a legacy from McClellan, who never felt that he was properly supported; the Army of the Potomac was irrational on the subject of its own strength. Then, too, some of the troops had an innate prejudice against the Pennsylvania "Dutch" and magnified every bad quality of the people. But it was true that many Northerners showed a lack of zeal during the invasion. The Lincoln administration was extremely unpopular at this time because it had introduced a military draft and had taken other arbitrary steps such as the arrest of the politician Clement L. Vallandigham. One officer, sent to organize the defenses of the Gettysburg area, was reported as saying that he would "first fight the Rebels, but, after the war, the Administration." His work in local defense was not outstanding and he was later discharged from the service. Some of the Potomac officers also had an abiding distrust of the Lincoln administration. But the invasion of the North was paramount to them. Duty lay in a solid front against the enemy and they were bitter against those who would not put shoulders to the wheel.[43]

Northern lack of enthusiasm made the soldiers anxious. General Alpheus S. Williams pictured Meade's force as this "small army," the only thing standing between the rebels and the capital. The Northern people, meanwhile, were sitting down "in search of the almighty dollar." Seeing the situation in these grave terms, Williams was naturally cautious about what the army should do. He felt that there were fearful risks in offering battle and he did not even consider the possibility that a smashing victory could be won on Northern soil with Lee's army trapped on alien ground. The best he hoped for was that the army would "do enough to preserve our honor and the safety of the Republic."[44]

There are some hints that the caution imposed by a sense that the army stood alone amid a welter of confusion was added to by a lack of complete confidence in the rank and file. Some officers would have found naive the comment of a professor at Gettysburg who said that the sight of the ragged rebels and "the filthy exhalations from their bodies" disabused him of the notion that they were "chivalrous Southerners, all from the first families of the South." Veterans did not judge the character of the rebels by their appearance. "Lee may well be proud of his infantry; I wish ours was equal to it," wrote Colonel Wainwright after the first day at Gettysburg. Even Meade may not have been entirely certain about the reliability of his men. In a circular to his corps commanders the general noted that "the army has fought well heretofore" but he added that commanders "are authorized to order the instant death of any soldier who fails to do his duty at this hour."[45]

The Confederate outlook on the march to Gettysburg was different.

Chancellorsville had appeared to offer additional proof of Lee's invincibility. Morale was high when Lee set off on his second invasion of the North. This is not to say that the rebels had no problems. The material resources of the Confederacy were becoming strained, and though Lee's men were confident of victory, morale was sagging elsewhere as the war dragged into its third hard year. Even in the Army of Northern Virginia there were times of melancholy in the quiet periods between marching and fighting. Stonewall Jackson had died on May 10 and this was a blow to the South as it was a relief to the North.[46]

Moreover, some Confederates were deeply troubled, like their conservative Northern opponents, about whether any lasting good could come from the war. Even Stonewall Jackson, who is usually thought of as a man deeply convinced of Southern righteousness, was reputed to have told General John Bell Hood in January of 1863 that he doubted he would survive the war and did not wish to. And just ten days before he made his famous charge, General George Edward Pickett wrote his wife that "when we've downed the enemy and won the victory, I don't want to hurrah. I want to go off all by myself and be sorry for them . . . and rest my soul and put my heart to sleep and get back something—I don't know what—but something I had that is gone from me."[47]

What kept men like Pickett going was a tremendous sense of identity within the army. Like the Army of the Potomac, the Army of Northern Virginia had a great deal of corporate pride. The one side fought only to endure, but the other fought to win. That the rebels expected to win in June of 1863 is clearly revealed by the diary of a visiting English soldier, Arthur Fremantle. He found that "Southerners generally appear to estimate highest the northwestern Federal troops," while the eastern soldiers "are not much esteemed." The feeling in Lee's army, he said, "was one of profound contempt for an enemy whom they have beaten so constantly, and under so many disadvantages."[48]

After Gettysburg was over, Fremantle returned to the theme, saying, "It is impossible to avoid seeing that the cause of this check to the Confederates lies in the utter contempt felt for the enemy by all ranks." He was right. When all is said and done about Longstreet's slowness, the failure of the artillery barrage, and so on, the fact remains that Lee felt his men could cross a mile of open ground, assault a prepared position, and drive an enemy who might be expected to strain every muscle to beat back what was obviously the major thrust. If the positions had been reversed— had Lee been defending Cemetery Ridge—there can be little doubt that he would have felt confident about his ability to hold the ground. From his contempt of the enemy, Lee attempted the impossible.[49]

The irony in the fact that the rebels were defeated by their own self-esteem is paralleled only by the fact that the Union commander was too inhibited by his view of the enemy to take advantage of their discomfiture. It is not true that the legend of Lee's invincibility was broken at Gettysburg. On the rebel side, many of the soldiers did not believe that they had lost the battle, for they had stood at bay after Pickett's charge, daring Meade to attack them, and he had not done so. In the Union ranks there was great jubilation because Lee had been stopped. Charles Francis Adams, Jr., wrote, "I really believe that we are learning to outfight the rebels on even fields, in spite of their dash and fanatical desperation." But it is doubtful whether the sense of relief implied any basic change of attitude.[50]

The Army of the Potomac fought on the defensive at Gettysburg. It did what General Alpheus S. Williams had hoped it would—it preserved honor and the republic—but it tried to do no more. There was no hard-pressed counterattack, no determined pursuit to show a realization that the enemy was reeling. The army fought as it had in the past: it simply tried to stave Lee off and push him away. This was the tenor of Meade's congratulatory address, delivered after the battle, in which he said that the enemy had been baffled and must next be driven off Northern soil. There was no mention of destroying him. At the end of July, Lee was allowed to cross the Rappahannock to safety, more or less unmolested.[51]

It could be argued that Meade did not have the fresh troops to press Lee closely. But his men were certainly as fresh as the rebels, who expected an attack daily. Anyway, the point is that no matter what the condition of the men, Meade's state of mind did not allow of aggressive action. T. Harry Williams, the historian, has demonstrated from Meade's dispatches that he wished to avoid a second encounter with Lee for fear that he might be beaten. Williams suggests that Meade's problem was that he was overly influenced by the fate of Pickett's charge. "He believed the same thing would happen to him if he attacked. His defensive victory at Gettysburg ruined him as an offensive general."[52]

This thesis places the ruin at too late a date. The army had never fought offensively. Meade fitted into a pattern older than Gettysburg. In that battle, Meade played the part of Hooker at Chancellorsville and of McClellan before him. Like previous generals, he could not conceive of offensive victory. *Wilkes' Spirit* had accused McClellan of having "mud on the brain" because of his slowness. General Patrick suspected that Meade sometimes got a case of "Lee on the Brain." Mud on the mind or Lee on the mind, either represented a sad lack of vigor on the part of men who put their main faith in the enemy. General Patrick, whose ideas were often closer to his commander's than he cared to admit, gave the most candid explanation of the failure to follow up after Gettysburg when he wrote, "We are satisfied with what has been accomplished and believe, as we did at Antietam, ten months ago, that it is a mercy to us that the Rebs left as they did—We could not attack them safely." It was, indeed, Antietam again.[53]

In terms of mental outlook, Gettysburg had changed very little. During the anticlimactic weeks following the battle, even young Charles Francis Adams revised his estimate of what had happened there. By July 23 he was writing that "Lee's army at Gettysburg was in every respect superior to the Army of the Potomac, superior in numbers, better officered, a better fighting material, as well armed, better clothed and as well fed." For those who had hoped that Gettysburg would be the prelude to the destruction of Lee's army, there was bitter disappointment. Lincoln was so shocked by the failure that he took up again the idea of a military conspiracy. "There is bad faith somewhere," he told Secretary Welles. The secretary was inclined to believe that the generals were deliberately trying to prolong the war. But General Wadsworth was closer to the mark when he charged that "there are a good many officers of the regular army who have not yet entirely lost the West Point idea of Southern superiority. That sometimes accounts for an otherwise unaccountable slowness of attack." It was not quite accurate to lump all the blame on West Pointers but Wadsworth made a point all the same.[54]

Whatever reason they ascribed to the failure, most critics agreed that it would not be surprising if Meade was outgeneraled again. General Alexander Hays wrote on July 18 that the war "ought to have been settled in Pennsylvania. We are tired of scientific leaders and regard strategy as it is called—a humbug. Next thing to cowardice. What we want is a leader who will go ahead." He later noted that he had little confidence in Meade. Further down the chain of command a young New England officer, John Chipman Gray, told his father in November that "looking at the matter in a purely military view" anyone's sympathies must be with the rebels, for "they have had the inferiority in numbers and equipment and the superiority in generalship."[55]

Some inkling of what the common soldiers were thinking may be gained from the words of a song popular in the Army of the Potomac during the fall of 1863. With wry humor the soldiers sang of the blunders made by their many commanders, including Burnside who "tried his luck, / But in the mud so fast got stuck" and Hooker who "was taken to fit the bill, / But he got a black eye at Chancellorsville." The last verse ran:

> Next came General Meade, a slow old plug,
> Hurrah! Hurrah!
> Next came General Meade, a slow old plug,
> For he let them away at Gettysburg.[56]

These comments go against the prevailing view of historians that Gettysburg marked the turning point of the war. For as Noah Brooks, a friend of Lincoln put it, "Gettysburg was not then regarded, as it is now, as the turning point." In modern nationalistic wars, morale plays a vital role and hence the outcome of the war may be dependent on sustaining the belief of the people in their ability to win. The materially stronger side may give up in despair of gaining the victory. Applying this to Gettysburg, the battle can only be seen as a turning point if we judge the contestants solely in terms of physical resources: if God is assumed to be necessarily on the side of the strongest battalions. In this case, Gettysburg would be "the high water mark" of the Confederacy, for after this point Lee's material assets declined steadily and he was never able to mount a full-scale invasion of the North.[57]

But the point is that the South could still win the war because the Northerners did not realize their advantage and were incapable of using it. The Union soldiers did not believe that Gettysburg had given them the whip hand of Lee. They would continue to act defensively. Some would not believe that the Confederacy was wearing down; others did not see that as the decisive factor. One Federal officer, studying dead rebel cavalrymen, noted that most of their equipment was homemade or makeshift. "How desperately in earnest must such a people be, who, after foreign supplies are exhausted, depend on their own fabrics rather than submit," he remarked.[58]

Gettysburg, then, was closer to the past and the defensive battles of the army than it was to the future. It belonged to a year in which, since the removal of McClellan, nothing positive had been achieved in the east. Of course, it would be a perversion to say that Gettysburg was entirely unfavorable to one side only. Gettysburg, and Vicksburg, had a depressing effect on civilian morale in the South. Some began to question the basic assumption of their superiority in war. The *Southern Literary Messenger*, which had much to say early in the war about the invincibility of Norman chivalry, now began to reject that chivalry as a useful quality. To break down their will to fight, said the *Messenger,* the Northern people must be shown the full rigors of war. The kind of gallantry Lee had shown in his merciful treatment of Northern civilians during the invasion of Pennsylvania, was self-defeating. "Cannonading with feathers is the equivalent of chivalry in this age" said the paper.[59]

However, the Confederacy still held a trump card in the fighting spirit of the Army of Northern Virginia. What was to tip the balance in favor of the North was the coming to maturity of a general who, while Gettysburg was being fought, successfully accomplished the fall of Vicksburg. The rise to prominence of him and his subordinates was crucial to the making of victory. If the war had any turning points they were these: the decision of Grant to march with the Army of the Potomac, for this ensured that Lee would be hit hard at last; and Sherman's taking of Atlanta, which gave the North stomach to carry on a little longer.

8

War in Earnest

The North and the Final Campaigns

Soon after midnight, May 3d–4th, the Army of the Potomac moved out from its position north of the Rapidan, to start upon that memorable campaign, destined to result in the capture of the Confederate capital and the army defending it. . . . The losses inflicted, and endured, were destined to be severe; but the armies now confronting each other had already been in deadly conflict for a period of three years, with immense losses in killed, by death from sickness, captured and wounded; and neither had made any real progress toward accomplishing the final end.

—U. S. GRANT, *Personal Memoirs of U. S. Grant*

Until we can repopulate Georgia, it is useless for us to occupy it; but the utter destruction of its roads, houses, and people, will cripple their military resources . . . I can make this march, and make Georgia howl!

—Telegram from Sherman to Grant, October 9, 1864

The appointment of Ulysses S. Grant to the position of general-in-chief in March 1864 successfully neutralized, even if it did not end, inferiority feelings at the highest level of army command. Grant's work in the last year or so of the war would make a neat ending to the story if it could be written up as a chronicle of mounting confidence with Grant emerging in the popular imagination as a fitting champion of Northern democracy—the plainly dressed, humble westerner triumphing over the haughty Southern aristocrat. But the actual picture is more complex than that.

For one thing, inferiority feelings in Virginia were never stilled; Grant simply rode over them. There never came to the army in the east the sense of superiority that inhabited Sherman's men. Many of the easterners never took to Grant. They could not see that the losses caused by his hard-fighting methods were necessary to winning the war. The general-in-chief, it seemed to them, never outfought the enemy, he simply clubbed him into the ground. This failure to appreciate Grant not only soured the taste of victory for some soldiers and helped the legend of Southern invincibility to continue after the war, it robbed Grant of his true stature among military figures until a foreigner, J. F. C. Fuller, retrieved his reputation.[1]

There must be some suspicion that certain officers not only failed to recognize Grant's ability, they did not want to see it. He was a common man, lacking in pedigree and social graces. His presence was an affront to certain soldiers who wished to be led to victory by a man of breeding, a McClellan, in whose success a gentleman might take pride. Moreover, by his hammering tactics Grant appeared to be killing off a large portion of the Southern ruling class which meant that in the postwar world Northern gentlemen would feel even more isolated and lacking in allies. Dislike for Grant as a butcher and a commoner largely accounts for why he did not become a symbol of Northern victory.

Of course, it would be wrong to argue that victory was due entirely to a few outstanding personalities like Grant. The failure of Southern morale and the related fact that the physical power of the Confederacy was wearing out are significant factors. By 1864 the South could no longer make good its losses in manpower and materials whereas it was apparent that its enemy could. It was the role of Sherman and Grant to aggressively exploit this physical advantage. In the terminology of the day, they were prepared to make war in earnest.

Despite a material advantage and the generals who knew how to use it, the North might still have lost had it not been for the continued willingness of the Northern people to endure the cost of war, a final point to be remembered when assessing why the North won. Even then it was a close run thing. The casualty lists sent north in the summer of 1864 brought many people to the point of despair. Sherman's successes in Georgia and Sheridan's victories over Early in the Valley helped alleviate the worst of the gloom and pull the North through. But there was still truth in Grant's comment that "anything that could have prolonged the war a year beyond the time it did finally close, would probably have exhausted the North to such an extent that they might have abandoned the contest and agreed to a separation." There were people in the North who did not realize until the end how close the rebels were to defeat.[2]

Following his victory at Vicksburg in July 1863, Grant was appointed to command the theater of the West and in November he defeated Braxton Bragg at Missionary Ridge, ending the Confederate threat to Chattanooga. Between the conclusion of this operation and the beginning of the spring campaigns in 1864 Grant worked out, in conjunction with Lincoln and Halleck, the grand strategy that was to result in Union victory. Some of Grant's first ideas were faulty—at one point he suggested that a force including substantial elements of the Potomac army should be shipped down to North Carolina, a move that would have left Washington open to assault by Lee. The final grand plan was, however, a good one.[3]

Essentially, the design specified a concentration of force against the two most powerful Confederate armies: Joseph E. Johnston's Army of the Tennessee in the west, Lee's Army of Northern Virginia in the east. In the west, Sherman would attack Johnston in front, and Nathaniel P. Banks, who was currently operating in Texas, would move upon the rebel from the rear, trapping him between the two Union forces. Meanwhile, in the east, the Army of the Potomac would advance against Lee. The primary intention was to pin him down so that he could send no help to Johnston but it was also hoped to destroy him if possible. At the same time, a smaller force under Benjamin Butler would approach Richmond and threaten Lee's rear from the direction of Fortress Monroe. A similar task was given to the forces under Franz Sigel in the Shenandoah Valley. Finally, when Johnston had been eliminated, Sherman would sweep through the South and come upon Lee, pinned in position by Meade, from the rear.[4]

The strength of the plan lay in its coordination of superior Northern resources to bring crushing power against the rebels. The principle seems obvious enough but Grant was the first of Lincoln's generals to fully appreciate the basic need for cooperative effort on the part of the Union armies. Essentially, the war was to follow the pattern outlined in this blueprint, though the movements of Butler and Banks were to prove abortive. These operations were not, however, crucial to success. If there were a potential threat to the success of the plan, a danger area where the design ran the risk of complete failure, that area was the main Virginia theater where the Army of the Potomac was slated to meet the forces of Lee. A glance at the picture around the beginning of 1864 will illuminate the point.[5]

A difference existed between the situations in the main western and eastern theaters. In the army under Sherman, who assumed command of the West in early 1864, steady achievement had built a sense of confidence. The Confederate victory at Chicamaugua in September of 1863 had been offset by Union successes at Lookout Mountain, Missionary Ridge, and latterly, in January 1864, at Meridian. In Meade's army the situation was different. The record of this force showed no decisive achievement. The major advances into Virginia under McClellan, Hooker, and Burnside had all ended in failure and retreat. The defensive victories at Antietam and Gettysburg had not been followed up. There was, therefore, a certain lack of confidence in success, at least among the senior ranks. General Patrick, for example, noted in his diary on October 9, 1863, that some movement had been observed among the enemy troops. He went on: "They are either making a feint, preparatory to an evacuation of our front, or they are preparing to give us our annual Bull Run Flogging and it is not yet known which."[6]

The past was an enemy to some officers in Virginia: it walled them in so that they could not act with sound confidence. Sometimes it was only by leaving the theater that men could achieve their full military potential. Joseph Hooker, defeated at Chancellorsville, fought with daring and skill a few months later at Missionary Ridge in the west. People transferred to other departments might develop a contempt for the enemy which they had found impossible in Virginia. Edward Hastings Ripley, a colonel from Vermont who was sent to North Carolina, came to believe that the people there "are as strongly Secesh as the Virginians, but have few of the high qualities which lead them to oppose us to the bitter end." And he admitted that "at all events I have learned to thoroughly despise them, while for the Virginia Rebels, I have the respect their bravery and fortitude demands."[7]

The "Virginia mentality," as it may be termed, posed a serious threat to the success of Grant's grand strategy. The Army of the Potomac had the job of hitting Lee hard and often. This was a tall order for an army some of whose officers were in awe of the enemy and whose policy, in the words of General Hancock before the Committee on the Conduct of the War, "has habitually been to seek a defensive position and receive an attack." To accomplish Grant's objective the army needed to break out of the pattern of the past. It needed a fresh inspiration but it is doubtful whether this inspiration could have come from the army commander, General Meade, who showed the same overcaution which had rendered his predecessors ineffective. The lack of drive that had been apparent in Meade's pursuit of Lee after Gettysburg continued to be exhibited in the following months. While trying to press Meade into action during the fall, Halleck wrote to another general that the Army of the Potomac seemed to fight well when attacked "but all its generals have been unwilling to attack, even very inferior numbers. It is certainly a very strange phenomenon." Meade did initiate two advances, in October and November, but neither resulted in a major clash and by the end of the year nothing had been gained.[8]

It is more than likely that if Meade had been left to his own devices, the cycle of advance and retreat would have gone on well into 1864. And if this had happened it is conceivable that the North would have given up the struggle in despair of ever hearing anything decisive from Virginia. Much, then, rested on Grant, who saw that it was important for him to be with the Army of the Potomac. And it is a considerable part of his achievement that he was able to impress the force of his personality on operations in Virginia and drive the war there into a new pattern.[9]

Grant never seems to have fallen prey to the common fear of Lee and he did not allow himself to consider the possibility of retreat. No longer did the Confederate leader dominate the thinking of both armies, as a consideration of the Battle of the Wilderness, fought May 5–7, will show. On May 4 the Army of the Potomac crossed the Rapidan and advanced into the Wilderness where Hooker had fought a year before. Grant hoped to avoid a battle in this jungle-like area where his heavy formations would not have room to manoeuver and where detailed knowledge of the terrain might count for more than troop numbers. But Lee attacked while the army was still within the Wilderness, confirming the belief of some Union officers that he was the master of every battlefield situation. By the sixth there was some danger that the rebels might work their way into the Northern rear and it was at this point that the moral strength of the new Union commander became critical.[10]

Meade had penetrated the fringe of the Wilderness during his 1863 Mine Run campaign but had quickly withdrawn. Now, some of his officers again thought of retreat. But Grant would not hear of it. He spoke sharply to one group of officers, who were worried that Lee would flank them, saying, "While Gen. Lee was getting into our rear we certainly ought to be able to get in the rear of Gen. Lee." A similar incident, which took place later in the day, is worth quoting at length as it reveals the basic difference in attitude. Apparently, a general came to headquarters and blurted out: "General Grant, this is a crisis that cannot be looked upon too seriously. I know Lee's methods well by past experience; he will throw his whole army between us and the Rapidan, and cut us off completely from our communications." Grant, who had listened to sufficient negative ideas, replied: "Oh, I am heartily tired of hearing about what Lee is going to do. Some of you always seem to think he is suddenly going to turn a double somersault, and land in our rear and on both flanks at the same time. Go back to your command, and try to think what we are going to do ourselves, instead of what Lee is going to do."[11]

If further evidence was needed that Grant was not going to follow the old pattern, it was given on the next day, May 7. The armies had fought each other to a standstill and Grant withdrew his men from the front. But instead of retreating, as previous commanders might have done, he continued the advance, heading towards Spotsylvania. This forward move must also have demonstrated to the rebel generals that they were playing a different kind of game from the one with McClellan, Hooker, and Meade. A shrewd observer might have sensed that here was the beginning of the end for an army that could no longer rely on the mental intimidation of its opponent to compensate for its own weakness in numerical strength.

Indeed, there is some evidence that from the beginning the new general gave the Southerners a touch of the dread that Northerners had long felt about Lee. Horace Porter, of Grant's staff, said that Longstreet told him after the war he had rebuked a rebel officer who, on hearing that Grant would fight in Virginia, "talked very confidently of being able to whip with all ease the western general who was to confront them." Longstreet apparently told the man that he knew Grant and that "in order to whip him we must outmanoeuvre him, and husband our strength as best we can."[12]

Grant's importance in the war of the mind was summed up in a perceptive paragraph written on June 24, 1864, by Charles Francis Adams, the American minister to Britain. "The imagination has a vast power in upholding human force, or in knocking it away," he wrote. "The self-reliance of the slaveholding rebel is the secret of the amount of his resistance thus far. He began the war with a full conviction that he was more than a match for half a dozen men. And in many instances that conviction acting against a feebler will made him what he thought he was. The progress of the war has done a good deal to correct these impressions. General Grant appears to be setting them right."[13]

There can be no certain explanation of why Grant remained immune to the awe of Lee and of the rebels in general. One factor may be that all of his service before 1864 was performed in the west where the soldiers had developed a confidence in themselves. Also, when Grant came to Virginia he was buoyed by his recent successes at Vicksburg and Chattanooga. It seems, however, that his basic attitude was formed prior to these victories. From the very beginning of the war he appears to have been remarkably free from the anxieties that troubled other generals. A good example occurred in January of 1862 when Grant was serving under Halleck in the Department of the West. Halleck was supposed to cooperate with Buell, commanding the Department of the Ohio, in a movement against the rebel forces in Kentucky. Both generals perpetually made excuses to avoid action. Buell wrote frankly to Lincoln, "My judgment from the first has been decidedly against it." By contrast, when Grant finally received orders to advance he responded with alacrity. He was not deterred by the bad state of the roads, which, he said, "will operate worse upon the enemy, if he should come out to meet us, than upon us." Such assumptions of Union advantage were rare among Northern generals in early 1862.[14]

Grant himself did not attempt much explanation of his outlook though he did suggest that a key factor in his attitude to Lee was that he had known the Confederate leader before the war. In his memoirs he said, "The natural disposition of most people is to clothe a commander of a large army whom they do not know, with almost superhuman abilities. A large part of the National Army, for instance, and most of the press of the country, clothed General Lee with just such qualities, but I had known him personally, and knew that he was mortal; and it was just as well that I felt this." Possibly there is some substance to the argument, though others including McClellan had known Lee, and the knowledge did not seem to help them.[15]

There is, perhaps, another reason why Grant did not attribute larger-than-life qualities to his enemies. Some of those who experienced most difficulties in their military role had some pretension to superior class or breeding: they were from, or identified with, the old leadership groups of bankers, lawyers, mercantile families, and landowners. The question of the role and significance of gentlemen in a republic was one with which they frequently wrestled. And they tended to be dissatisfied with the performance of Northern democracy, seeing Southern wartime arrangements as stronger by virtue of their seemingly greater reliance on leadership by gentlemen.

Grant was not of this group. His memoirs, for example, reveal hardly any speculation on such common themes as the class composition of the Northern officer corps. Why Grant did not fit the pattern is hard to say. Perhaps part of the answer lies in the fact that his family background was relatively undistinguished. His father eventually rose to be mayor of Bethel, Ohio, but he was a tanner by trade. Grant's own career before the war had been rather dismal. In 1854 he had to resign from the army to avoid a court-martial for excessive drinking. In private business he was largely a failure and had it not been for secession his record might have been one of increasing decline. Such a man could make few claims to privilege on the basis of birth or background.[16]

At any rate, whatever the reasons, Grant apparently saw no special virtue in the aristocratic way. This could explain his moral unshakability in the face of the rebels. Having no gentlemanly pretensions, he presumably felt no particular awe for the gentleman image of the Southerner. As opposed to more well-born types, he computed the skill and strength of his opponent on rational probabilities and not on preconceptions about the superiority of aristocracy in war. Grant's freedom from acute awareness of class may also partially explain his excellent working relationship with Lincoln. Grant was one of the few top generals who managed to avoid looking down on the common-man President. He took his suggestions seriously and benefited accordingly.[17]

Grant, then, was the first general to remain immune to what we have termed the "Virginia mentality." He was also the first commander to achieve his strategic purpose in this theater. This fact has often been obscured by misunderstanding of Grant's primary aim. Grant was not able to bring Lee into the open and destroy his army in pitched battle. The Confederate commander could not be flushed from his entrenchments. This has led many people to argue that Lee was the superior general. However, J. F. C. Fuller has pointed out that to destroy Lee was not Grant's primary aim. His main wish was to pin the rebels down and in this he was successful from the beginning. In the first battle, that of the Wilderness, Lee was forced onto the defensive. Fuller sums up the point thus: "Strategically it was the greatest Federal victory yet won in the East, for Lee was now thrown on the defensive—he was held. Thus, within forty-eight hours of crossing the Rapidan, did Grant gain his objective—the fixing of Lee."[18]

This purpose was not achieved without a cost—between May 7 and June 3 Grant lost as many men as were in the whole Confederate army. Could the price have been less? Possibly so, if the Army of the Potomac had done more to weaken Lee and end the war in Virginia before 1864. But as Grant pointed out in his memoirs, "The opposing forces stood in substantially the same relations toward each other as three years before, or when the war began; they were both between the Federal and Confederate capitals." Thus the main work of destroying the Army of Northern Virginia as a powerful and dangerous field force had still to be done. Incessant fighting was necessary to make up for the failures of the past years. Grant concludes: "The campaign now begun was destined to result in heavier losses, to both armies, in a given time, than any previously suffered; but the carnage was to be limited to a single year, and to accomplish all that had been anticipated or desired at the beginning in that time. We had to have hard fighting to achieve this."[19]

Finally, while the real losses were high because of the large number of battles fought, Fuller has argued convincingly that Grant's average loss per battle was not excessively high by Civil War standards. In the eight major battles fought between the Wilderness and Appomattox, his average of killed and wounded per engagement was 10.42 percent of men present. This is slightly lower than the Federal average for the whole war (11.07 percent) and decidedly below Lee's average of 16.02 percent for the period 1862–1863 (the only years for which accurate figures are available.) The only battle in which Grant may have been guilty of needless slaughter is Cold Harbor. And even here the situation is not entirely unfavorable to him, for while he may have been culpable in not stopping the assaults, it appears to have been Meade who actually organized and directed the attacks.[20]

The overall impression of Grant is of a man who was not superior to his opponent in battlefield tactics but whose strategic reasoning was sound and who carried out his task without excessive cost. There was of course a gamble involved in what Grant was doing. On the one hand, the stalemate in Virginia had to be broken to show the North that the war could be won. On the other, the concentrated losses might cripple Northern morale before the inevitability of victory could become clear. The balance was a fine one and for a period in the summer of 1864 Grant, together with the administration that supported him, trod a fine line between success and failure.

The North reeled under the weight of the casualty lists from Virginia. Noah Brooks wrote that these were "the darkest of many dark days through which passed the friends and lovers of the Federal Union." General Martindale, in New York, found that "there is very great discouragement over the North, great reluctance to recruiting, strong disposition for peace, and even among Republicans of long standing inclination for a *change of rulers."* Wendell Phillips was so depressed as to fear that "we shall be obliged either to acknowledge the Southern Confederacy or to reconstruct the Union on terms grossly unjust, intolerable to the masses, and sure soon to result in another war."[21]

There were those who realized that the killing was necessary to retrieve the time lost in Virginia. Adam Gurowski wrote that Grant was trying to make up for the criminal imbecility in the conduct of the war since the time of Winfield Scott, which had allowed the rebellion to grow roots so deep that only a superhuman effort could pull them up. But many people could not see this far; they felt only the suffering. "I am very dull tonight," wrote Mrs. Benjamin Butler. "What is all this struggling and fighting for? This ruin and death to thousands of families? What is to come out of it? What advancement of mankind to compensate for the present horrible calamities?"[22]

The anguish was increased by the fact that, on April 17, Grant had halted the exchange of prisoners in order to further his policy of fatally weakening the rebel armies. As with his other plans, a certain risk was involved. Though the move damaged the rebel armies, it also produced a great deal of bitterness against the Federal government among Northerners. Morale was hurt, not only among Northern prisoners like John Ransom, who engaged in "cursing their government for its refusal to exchange," but among civilians like the woman who said, "There is nothing so discourages enlisting as the fact of the government allowing her men to endure the barbarous treatment."[23]

The anxiety was inadvertently intensified by Northern propagandists. Basing their sketches on abolitionist stereotypes of the vicious slaveocrat, certain Northern editors and public men had, throughout the war, stressed that Southerners were a fiendish race. The aim of this propaganda was to make people hate the rebels and thus keep up the war spirit. But in the case of the prisons it backfired: portraits of the rebel camps as hellholes discouraged enlistment and sapped the morale of those who had relatives in the army. As Isabelle S. Parker put it, "The mother's heart shrinks from exposing her son to the possibilities of such a fate as here portrayed."[24]

Finally, the floundering confidence of the North reached a nadir when, in July, Lee sent Jubal A. Early with 14,000 troops on a raid into the Shenandoah Valley to draw pressure off the Army of Northern Virginia. By July 11 Early was in the suburbs of Washington and though he was not able to maintain his position he demonstrated graphically that the Confederacy was not yet dead. The administration stood disgraced and had there not been some improvement in affairs Lincoln would almost certainly have lost the November election to McClellan. As it was, he received only some 400,000 popular votes more than his opponent. If McClellan had won, the war might have been lost, for though he pledged himself to carry on the struggle, many votes for him represented a desire for peace that might have become too powerful to resist. Undoubtedly, too, McClellan would have interfered with military policy and might have spoiled the grand plan.[25]

Two generals played key roles in bringing the North up from the depths of depression. These were Sheridan, who between August and October ended the Confederate threat in the Shenandoah, and Sherman, who took the key rail center of Atlanta in September and then plunged through the heart of the Confederacy, showing both sides that the end was near.

Sheridan resembled Grant in many ways (it may be significant that his background was also a humble one: his father was a laborer). In Virginia, he demonstrated the same level-headed approach as his chief. When he took over the cavalry of the Army of the Potomac in 1864 it "had not done all it might have done," as Lincoln phrased it. On more than one occasion it had held the field against Stuart but it had not established a moral superiority any more than had the rest of the army. As George Hughes Hepworth, an anti-slavery minister, noted in a book published in 1864, "Wherever Stuart rides, he carries terror with him. His victories are half won before he strikes a blow. Our soldiers feel that he may pounce on them at any minute, and that he is as resistless as a hawk in a fowlyard."[26]

The situation changed quickly under Sheridan. On May 8 he set out for Richmond with 10,000 men. On May 11 he fought Stuart at Yellow Tavern. The attack was pressed with the same kind of remorseless vigor shown by Grant in his battles with Lee. At the end of the day Stuart was dead and the Confederates had suffered irreparable damage. The rebel cavalry, said Sheridan, "had acquired such prestige that it thought itself wellnigh invincible; indeed, in the early years of the war it had proved to be so. This was now dispelled by the successful march we made in Lee's rear; and the discomfiture of Stuart at Yellow Tavern had inflicted a blow from which entire recovery was impossible."[27]

Even men like Colonel Theodore Lyman of Meade's staff, who were not particularly friendly to the newcomers from the west, had to admit that "the Southern cavalry cannot now cope with ours. We have beaten them every time this campaign; whereas their infantry are a full match for ours." Not all the credit was Sheridan's. The Confederates no longer had the numbers, mounts, or equipment to deal with the well-led Union horse. Also, Sheridan's predecessors labored under the disability of having their men and horses worn out by secondary duties such as picketing the infantry camps. Grant, with Sheridan's prodding, prevented much of this. However, no matter what advantages Sheridan enjoyed, the driving force, the "earnestness," was his. He showed the same trait when sent by Grant to stop Early's raids and to ravage the Shenandoah so that it could no longer give succor to the Confederates. Like Grant accepting the necessary losses in Virginia he saw what had to be done and did it without either reveling in the destruction or allowing himself to be deflected from his course by doubts about the rightness of his actions.[28]

Sherman, the third of these men who made hard war, is perhaps the most intriguing of all for his wartime career remains something of an enigma. Of the generals who suffered from an acute sense of enemy superiority he is the only one who eventually achieved a sustained aggressive mentality. In late 1861, lack of confidence drove him to the point of exhaustion, yet he went on to conduct one of the most daring campaigns in the history of warfare. I have found no certain explanation of this phenomenon. But perhaps it is possible to throw a little light on Sherman's mental process.

The seemingly abrupt change from timid to aggressive has led certain writers to suggest that Sherman's personality changed drastically and they hint that this may indicate a certain mental instability. Edmund Wilson, for example, points to a comment by Sherman's wife about insanity in the family and goes on to say that as the war progressed the general became gripped by "a 'manic' elation," by "the strong throb of the lust to dominate and the ecstasy of its satisfaction which in the past made people believe that they were fighting as instruments of God and in our own times as instruments of 'History.'" Otto Eisenschiml in "Sherman: Hero or War Criminal?" also discusses the seeming change in Sherman's attitude. Eisenschiml says that he rejects the idea of madness but he seems to imply that Sherman had a kind of split personality. He believes that there was in the general a latent fanaticism which surfaced during the war; Sherman became obsessed with the idea that he was an avenging angel sent to scourge the South.[29]

Each of these theories stresses the element of change. Both have something to recommend them, especially in their emphasis on a certain strange quality in Sherman's later behavior. This will be returned to later. For the moment, perhaps something can be gained by changing the angle of vision—by stressing the element of continuity rather than change. It is important to realize, first of all, that the paradox in Sherman's career can be overstated: his basic view of the enemy never changed that much. For example, he retained a tendency to overstate their powers and resources. Late in the Atlanta campaign he was still magnifying the numbers of his opponents. On August 2, 1864, he wrote, "I doubt if our army much exceeds that of Hood," and by the eleventh he was inclined to "think to-day Hood's army is larger than mine, and he is strongly fortified." In fact, at the beginning of August Hood was holding Atlanta with 37,000 infantry and 5,000 Georgia State Militia while Sherman had 85,000 infantry.[30]

If this sounds reminiscent of McClellan, the likeness is not entirely coincidental. Sherman had a certain sympathy for that fallen general. As late as October 1864 he wrote that the howl against McClellan had been in a measure unjust for he never had the number of soldiers accredited to him. That he always had more than the rebels was a fact that escaped Sherman as it had McClellan.[31]

The tendency to exaggeration that had betrayed him in 1861 was still in Sherman; what had changed was his ability to prevent it from destroying his usefulness. It was more under control. How Sherman achieved this is a puzzle but one factor may be that after 1861 all his service was in the west where there was generally less respect for the rebels than in the east. If he had been posted to Virginia in 1862 it is more than possible that he would have gone the way of the other generals there. Instead of participating in the unsatisfying Gettysburg campaign he was in at the capture of Vicksburg, which pleased him enough to elicit the remark that "though full of corruption and base materials, our country is a majestic one, full of natural wealth and good people."[32]

The fact that Sherman served under Grant must also be significant. Grant was preeminently the man of reason, the pragmatic mind. There seems to have been no midnight hour when visions of the enemy host could strike terror through his soul. Sherman must have learned something from Grant on this score, though he was aware that he never achieved his chief's equanimity, remarking on one occasion that Grant "don't care a damn for what the enemy does out of his sight, but it scares me like hell! I am more nervous than he is."[33]

Service under Grant in the west helped Sherman gain in confidence. But it appears to have been the fall of Atlanta that finally made him realize the enemy was significantly weaker than himself. However, it must again be stressed that Sherman's view of the enemy soldier's character had not altered; he simply saw the rebel army as failing in numerical power. He continued to use the old stereotype of the Southerner as a hotheaded fellow, proud and daring, who preferred fighting to earning a decent living. Forrest's cavalry seemed to him typical of the breed—"young bloods of the South: sons of planters, lawyers about towns, good billiard-players and sportsmen, men who never did work and never will. War suits them, and the rascals are brave, fine riders, bold to rashness, and dangerous subjects in every sense." They were to him a "whole batch of devils."[34]

Ironically, the general who has come down through history as the hard-headed pragmatist—the man who ripped the veil of illusion surrounding modern war—may have based his military thinking partly on these highly fanciful characterizations of the enemy. In Sherman's thesis that the South must be made to feel the heavy hand of war, his idea of the rebels as a devil's brood played a significant role. Looking forward to the end of hostilities, Sherman could see no hope for a lasting peace until these blooded Southerners were broken in spirit or killed in mass. They were far too dangerous to be treated with kid gloves: their warlike energy must be extinguished through a ruthless harrying of the South. Unless such a policy was carried out, what was to prevent the young men of the South, who despised peaceful pursuits, from carrying on indefinite guerrilla war?[35]

The Sherman of the march to the sea was not so different from the Sherman of 1861. He was more confident, more aggressive, but he still felt that he faced an enemy who was tougher, more wily, and more artful than most the world had seen. Paradoxically, this may in part explain the evolvement of his highly pragmatic scorched-earth policy. Facing a perhaps still dangerous foe, he came to a ruthless policy. Indeed, he was one of the few senior officers to advocate killing the whole Southern ruling class.[36]

So far, Sherman's behavior may be explained without posing a vast personality change; his ideas are a natural product of his experience. There remains, however, a disturbing quality about Sherman, one that previous writers have pointed to. And it is here that they find their strongest evidence for suggesting that Sherman was mentally unsound. For Sherman not only came to make hard war, he seems to have actually gained some emotional satisfaction from the suffering. The point may be made by comparing an incident on the eve of war with one which occurred in 1864. Sherman liked most of the Southerners he met before the war and was overcome with emotion at having to leave his Louisiana cadets in the Secession Crisis. By 1863 signs of a less sentimental approach to the rebels were developing and by 1864, when he was ordering enemy prisoners to dig up mines planted in the road, he "could hardly help laughing" at their frightened antics while on the job.[37]

In pointing to this phenomenon, Wilson and others have performed a service. But there seems little reason to resort to speculation on insanity in the family or to theories about split personality to explain the case. Sherman was under a great deal of strain. While he achieved an aggressive mentality, he never quite lost his awe of the enemy soldier. To contain his own fears and imaginings must have taken a great deal of self-control. And this in turn must have had a terribly wearing effect on Sherman's nerves. It may be suggested that this strain ultimately produced a tremendous rage against those who had rebelled in 1861 and thus forced him into his present position.[38]

There was further mental pressure on Sherman. The Northern people, he believed, had never understood fully the huge dimensions of the struggle. Not only this, but when he tried to tell them, they had laughed at him. In 1861 the press had hounded him unmercifully and this was partly responsible for his mental exhaustion in that year. The seeming failure of the North to grasp the true situation remained a tremendous source of frustration to him. He was staggered by the draft laws which allowed men to buy substitutes to do their military service. On August 2, 1864, he wrote, "On the other side they have everybody, old and young," in the ranks, while the best the Northern armies could expect were "niggers and bought recruits that must be kept well to the rear." Sherman's unawareness of loopholes in Southern legislation that also allowed the wealthy to evade the draft is another indication of his continuing awe of the foe.[39]

If the general was not happy with the North as a whole, he reserved his most intense hatred for the press. In a letter of June 9, 1864, he accused the "mischievous scribblers for newspapers" of causing the war and continuing it by fanning "the flames of discord and hostility." If he could have got away with it, he would have had all the reporters shot. As it was, this pent-up aggression had to be released somehow. In the case of McClellan's officers, who had also felt themselves to be persecuted by a stupid and unseeing public, these aggressions might have been converted into a military coup against Washington. Sherman, it may be speculated, transferred his frustrations onto the enemy and reaped vengeance from them.[40]

To conclude, although the exact process of change from the timid general of 1861 to the bold warrior of 1864 will probably remain partially a mystery, the development is made intelligible if we concentrate on the element of continuity. Paradoxically, awe of the enemy's power was a factor that drove Sherman to a policy of ruthless, all-out war. Even the enjoyment of suffering, which seemed to inhabit the man in the later period, may be explained in terms of the strain produced by fighting an enemy seemingly superior to one's own side. Thus, Sherman does not appear to have been the Jekyll and Hyde figure portrayed by Wilson. He was not a man with an intrinsic bent to destruction but a victim of the strains of war.

His case was not entirely abnormal. Wars, by their very nature, seem to have a brutalizing influence on those involved. The longer a war continues, the stronger is the impulse away from humane feeling. In the Civil War it was apparent at least by 1862 that the conflict was starting to turn savage. Pope's orders regarding the treatment of civilians are symptomatic of the change as was the increasing frequency with which both sides hung spies. Some who began the war with a warm regard for the South turned cold as the killing mounted. George Armstrong Custer, who in 1862 enjoyed singing with avowed rebels around the piano, was by 1864 hanging Mosby's partisan rangers and is reputed to have ordered a boy dragged through the streets and shot in front of his mother.[41]

Stories of atrocities such as this, whether true or untrue, had an important influence in heightening feeling. For example, rumors of rebel atrocities at Fort Pillow, where Forrest's men supposedly killed women and children, produced a violent reaction. General Alexander Hays wrote, "I almost feel like announcing, 'Boys, I do not wish to be encumbered with prisoners.'" Like Sherman, some men came to talk of mass killing. The slaughter of 1864 so shocked certain types that they were willing to use the threat of extermination to force the South into surrender and end the killing. Others wished to depopulate the region so that no such rebellion could ever occur again. Again like Sherman, the most ruthless were sometimes those who had been most humiliated by apparent rebel superiority. Thus David Hunter Strother, who had served under a series of undistinguished Union commanders, was largely responsible for the burning of the Virginia Military Institute.[42]

Of course, not all men became hateful. Soldiers were often nauseated by the fighting. It will be seen later that this was particularly true in Virginia where respect for the quality of the enemy acted as a bar on the deepening of feeling. In the west too, there were men who balked at all-out war. Harvey Reid, a soldier with Sherman, wrote on November 15, 1864, "The cruelties practiced on this campaign toward citizens have been enough to blast a more sacred cause than ours." Others became caught up in the mood of Sherman's march only reluctantly. On November 13 Major James A. Connolly recorded that he had tried to prevent the burning of a village. But by the twenty-sixth he had decided that the army had gone so far in antagonizing the citizens that the only way it could survive was to continue the policy and mercilessly crush all resistance. "It is a question of life or death with us, and all considerations of mercy and humanity must bow before the inexorable demands of self-preservation."[43]

In terms of humanity, the deepening anger of the war was unfortunate but in a military sense it may have greatly helped the North. It had lacked aggressiveness. There had been reluctance to fight and fear of the South. Perhaps anger helped overcome both. At any rate, by the end of 1864 it was becoming clear to many that the generalships of Grant and Sherman had been effective. Even Sherman grasped that the enemy power was utterly broken. "It seemed to me then," he wrote later, "that the terrible energy they had displayed in the earlier stages of the war was beginning to yield to the slower but more certain industry and discipline of our Northern men." He continued: "It seems to me manifest that the soldiers and people of the South entertained an undue fear of our Western men, and like children, they had invented such ghostlike stories of our prowess in Georgia, that they were scared by their own inventions." So had the terrorized become the terrorizer.[44]

Lee surrendered on April 9 and Johnston on April 26, 1865. With this end of the main Confederate resistance there was tremendous rejoicing in the North. Inevitably, some of this took the form of boasting that Southern military claims had been disproved. James T. Ayers, a recruiting officer, said the war had taught that "being Southerners don't necessarily make them better than other men and there fighting qualities far superior to Any other people." Secretary Welles wrote, with rather more polish, that through reading Sir Walter Scott and others, Southerners "came ultimately to believe themselves a superior and better race . . . Only a war could wipe out this arrogance and folly." "We all remember one type of the traditional Southerner," wrote Colonel James Fowler Rusling in the

United States Service Magazine, "a fiery-eyed, long-haired, neglige individual, great upon juleps and cocktails, fond of fast horses and faster
women, a barbaric compound of ignorance and cruelty." These people
had boasted that they could each whip five Yankees, who "were only canting Puritans, snivelling Roundheads." But the rebels forgot the lessons
of a Naseby, Marston Moore, Lexington, and Bunker Hill. James Russell
Lowell was thinking along much the same lines. At the Harvard Commemoration on July 21 he recited an ode which asked, "Who now shall
sneer?/Who dare again to say we trace/Our lines to a plebian race?/
Roundhead and Cavalier!"[45]

As well as a victory of the Puritan over the Cavalier, the war could be
seen as the triumph of democracy over aristocracy. James T. Robinson, a
Baptist speaker, proclaimed that "Aristocracy and despotism are over-
whelmed, . . . The greatest conspiracy against the Free Institutions, and
the progress of mankind, is annihilated." The American experiment in
popular government was complete, said *Harper's Weekly.* Democratic
principles had been found sufficient to suppress an unprecedented rebellion. And the soldiers of the Army of the Cumberland, in adopting a
corps badge, noted in their resolve that each man had "done his part in
proving to the world that republics have the ability to maintain and per-
petuate themselves."[46]

The predominant spirit of the times may be sampled through the
works of the Reverend George Hughes Hepworth, a minister of strong
anti-slavery sentiments. His sermons present a comprehensive view of the
history of the rebellion. He recalled the years before the war when it had
seemed that Northern public men allowed themselves to be bullied by
Southerners. "Do you recall those shameful scenes in Washington," he
asked, "when the Northern statesman was continually under the censorship of the braggadocio's duelling-pistol or bowie-knife?" It seemed, said
Hepworth, that "we almost saw the spectral shapes of our dead forefathers
coming from their graves to accuse us of cowardice." But four years of war
had shown that the earlier tolerance was not cowardice but love of country and desire to save the Union, for the North had fought well when the
time came.[47]

Indeed, said the minister, the Union achievement in the war was no
mean one. In the beginning of the war it had been unprepared while the
South was ready to fight. Reverting to the idea of a military conspiracy,
Hepworth pictured in the South an army of one hundred thousand men
"frenzied with hatred of the North, their lips trembling with vows of
sacriligeous allegiance to slavery, . . . Our Treasury had been robbed; our
arsenals were empty; our navy was at the uttermost parts of the earth; our

army was on the farm, in the workshop, office, and pulpit." The frenzy of the rebels carried them to victories but in the end they were ruined "by the Union army, aided and encouraged by the irresistible spirit of the century." The South, he concluded, had shown by its cruelties and by its ultimate failure that it was not really chivalric or superior. "The best society—I mean the society which gives us the greatest number of generous, devoted, and brave men—is always that in which the citizen is at once humbled and ennobled by labor." For the epitaph of the Confederacy Hepworth suggested "a petticoat and a bowie-knife. These are the symbols of weakness and cruelty."[48]

This was the dominant theme in Northern thought. But beneath the trumpet blasts a dissonant note could be heard occasionally. Perhaps an article in *Wilkes' Spirit* for April 15, 1865, gives a hint of this. In extolling the virtues of a democratic people the editor commented, "The war has produced a great people, but no great men, and that perhaps is the best boon to liberty and true democracy, of all the blessings of the crisis." Did *Wilkes'* simply mean that the war had produced no "men on horseback," no dictators, or did it mean that Lincoln, Grant, and Sherman were not to be considered great men?"[49]

A second intriguing point is that the kind of symbolism that can be found in the meeting of Grant and Lee at Appomattox—the aristocrat immaculate in a fresh uniform; the representative of democracy muddy and without a sword—has appealed more to later generations than to the men who fought the war. There is a conspicuous lack of comment on Grant as the symbol of conquering democracy in the letters and diaries of the time. Further, some soldiers in the Army of the Potomac do not seem to have found victory as satisfying as one might expect. There was relief but, at the same time, a certain lack of exuberance. An anecdote told by a Confederate veteran illustrates the point. After the surrender a group of rebels were accosted by Union soldiers who, to relieve their pent-up feelings, "began to curse and use the most approbrious language" toward them. The cursing was stopped by a Federal major who rode up and said to the Union men, "These Confederate soldiers are brave men. If you were half as brave as they are, you'd have conquered them long ago." Evidently, the Virginia mentality was not quite dead.[50]

Many Union soldiers might well have agreed with the officer for they deeply respected their late opponents. It is reputed that when the time came for the last Confederate brigade to surrender its arms, someone in the Union ranks raised three cheers for the rebels. Henry Kyd Douglas, commanding the brigade, remembered "how that line of blue broke its respectful silence to pay such tribute, at Appomattox, to the little line in grey that had fought them to the finish and only surrendered because it was destroyed."[51]

Douglas' comment is not only of interest for the light it throws on Northern feeling but also for its emotionally charged reference to "the little line in grey." This smacks of that myth which helped insulate Southerners against the raw pain of defeat—the myth that the South only surrendered when its manpower was gone. In fact, there were plenty of able-bodied men in the Confederacy, some of whom had deserted, some who joined local military units to avoid service at the front, and some who were never called. But many Southerners could not admit this: even before the surrender they began to cocoon themselves in the idea that they had been whipped by numbers alone and not by skill or determination. On April 3, 1865, William Graham, a soldier from Georgia, wrote in his diary, "Our gallant and hitherto invincible Army of Northern Virginia has been overcome by mere brute force of numbers." And on May 20 Private Henry Robinson Berkeley noted that the South was beaten only " 'by overpowering numbers and resources,' as Gen. Lee puts it in his good-bye order to the Army of Northern Virginia. We put up a bully fight if we did go under." The interesting point is that something of the same feeling could be found among Union soldiers. As with most myths about the South, Northerners had a hand in the making. Colonel Wainwright, for example, wrote on April 9 that though Lee's surrender made this "a day forever to be remembered," it would have been more glorious if there had been a grand battle —a Gettysburg. "As it is," he said, "the rebellion has been worn out rather than suppressed."[52]

Victory did not seem quite so sweet as it might have been: there was something lacking. Of course, it would be unwise to draw too much from the scattered comments of soldiers but they do point to a lurking disgust with the last year of fighting in Virginia. This disgust was born partially of antipathy to Grant and his methods, and it is worth looking at the reaction of the soldiers to their new commander both for what it reveals about their philosophy and as a background to the continuation of the martial South idea after Appomattox.

A negative attitude to Grant began to form in the Army of the Potomac even before it met him. He came east to be made lieutenant general and, as Bruce Catton pointed out, this elevation to special rank implied a criticism of everything the eastern army had done. In self-defense, eastern soldiers called Grant a second John Pope, who might be coming to Virginia full of confidence but who would quickly crumple before the rebels. Grant was told that "he had not so far met either the Confederacy's best generals or its best troops, and good patriotic officers openly expressed the opinion that Grant would find Lee a very much more difficult man to beat than Buckner, Joe Johnston, or Bragg." So far as the feeling of the average soldier was concerned, Major Hyde of the Sixth Corps admitted that the troops did not like it much when they heard a rumor that Grant was to take command, for they had experienced Pope, another western general. There was never enthusiasm for Grant, he said, "as we had exhausted much of our early fervor, and envied the Confederates their great captain." Finally, Hyde remarked, "We thought people North hardly comprehended that the Army of the Potomac had been fighting the choicest leadership and the best army by far of the Confederacy."[53]

The easterners were probably right in thinking that they had faced some of the best rebel generals and that the men opposed to Grant had often been mediocre. But they were blind to the fact that Grant's victories had been won with less resources than were available to generals in Virginia. One biographer points out that "when he won his first important victory at Fort Donelson, Grant had just three West Point men in his army." It was not a new thing for the Potomac soldiers to stress that they faced the strongest opposition; the idea was at the base of the Virginia mentality. There was a certain inverted arrogance in the attitude. While they were overawed by the enemy, these soldiers were condescending to outsiders. As one officer put it, "When Lee takes command of both armies, as he has done several times before, we shall go rattling back to the Potomac."[54]

In the weeks of hard fighting that followed the opening of the 1864 campaign, the reservations turned to horror and revulsion. Augustus Meyers, a private soldier, wrote later that "this sanguine campaign, its awful sacrifices without any advantages, caused mutterings of discontent and had a gloomy and depressing effect." And Warren Lee Goss recalled that by the time of Cold Harbor many soldiers "began to say among themselves that Grant was simply 'bull-headed and stubborn, not skilful and great.'" It was thought that he compared unfavorably with McClellan, who had reached the same point in 1862 with less loss of life.[55]

Similar feelings were to be found among the officers. Oliver Wendell Holmes, Jr., told his parents on June 24 that "many a man has gone crazy since this campaign begun from the terrible pressure on mind & body" and that "there's no use in disguising that the feeling for McClellan has grown this campaign." John William De Forest, coming up from the Department of the Gulf in August was astonished by the negative attitude of the officers in the Army of the Potomac. After listening to the gloomy predictions of one group he finally asked, "But don't you believe in Grant at all?" "Yes, we believe in Grant," said a colonel, "but we believe a great deal more in Lee and in that Army of Virginia." Colonel Wainwright, who had never thought much of Grant, felt that "his only dependence is on being able to furnish the most men to be killed."[56]

Such comments by soldiers molded the image of Grant as a butcher. It was, as pointed out earlier in the chapter, an erroneous idea. Comparing the generalship of Lee and Grant, while the Union man could not force his opponent out from behind entrenchments, he did achieve his primary object of pinning him down. And given the magnitude of the task, he accomplished his objective without excessive cost. It may be added in Grant's favor that while his actions were part of a larger strategic concept that embraced the winning of the whole war, Lee restricted his vision largely to Virginia and hence contributed to the Confederate failure to develop a viable overall plan of defense. Why could the Union soldiers see none of this? For one thing, to confess that Grant's style of heavy fighting was necessary would have been to admit that for three years they had failed to do their job in Virginia. This was psychologically impossible for them.[57]

Equally important was the fact that most of the soldiers were not on Grant's military level. The majority of Civil War generals had read or had otherwise become familiar with the writings of Antoine Henri Jomini, a Frenchman who had served with Napoleon I. Appalled by the slaughter of the wars following the French Revolution, he had attempted to take the methods of warfare back to the style of the eighteenth century, when armies had been largely tools of foreign policy, used to gain limited objectives. Because these armies were professional bodies, expensive to raise and maintain, manoeuvring for position and the taking of cities or other key locations rather than the destruction of enemy forces was emphasized. If there was a major pitched battle it would often be taken as decisive and a peace would be arranged on its basis.[58]

This concept of limited war had a tremendous influence on Civil War generals. McClellan, for instance, usually thought in terms of taking Richmond rather than of destroying the Army of Northern Virginia and he considered his greatest successes to be those in which there was the least fighting. It was part of the genius of Grant and Sherman to realize that this method of warfare was out of place; that they were not fighting for limited gains in foreign policy but to subdue a whole people and that to achieve success enemy armies must be wasted and civilian morale broken. The point seems obvious now but it was hidden to most of the soldiers and this partly explains why there was nostalgia for McClellan. Thinking in terms of taking Richmond rather than of smashing Lee, they measured the two generals by miles covered rather than by enemy power destroyed. And because Grant was not able to give them a single climactic battle—a Waterloo—they thought the victory poorly won.[59]

Even if some of the soldiers had understood Grant, they would still have been appalled because for them, as for Jomini, the concept of limited war was part of a larger view of the world and it was a world in which Grant had no place. Their ideal society was one in which gentlemen of background and education took a leading role and settled disputes according to well-established principles. Emancipation, with its revolutionary implications, had been a great shock and McClellan's refusal to countenance a coup had ended any real chance of a counterrevolutionary thrust. But hope that the old way would ultimately triumph had continued. General Meade was still insisting late in the conflict that the war could be ended if the better men on both sides were allowed to sort things out through the exercise of a little Christian charity. But in the triumph of Grant could be sensed the fact that there would be no turning back to an older and more gentlemanly way of doing things.[60]

For Grant neither looked nor acted the part of a gentleman. He was awkward in manner and lacking in social graces. When he first arrived in Washington, people did not recognize him as the great war captain about whom they had read. The New Englander, Richard Henry Dana, Jr., wrote disdainfully that Grant "had no gait, no station, no manner." And he thought it improper that the general should stand talking and smoking in the entrance to Willard's hotel. When the President and his leading general met publicly there was a display of democratic informality among the guests sufficient to make any gentleman shudder and to remind him of the rude crowds at the inaugural of Andrew Jackson, the so-called democratic king. "So great was the crowd," wrote the journalist Noah Brooks, "and so wild the rush to get near the general, that he was obliged at last to mount a sofa," while "ladies suffered dire disaster in the crush and confusion; their laces were torn and crinolines mashed." Secretary Welles, who believed that the administration's public receptions had never been to its credit, could only think the whole business "rowdy and unseemly."[61]

Some Potomac officers inevitably found Grant's personality not to their taste. Colonel Wainwright, who believed that officers should be drawn from the upper levels, found him "stumpy, unmilitary, slouchy and western-looking; very ordinary, in fact." It was partly disapproval on the part of some of the most articulate men in the army that prevented the symbolic interpretation of the meeting at Appomattox from gaining wide currency. They did not like to think of their representative as being a mud-stained, common-looking fellow.[62]

If Grant represented anything to them, it must have been the triumph of new men whose major talent appeared to be an aggressive ability to survive in the hard milieu of the modern world. Probably such symbolism was not fully articulated or even understood but it must partially stand back of that refusal to take to Grant. It may not be stretching the point too far to say that in Grant's methods—his hard-nosed approach, his use of superior numbers to wear down the enemy—could be sensed the triumph of the mass, the victory of quantity over quality, of technology over taste.

There was a more concrete threat inherent in Grant's war. As gentlemen glimpsed the road leading into the postwar world, they might sense that it pointed not toward their stable society but toward greater popular participation in government, even more social and economic mobility. They might realize too that in the war they had been fighting their potentially strongest future ally—the Southern planter class. But Grant was decimating this class in Virginia. Colonel Lyman, a gentleman on Meade's staff, had a certain fellow feeling for men of equal social rank on the other side. He praised the bearing of rebel officers which, he felt, was superior to that of Union men. Thus the slaughter of the 1864 campaign troubled him, for, he said, "It is not a gain to kill off these people . . . They are a valuable people, capable of a heroism that is too rare to be lost." Reading between the lines, it can be seen that Lyman was perturbed about what America was to do for gentlemen in the future. For such men, victory must also have had a tinge of defeat.[63]

9

Losing the Peace
The Idea of a Martial South Revisited

Our perceptions of reality are crystallized in a collection of stereotypes; and people become so fond of the stereotypes, so much at home with them, that they stop looking at actuality.

— ARTHUR M.
SCHLESINGER, JR.,
The Bitter Heritage

A photograph of any one of them, covered with yellow dust or mosaics of mud, would have served any relation, North or South, and ornamented a mantel, as a true picture of "Our Boy."

— ABNER R. SMALL,
The Road to Richmond

John William De Forest, from New Haven, Connecticut, was commissioned a captain in the 12th Connecticut Volunteers early in 1862. He served at this rank until the expiration of his term in December 1864. Before joining the Bureau of Freedmen and Refugees at Greenville, South Carolina, he spent a period recuperating from the exhaustion of campaign life. During this time he began writing his war novel, *Miss Ravenel's Conversion from Secession to Loyalty,* which appeared early in 1867. In many ways, the book expresses the proud spirit of the victorious North.[1]

This reading of the work rests primarily on an interpretation of the two leading male characters as types representing the qualities of the North, or more specifically, New England and the South. The characters are Edward Colburne and Colonel Carter.

All the traits that Northerners associated with the Southern upper class are to be found in Carter. Introducing him, De Forest notes that he was from Virginia and no family there "boasted a purer strain of old Colonial blue blood than the Carters." The colonel was also "a gentleman by right of a graduation from West Point, and of a commission in the regular service." Carter is thus the Southern-gentleman image personified —an officer and a man of mature breeding. The typing of the colonel is completed when he remarks that he might have been a slaveholder. "Splendid life, that of a Southern planter," he says, "if I hadn't been in the Army—or rather, if I could have done everything that I fancied, I should have been a sugar planter."[2]

Colburne is from New Boston, which, says the author, "is not a lively nor sociable place. The principle reason for this is that it is inhabited chiefly by New Englanders. Puritanism, the prevailing faith of that land and race, is not only not favorable but is absolutely noxious to social gayeties, amenities, and graces." This is a portrait of New England as it had appeared before the war—a rather bleak, unwholesome place. The kind of man who might be produced by this environment was John Whitewood, Jr., the son of a professor, whom De Forest describes as "thin, pale, and almost sallow, with pinched features surmounted by a high and roomy forehead, tall, slender, narrow-chested and fragile in form, shy, silent, and pure as the timidest of girls, he was an example of what can be done with youthful blood, muscle, mind and feeling by the studious severities of a

176

Puritan university." Colburne, while comparing favorably with this specimen, is still only half-developed in character "in consequence of youth,
modesty and Puritan education." He is the sort of person whom Parkman wished to rejuvenate.[3]

Both Carter and Colburne are enamored of Miss Ravenel, daughter
of a Unionist refugee from the South. Because Carter, in the martial
atmosphere of 1861 when military men were in demand, appears to be the
more impressive of the two figures, he gets the girl and they are married.
Colburne, disappointed, goes off to the war and becomes a man. He is in
the end an excellent soldier, exhibiting such qualities as a sense of duty,
loyalty, and manly endurance. He is physically and mentally matured;
"his body and even his mind are in the soundest and most enviable health."
It turns out that Colburne had all the makings of a strong character; he
only needed the challenge of war to develop fully. De Forest concludes
that "he is a stronger and better man for having fought three years, out-
facing death and suffering. Like the nation, he has developed and learned
his powers."[4]

Carter, on the other hand, quickly reveals grave character defects.
Like the slaveholders described before the war by people like J. S. Buckingham, Frederick Law Olmsted, and Fanny Kemble, he is unable to control his passions. He drinks too heavily and spends money beyond his
means. To cover himself he is forced to make a fraudulent deal by which
the army loses a great deal of money. Carter thus sacrifices his honor as
an officer, which is the only kind of honor about which he truly cares.
Finally, he has an affair with a Mrs. Larue. The Southerner has been
shown to be the lesser of the two men. De Forest refrains from degrading
him completely. Carter still has military courage and, like Shakespeare's
Richard III, he is allowed to die valiantly on the field of battle. Nevertheless, the point has been made. Northern blood has the most mettle in it
and Colburne now gets the girl. It has been said that the marriage between Colburne and Miss Ravenel represents the reconciliation of North
and South. But the point is that the reunification is made on Northern
terms.[5]

This was in 1867. In 1881 De Forest published *The Bloody Chasm*.
In this novel a change of tone is apparent. Now, Edmund Wilson points
out, "De Forest is treating ironically the complacency of the winning
North which he had seemed in some degree to share at the time of his
writing *Miss Ravenel*." For instance, a New Englander in the novel, Silas
Mather, visits old Southern friends in Charleston. The men whom the
Northerner meets have been humbled, even ruined by the war; the city
wears an aspect of destruction. The New Englander, instead of being

magnanimous to the defeated, adopts an air of "I told you so." When an ex-rebel general tells him that four acquaintances fell in the war, Mather remarks uncharitably, "May God forgive them." The Southerner, apparently speaking for De Forest, replies, "God may find it easier to forgive than a New England Yankee can."[6]

Evidence that De Forest was turning away from a self-congratulatory air is to be found in a much earlier piece, his "Chivalrous and Semi-Chivalrous Southrons," published in *Harper's New Monthly Magazine* during 1869. Here, De Forest stereotyped Southern character as he had in *Miss Ravenel's Conversion*. Southerners all appear as duelists and street fighters. The extraordinary courage of the rebels during the war could be explained by this pugnacity, said De Forest, for "a man might as well be shot doing soldierly service at Bull Run or the Wilderness as to go back to Abbeville and be shot there." The Northerner found a certain humor in Southern sensitivity to honor. A Southerner in New York was nearly driven mad, he said, by being bumped and hustled on the sidewalk by people who moved on before he could cane them. "If you ever see a tall man in Broadway, standing stock-still, glaring about him, and swearing, you may be sure that he is a Southerner, and that some one whom he can not find has run against him."[7]

At the same time that he was amused by them, De Forest respected the Southerners' style. They were more individualistic than Northerners, he said, and had "a very pleasing manner, an ease which is not assumption, a dignity which is not hauteur, consideration for the vanity of others, grace of bearing and fluency of speech." A strong military tone was apparent in their character, he thought. "Notably brave, punctilious as to honor, pugnacious to quarrelsomeness, authoritative to imperiousness, generous to extravagance, somewhat formal in his courtesy, somewhat grandiose in his self-respect, there is hardly an agreeable or disagreeable trait in him which you can not find in the officers of most armies." The intriguing point is that while the 1867 novel seemed to imply that the Northerner had become self-sufficient through war, this shorter piece was, in part, an argument that Northern character might benefit from a copying of Southern manners. He remarked, "We shall do well to study this peculiar people, . . . we shall do better to engraft upon ourselves its nobler qualities."[8]

In these final pages it will be suggested that Northerners reverted very quickly after the war to the old views of Southern society. Looking back on the war, they felt that Southerners had been better soldiers after all. If there is a larger significance to this, it is that in conceding that Southerners were usually right on the battlefield, people tended to assume that they were right about other things also, including the proper place of blacks in society. It has often been argued that Northerners who gave up the struggle for black rights after 1865 were revealing a latent racism or were innocents who failed to realize the economic base of freedom. No doubt all this was true. But it may also be that much genuine concern for the ex-slaves was simply swamped by a surge of emotional adoration focused on the heroes of the Lost Cause.

In no sense does the discussion presented in this chapter pretend to be definitive. It is simply hoped to round out the Civil War picture by presenting some lines for further thought on the continuing belief that the South had a peculiarly martial culture in the nineteenth century.

Even before the surrender of the Confederate armies, Southerners had begun to build their defense mechanisms against the sharp pain of defeat. They turned to the idea that their armies had only been beaten by numbers —that their generals and troops had never been outfought, only overpowered. The building of this rationale continued after the war. John Esten Cooke, in his *Wearing of the Gray*, published in 1867, spoke of the Confederate leaders as "noble types, of the great Norman race of which the Southern people come—brave, honorable, courteous, social; quick in resentment, proud but placable." These men led an army that was never routed, he said. "It was *starved*, and it surrendered." George Cary Eggleston, another Confederate veteran, painted a similar picture of Southern chivalry in his *A Rebel's Recollections*, published during the 1870s. Eggleston's interest lay mainly in portraying the part played by the Virginia gentry in the war. Every one of them, he said, who was "not wholly incapable of rendering service, enlisted at the beginning of the war." He rationalized Confederate defeat by saying that the Virginians had never expected to win. They knew that war would ruin them but honor impelled them to take a stand against Federal invasion of sovereign states. "Should Virginia seek safety in dishonor," wrote Eggleston, "or should she meet destruction in doing that which she believed to be right?" Such a question was not long to be debated, he concluded.[9]

There were, of course, writers who took a different view of past affairs. When Cooke's work appeared, the Richmond *Whig* commented that his "eyes are not only in the back of his head, but they are also afflicted with a pair of rose-colored goggles of enormous magnifying powers." A year earlier, in 1866, Edward A. Pollard, a Southern journalist, had bluntly attacked the notion that Southerners had not expected to win the war when they enlisted in 1861. Rather, he said, the belief that the Yankees could be speedily whipped helped defeat the South because the government, in its complacency, failed to make long-range preparations. In the final analysis, he wrote, the loss of the war was due to mismanagement by the Confederate government and to lack of the "virtue of endurance" among the people. An equally critical view was given by Sam R. Watkins, a crusty Confederate veteran. In his memoirs, he claimed, "Our cause was lost from the beginning . . . Our people were divided upon the question of Union and secession. Our generals were scrambling for 'Who ranked.' "[10]

Nevertheless, the glorification of the Southern past continued. A tremendous amount of energy was devoted to the task, the result of which was to complete the planter image of Southern life that was begun during the antebellum period. The finished portrait was of a genteel Old South culture that had gone down fighting nobly in a lost cause. A typical statement is to be found in Howard Melancthon Hamill's *The Old South: A Monograph,* published in 1905.[11]

Hamill was a boy during the Civil War but, at the age of sixteen, he had enlisted and served one year under Lee. The Old South culture he remembered was one where the Cavalier gentry were men of good breeding, wealth, and honor. These people had contributed most of what was good and significant in American life. He was confident, said Hamill, "that deeper down at the foundation of our greatness as a people than all other influences are the qualities and spirit that have marked the Cavalier in the Old World or the New." Southern statesmen led the independence movement from Britain and nurtured the young republic into strength. "As with statesmanship, so with the military leadership of the Old South. The genius for war has been one of the gifts of the sons of the South from the beginning, not only as fighters . . . but as born commanders, tacticians, and strategists." Ultimately, the civilization had succumbed but in its last moments it had "confronted the soldiery and resources of the world."[12]

That Southerners should have wished to embrace this romanticized picture of the past is understandable. Something had to be salvaged from the ruins; there had to be a rationale for what had been. The more intriguing point is why Northerners, after they had won the war, came to accept much of the Southern view of things.

To begin with, Northern victory was tarnished for some people by the way in which it seemed to have been won. Once passions had cooled, there was a certain uneasiness about the devastation of the South in the last years of the war. A picture of the ruined regions was given to the public in 1866 by John T. Trowbridge in "A Picture of the Desolated States." In this piece, Trowbridge talked of the Union forces not as the North's heroic armies but as its destroying armies. Perhaps this sense of disgust, of guilt, bred a magnanimous attitude toward the foe—a willingness to accept many of their claims to heroism as a way of assuaging conscience. Possibly Sherman himself felt uncomfortable with the past for it is said that he developed a distinct aversion to the song "Marching through Georgia."[13]

It seems that as soon as war neared its end and the tremendous pressure was released from Sherman, his attitude to the South began to mellow. As early as May of 1865, the man who had said that the South must be depopulated now "desired to see all restored to the rights of citizenship who were willing to return to their allegiance, and obey the laws." At least this is what he told Orville Hickman Browning. He also paid the rebels a generous compliment, saying that they "were very fine soldiers and fought gallantly, that all the best and most earnest men in the South were rebels." And according to Joseph Pearson Farley, a Federal soldier, Sherman advised all his officers to see *Shenandoah*, a play produced in 1888. Farley himself was most affected by the performance.[14]

Written by Bronson Howard, who was originally from Detroit, the play achieved great success in the nineteenth century though it now seems rather dull and heavy-handed. It appealed particularly to army men because it dealt with the trials of two regulars, one from the North and one from the South. They are friends who are placed on opposite sides by the war. All comes right in the end with the Union man marrying the Confederate's sister. The one interesting point about the play is that it used, as had works like *Uncle Tom's Cabin* and *The Octoroon*, a Northerner in the role of villain. His name is Edward Thornton and he is described in the first act as one who "came to Charleston some years ago, from the North, but if there are any vices and passions peculiarly strong in the South, he has carried them all to the extreme." He becomes a captain in the Confederate Secret Service, a role that allows him to become a vehicle for all the mean traits the author preferred not to attribute to rebels of Southern birth.[15]

The costly nature of victory in Virginia also seemed apparent to Northerners looking back on Grant's campaign in Virginia. Charles A. Dana, who had been assistant secretary of war during the conflict and had approved of Grant's methods, wrote in his recollections that by the end of May, 1864, "even our officers had ceased to regard Lee as an invincible military genius." In fact, as we saw in the preceding chapter, this was far from the case. Many of the senior officers were disgusted by what they saw as uninspired generalship producing needless slaughter. And for them, Lee remained an unbeaten leader.[16]

The belief lived on after the war. A history critical of Grant was written by John Codman Ropes, a professor at Harvard, whose friend John Chipman Gray had written from the army in 1864 to say, "I still have faith in Grant's grit, though I think we must acknowledge Lee his superior, and indeed to whom is Lee inferior?" Francis Winthrop Palfrey, a Union veteran, wrote in 1882 that "as for Grant, with his grim tenacity, his hard sense, and his absolute insensibility to wounds and death, it may well be admitted that he was a good general for a rich and populous country in a contest with a poor and thinly peopled land, but let any educated soldier ask himself what the result would have been if Grant had had only Southern resources and Southern numbers to rely on and use."[17]

It is perhaps more than coincidence that both these postwar critics were New England men for the soldiers of this area had been especially concerned to lay the idea of Yankee weakness to rest. Grant's hammering tactics had thwarted them by making it appear that only numbers had brought the North victory. There is also reason to suspect that Grant was rejected because he was not from New England—not, indeed, from the east at all but from Ohio, a western state. When, in 1868, Harriet Beecher Stowe wrote a book on leading patriots of the day she felt it necessary to stress time and again that Grant could really be regarded as a New Englander because his family was originally from there. She wrote: "Gen. Grant is a genuine son of New England, therefore to be looked on as a vigorous offshoot of the old Puritan stock." As the Grant family had actually moved west shortly after the Revolution, the claim said more about the author than the subject.[18]

Mrs. Stowe did feel able to allow that Lincoln was a common man and a westerner but Lincoln's assassination had lifted him out of the arena of partisan politics and onto the plane of American martyrs. Now that he was dead, many people who had despised Lincoln for his policies or his seeming uncouthness could give lip service to the idea of him as the great commoner. But Grant was still on the scene and was elected President in the year Mrs. Stowe's book was published. The scandals of Grant's administration would increase the distaste for him.[19]

Examples of corruption during the postwar period, not only among those close to Grant but in politics generally and in business, also helped sour the taste of victory. Selfishness and money lust had seemed to be key problems during the antebellum period. People had hoped that the war would cleanse them through its purifying call to duty and sacrifice. There was consequently deep disappointment when the disease reappeared with even greater force. Again, this helped draw Northerners toward respect for Southern character. Before the war, the planters had been held up as examples of men free from money lust. C. Vann Woodward demonstrates in his excellent essay, "A Southern Critique for the Gilded Age," that at least three authors of the postwar period—Herman Melville, Henry Adams, and Henry James—also used Southern figures to point out failings in the society around them.[20]

To take one of these as an example, Henry Adams, in his book *Democracy: An American Novel,* makes the hero a Virginian whose integrity is used as a foil to reveal the corruption of a Northerner, Senator Silas P. Ratcliffe of Illinois. As in *Miss Ravenel's Conversion,* there is a woman who must choose between the two men but this time it is the Northerner who is shunned. The girl is nearly convinced that she should accept the standards and the hand of the man whose only concern is self and party. But the Southerner opens her eyes to the wrongdoings of the senator and the ugliness of politics. For the first time, says Adams, "she really felt as though she had got to the heart of politics so that she could, like a physician with his stethoscope, measure the organic disease."[21]

Why did Adams choose a Southerner? The simple answer is that the notion of honor seemed as relevant after the war as it had before. More specifically, Eggleston and others claimed that the Virginian had gone to war in defense of principle, knowing that he would lose and would be ruined in the process. There could hardly have been a better model of the man who, in contrast to the corrupt public figures of the time, put duty before profit and even before life itself. Adams' hero is a Virginian whose sense of duty impelled him to enter the rebel army, though "he had seen from the first that, whatever issue the war took, Virginia and he must be ruined."[22]

Other examples can be found. There was Ambrose Bierce, a writer originally from Ohio, who had served in the Civil War. He, like other Northerners, was disillusioned with the tone of postwar society and may have come to feel that the war had been in vain. He wrote to a friend that "They found a Confederate soldier the other day with his rifle alongside. I'm going over to beg his pardon." The theme of respect for Southern character is less easy to trace in Bierce but it is notable that in his short stories, most of which treat human nature with contempt and the human condition as something of a macabre joke, the only characters who seem to be allowed a heroic, or even a genuinely tragic status are Southerners. In one of his best-realized stories, "An Occurrence at Owl Creek Bridge" (in which a man is hanged by Federal soldiers and during the death plunge believes that he has escaped and returned to his wife), the central character, Payton Farquhar, was "a well-to-do planter of an old and highly respected Alabama family." Again, in "A Horseman in the Sky," another of Bierce's better stories, in which a sentinel has to shoot his own father, the main figure is a Virginian. The point is not absolutely certain but it does appear that Bierce saw his old opponents as deserving a little more sympathy than he accorded his own kind.[23]

Robert Penn Warren, in his stimulating little book *The Legacy of the Civil War,* suggested that those who used Southern types as vehicles for criticism "stood outside their age, and the age swept by them oblivious of their criticism, with little concern to do justice to anything except the demands of double-entry book-keeping." In a sense he was right, for the most bitter critics of political life were New England intellectuals. And it was precisely because society seemed oblivious to them that they took their stand. It will be recalled that in the prewar period upper class people had hoped that in some way the most educated and well-born could be returned to power. In the Civil War it was anticipated that through military life the gentleman would become tougher and fit to lead while the common people would become used, through army discipline, to accepting the guidance of their betters.[24]

The kinds of ideas entertained by New Englanders were expressed in a series of letters which Francis Parkman wrote during the war to the *Boston Daily Advertiser.* The onset of the struggle pleased him in many ways because he had been looking for some method of reinvigorating the New England stock. In September 1861, he wrote, "Our position . . . is one not to be lamented." Peace, he thought, had corrupted the nation.

"A too exclusive pursuit of material success has notoriously cramped and vitiated our growth." Without any crisis to call it forth, "the best character and culture of the nation has remained for the most part in privacy, while a scum of reckless politicians has choked all the avenues of power." But the time had come when the nation might stand "at length clarified and pure in a renewed and strengthened life." Presumably, this strengthening meant that the best character would replace the scum.[25]

The point was made clear in two letters to the *Advertiser*. In one, written during June of 1863, Parkman tried to explain why the North was not making better progress toward winning the war. He suggested that the fault lay neither with the mass of soldiers nor with the commanding generals who, if not Napoleons, were good enough. The problem was "a deficiency in character and qualification in a vast proportion of our junior officers." The reason for this was that politics controlled appointments; "Bowery boys are made brigadiers," and regimental officers "appointed, not because they are fit for the work, but because they are able and willing to serve the ends of some unworthy politician." Better material was available, he had said in an earlier letter. There was a type whom the soldiers could recognize as having an inherent claim to their respect "by nurture, by associations, by acquirements, by character." New England had more than its share of such men. "New England nurture has been of anything but a martial stamp," he said, "and yet she has drawn a most efficient, faithful, and brave body of officers from the ranks of her educated young men." The key argument came a few lines later when Parkman advised that these men must be advanced to positions of importance: "Democracy has learned the weak points of her armor. At least she has ample means to learn them. In peace, as in war, she cannot dispense with competent and right minded leaders. If she demands them, they will come in time." The best must rule.[26]

By 1865, it might have seemed that the New Englanders had earned a place in the foremost ranks of the nation's leadership. Like De Forest's Colburne, they had withstood the test of war. "Possessing more physical and intellectual vigor than is merely necessary to exist," said De Forest of his hero, "he will succeed in the duties of life and control other men's lives, labors, opinions, successes." But it soon appeared that there was to be as little recognition as ever of the peculiar talents of gentlemen. Political power was in the hands of men like Grant and the city machines of New York and Chicago. The North, it seemed, was determined to accept standards of democratic mediocrity.[27]

In the South things were different. Or at least according to De Forest,

who said that the Southern gentleman would not remain in any place where
he was not recognized. In his "Chivalrous and Semi-Chivalrous Southrons," he related the case of a Virginian who left New York, saying, "I de-
test a city where seven hundred thousand people tread on my toes, and
haven't a moment's leisure to apologize, and don't even know my name is
Peyton." De Forest must have felt a certain sympathy for him as the
article was written as a plea that Northerners, "cowed as we are by . . .
democracy; moulded into tame similarity by a general education, remarkably uniform in degree and nature," should try to learn something from
the South.[28]

The quality De Forest felt he saw in the Southern gentleman—a determination to retain control of his environment—had long been admired by
Northerners. Travelers in the Old South had commented on the commanding presence of the slaveholders. Respect for this quality may be one
reason for Northern acquiescence in the failure of Reconstruction: if the
Southerner had an unusual ability to direct society, why should he be denied through outside interference the use of this talent?

At any rate, whatever the causes, Southerners did quickly reassert
control of their society after the war. Testimony to the effectiveness of
the whites in reconquering their domain was given in *A Fool's Errand,*
written by Albion W. Tourgée and published in 1879. Tourgée was
originally from Ohio, spent two years in Massachusetts, served intermit-
tently during the war, and in 1865 left for North Carolina. Originally
concerned only about gaining financial advancement in the seemingly
wide-open economic field of the South, he quickly became involved in Reconstruction efforts. Believing that the South was a land where wealth
and position held down the poor of both races, he worked to raise the status
of underprivileged whites and blacks, risking physical violence to state his
views. In 1879, after most of his efforts had failed, Tourgée returned
north.[29]

In *A Fool's Errand,* Tourgée vented his bitterness at defeat. But,
interestingly, his attack was aimed as much at the North as at the South.
He accused his own people of allowing the Reconstruction experiment to

fail through their silly romanticizing of the rebel veterans. Instead of ruling with the iron hand necessary for success in implementing new programs, the North had become lost in mawkish sentimentality. The Northern people, he said, were getting "the notion that rebellion has transformed those engaged in it into sanctified and glorified saints." While Southerners were reestablishing their rule through the Ku Klux Klan, Northerners talked of it as a good jest. "What could be funnier, or a more appropriate subject of mirth, than that the chivalric but humorous and jocose Southerners should organize a ghostly police to play upon the superstitious fears of the colored people, who were no doubt very trifling, and needed a good deal of regulation and restraint?"[30]

Like other radicals before him, Tourgée had to admit contempt for the North and a grudging respect for Southern character. He felt "fear that the North lacks virility." If the South had won the war "there would have been no hesitation, no subterfuge, no pretense of restoration, because the people of the South are born rulers,—aggressives, who, having made up their minds to attain a certain end, adopt the means most likely to secure it." He concluded that the bravery of the South after the war had allowed it to turn the tables on the North. In the United States, he said, existed two irreconcilable cultures, one of which must dominate the other. The South seemed likely to win, for it "is the most intense, vigorous and aggressive." He viewed the prospect with a certain equanimity because, like other Northerners, he found much to admire in his Southern opponents. "He looked forward," said Tourgée through the hero of the novel, "to see them regain the proud supremacy of ante bellum days,—not indeed with satisfaction; . . . but at least with admiring pride in the capabilities of that branch of the American stock."[31]

There was some truth in Tourgée's argument that the North allowed Reconstruction to die by default. Even some abolitionists had mellowed in their opposition to the South. This is not so surprising if we recall that some radical anti-slavery people were members of the older upper class who found in reform an alternative to participation in democratic politics. Such people had sometimes revealed a grudging respect for the slaveholders, who were, after all, supposed to be gentlemen like themselves and ones who had managed to retain control of their society. This fellow feeling naturally increased after the war when the planter became, like themselves, a struggler against forces that might destroy his place and role. With the bar of slavery gone, the sense of kinship could penetrate more deeply. Small wonder, then, that according to legend, Thomas Wentworth Higginson, who had led a mob to free a fugitive slave and commanded a black regiment in the war, sat in his study years later weeping over the romanticized picture of plantation life in "Marse Chan."[32]

By no means all those who enjoyed Southern postwar romanticizations of plantation life were abolitionists; nor did they have deep psychological reasons for their interest. It was true after the war as it had been before that many simply found the plantation image attractive as a colorful addition to the dull round of daily life. They read the novels of men like Thomas Nelson Page and even tried to ape what they saw as Southern chivalric ways. As early as October 1865, *Harper's Weekly* suggested that Northerners maintain the manly qualities bred during the war by holding jousting tournaments like the ones in Virginia.[33]

For a young nation short of romantic heroes, the leading soldiers of the South quickly acquired a strong appeal. When Beauregard visited the North in 1867, crowds came out to catch a glimpse of him and reporters sought interviews. They described him as one of the great captains of war. According to T. Harry Williams, at least one Southern newspaper became irritated by what it saw as a Northern tendency to appropriate the "valor of Southern arms, the skill of Southern generals, the vastness of Southern rebellion—and boastfully credit them to 'the national account.' "[34]

Respect for Lee was even more pronounced. He was a Virginian and the awe-inspiring figure who had kept the Army of the Potomac at bay for so long. In 1869 the New York *Herald* commented, "The name of Lee is identified with the most heroic deeds of the war for independence." Again, while discussing Lee's educational plans for Washington College, the school where he was president after the war, the paper commented that he might "make as great an impression upon our old fogy schools and colleges as did his military tactics upon our fogy commanders in the palmy days of the rebellion."[35]

To conclude, it had seemed to many people in 1865 that Southern claims to superior breeding and character had been vanquished. But Northern interest in Southern styles quickly blossomed again. As before the war, there was fascination with the romantic possibilities of the region. At a deeper level, alienated Northerners again examined Southern character for its special virtues. The corruption of the period gave them an uneasy feeling that in the war they had destroyed a valuable part of the nation's human resources and now they might pay the penalty. There were echoes of Colonel Lyman's unhappy remark during the 1864 campaigns that the Southerners "are a valuable people, capable of a heroism that is too rare to be lost."[36]

Inevitably, renewed involvement with the idea of the South entailed accepting that the Southerner had indeed shown the peculiar bravery and other noble qualities to which he laid claim. Acceptance of the notion that Southerners were more martial was encouraged by guilt about the nature of Northern victory, especially about Grant's methods in Virginia. Perhaps, too, on such matters as the question of ability with a rifle, Northerners acquiesced in Southern claims because there seemed no tangible method of proving or disproving them. Having won the war, Union men could be magnanimous and allow Southerners the benefit of the doubt.

Finally, the idea that an industrial, commercial society is almost inevitably weaker in war took a long time to die. This too must have reinforced the contention that Southern culture had been more martial. As late as 1909, Homer Lea, an American military writer, stated that wealthy, industrial nations tended to lose the manly qualities. "Opulence, instead of being a foundation of national strength is liable to be the most potent factor in its destruction," he asserted.[37]

Much has been left unsaid in this discussion of the postwar period. Those who were not willing to forget Southern treason and bathe in sentimental reconciliation have been largely ignored. One reason for this is that their role, including that of the politicians who "waved the bloody shirt," has been well documented in other works; so well documented in fact that the numbers and significance of these people may have been overstated. However, one point about postwar attacks on the South is worth mentioning here. This was the continued attempt to document the belief that the South had made deliberate military plans for secession. This was part of the old plot thesis and it found expression in such works as John A. Logan's *The Great Conspiracy*, published in 1886. (The reason for this interest is clear: if military conspiracy could be proved, an alienated North would refuse to sanction the triumph of white supremacists.)[38]

One of the charges laid against Southern leaders was that they had trained cadets at West Point in secessionist principles. Evidence of a kind was not hard to find, as some Confederate soldiers believed that their teachers had taught State Rights and used this as a defense of their actions in fighting for the South. In a letter of September 17, 1861, for example, George Edward Pickett remarked that he did not doubt "the right of secession, which was taught in our text-book at West Point." Some Northern officers agreed. Joseph Pearson Farley said that his law instructor at the Point, a Southern man, believed that soldiers had a duty to fight for their native state. The bluntest statement against the academy was made by Robert Bingham in the *North American Review* for September 1904. Evidence showed, he said, that "the right of secession was distinctly taught at West Point up to about 1850."[39]

The thesis was effectively rebutted in 1909 by Colonel Edgar S. Dudley. The pivot of Bingham's argument had been that the law text used at West Point was Rawle's *A View of the Constitution of the United States,* which definitely supported State Rights. But Dudley pointed out that the text was changed around the year 1828 to James Kent's *Commentaries on American Law.* This work did not endorse state sovereignty though it did support the right of revolution (a right to which the South did not appeal). This subtlety of difference may have escaped some students or have become blurred in recollection. It is possible also, as Dudley pointed out, that Rawle's work was cited during student debates over State Rights. Over the years, graduates might have come to believe that they had been taught from the book.[40]

Many other pieces of the Southern legend have been chipped away. Yet there remains a feeling that the South did have a uniquely military culture in the nineteenth century. John Steinbeck, in a little book, *America and Americans,* says that "Southern Americans have throughout our history shown a gift for the military. They fought the Civil War with incredible bravery and ingenuity, and held out with pure spirit against the overwhelming Northern superiority in numbers, equipment and supplies."[41]

Military wirters have also accepted the idea of a martial South. G. F. R. Henderson, the influential biographer of Stonewall Jackson, wrote that "the Confederate soldiers were drawn from the farm and the plantation, for there were few large towns in the seceded States. They were consequently trained from childhood to the use of fire-arms, excellent marksmen, practised horsemen and of hardy constitution. Habituated to a life of sport and adventure in the wilderness and forests of the South, it was easier for them to become soldiers, and they were more reliable in the emergencies of battle than their city-bred opponents." As a final example,

Francis Butler Simkins, in his history of the Old South, said that "at the beginning of the war, at least, Southerners were better equipped for military life than their Northern rivals. Their outdoor activities had accustomed them to field exercises and they were trained in the use of firearms because they had followed the chase and guarded against slave insurrections."[42]

In view of this weighty opinion in favor of the notion that the Southerner did possess superior military qualities, it is worth drawing together some points from the body of this work that tend to a different conclusion. The important questions to discuss seem to be ability to ride and shoot, discipline, outstanding excellence in military and political leadership.

On the cavalry, it was noted in Chapter 2 that the South may have had some advantage here in terms of trained officers. But it was also pointed out that the main disadvantage of the North may well have been lack of self-confidence compounded by abusive treatment at the hands of army commanders. Tedious and unnecessary work on minor details not only prevented the growth of military competence, it must also have lowered the self-image of the troopers.

This is only a suggestion. But on the question of shooting ability a more concrete statement can be made. It was said earlier that at Bull Run the Northern forces scored a higher kill rate than their opponents. A sampling of other earlier battles shows the same phenomenon. At Wilson's Creek, one of the first encounters in the west and one in which native ability would have been at a premium, the Union performance was by far the more impressive, even though the Federals finally lost the battle. In the east, no rebel superiority is apparent before Second Manassas. (A number of factors might explain the Southern improvement after this time. One might be the steady drop in Union morale and hence also efficiency after the failure of McClellan's Peninsula Campaign.) At any rate, the rebel claim to innate superiority in marksmanship remains unproven.[43]

Much the same can be said on the score of discipline. Union soldiers were prone to believe that their enemy had an advantage here because the Southern poor white was supposedly used to a position of defference, but the evidence tends to show that discipline was a severe problem on both sides. Northern and Southern veterans apparently had a habit of retreating without orders if they felt that further fighting was futile. The Confederacy may even have suffered somewhat more than the Union from lack of proper subordination among the soldiers. For the democratic election of junior officers, a system which could mean that popular rather than efficient men were chosen, continued longer among the rebels than the Federals.[44]

It was the belief that Southern planters brooked no opposition from the lower classes which also led Northerners to assume that Southern political leadership was more efficient. In the South, they said, men did not have to worry about politics whereas in the democratic North, party had to take precedence over military interests. Lincoln had to give military office to politicians whose support he needed, while Davis could appoint men strictly on their service record. The contrast between a despotic South and a democratic North is a clumsy and inaccurate one, but there is some point to the argument. The Confederacy did not have a mature political system with defined parties and Davis was free to approach men on the basis of their military credentials alone. In the North commands were given to politicians like Nathaniel P. Banks, who were militarily incompetent.[45]

However, Eric L. McKitrick and others have argued that the party system was actually a source of strength. For one thing, the existence of clearly defined political groups with recognized leaders meant that Lincoln had a fairly accurate checklist of the men he must humor in order to keep particular sectors of the public behind the war effort. In the South, where special interests were less easily defined, the resentments of those who felt that they were ignored by the government proved a source of fierce division.[46]

Many Northerners believed that the South had established a dictatorship, yet the central government was never able to gain adequate control of the human and material resources of the section. Until the end of the war, localism and the State Rights philosophy kept valuable men and supplies from the Confederate army. Finally, although Northerners often saw Lincoln as a man of few talents, T. Harry Williams has demonstrated that he had one of the best military minds on the Union side.[47]

All that remains to be dealt with is the question of whether the South had more able generals than the North. Two points need to be dealt with here. First, did the South have a special relationship with the United States Army and, second, did Southern generals actually display more competence on the battlefield?

Regarding the army, it was shown earlier that there was not a higher percentage of Southern cadets graduated from West Point. Nor did the South have an unusually large number of officers serving in the army, excepting the cavalry branch of the service. And the idea that West Point cadets were trained on secessionist principles was exploded long ago. It is true, however, that some Northern officers did show distaste for their cause and a lack of attachment to the democratic form of government they purported to serve. During the McClellan days, this disaffection might have resulted in a march on Washington. It could be said that West Point failed to educate officers in the principles of national allegiance. But the problem of alienation in the war went beyond this and volunteers as well as regulars were affected. Distaste for politics, a certain respect and sympathy for the gentlemen of the South, these were characteristics of conservative upper class people both in and out of the army.

Even if the South did not have a more significant tradition of association with the regular army upon which to build, it is still possible that its generals were men of unusual native talents in the military line. Thus Bruce Catton says that one asset of the Confederacy was that the regulars who went South "included some of the most capable men on the army roster." But after noting Lee, Jackson, and possibly Stuart, the South seems to have acquired few outstanding talents. Joseph E. Johnston, while competent, was not better than Meade or Reynolds. Indeed, he much resembled George H. Thomas. Albert Sidney Johnston was killed before his abilities could be demonstrated one way or the other. Bragg, Hood, and the like showed no fitness for high command and the South produced no generals with the original genius of Sherman and Grant.[48]

The battle over the generalship of Grant and Lee will probably continue indefinitely but it is noteworthy that though Lee won battles his army lost the war; Grant's strategy succeeded. Even generals like Hooker and McClellan were not greatly if at all inferior to Lee in terms of strategic thinking. The one real advantage that Lee and his army had over their opponents was self-confidence. This allowed the Confederate generals to beat men who lost their nerve. The esprit or élan with which the Confederates fought is illustrated by the fact that though they formed the defensive side in the war, they attacked in half of the twenty-two major battles.[49]

But why have the other claims to Southern martial superiority been so generally accepted if, as claimed here, there was little truth to them? On one side, dislike of more recent developments in the South seems to have colored thinking about the antebellum period. It may be significant that John Hope Franklin notes, in the preface to *The Militant South,* a study of the antebellum period, the large number of lynchings which occurred in the region between 1900 and 1930. A black historian who recalls the sadistic killing of his people may be forgiven for believing that the South has always revealed an unusually militant character. W. J. Cash, who also portrayed the antebellum South in terms of violence, grew up during the period when savage acts against blacks were frequent.[50]

At the other pole are those who still are attracted by the romantic image of the South. An obvious indication of this attraction may be found in the enormous popularity of *Gone With the Wind* by Margaret Mitchell. Other lesser examples include James Warner Bellah's *The Valiant Virginians*, a collection of stories about three young Confederates who embody all the noble martial traits associated with Old South culture. In a preface to the book, Richard H. Tyre listed a number of possible reasons "why the South is the hero of so many Civil War books." Among the factors he cited was the image of the South as gallant underdog, fighting "brute force of numbers and matériel, . . . with the only commodity she produced in quantity: proud and courageous boys." Another motive for interest, he thought, might be the fact that the North won the war and carried America away from rural life toward a highly industrialized, technologically complex society. Thus the South acts as "a never-never land to us now, a dream of a way of life that we could have had." If Tyre is right, then Americans still wish to use the South in imagination as a colorful alternative to the gray tones of modern life.[51]

It is perhaps this determination of the people that they will have a romantic South which has been most responsible for the inability of historians to get beyond the stereotype of a soldier's South to a more realistic picture. Unless one is particularly concerned to dig into the issue, and to dig deep, there is little encouragement to question the popular belief that the Old South did indeed produce a peculiarly martial breed.

Notes

Notes

1. North and South

1. Philip Schaff, *America: A Sketch of Its Political, Social and Religious Character,* ed. Perry Miller (Cambridge, Mass.: Harvard University Press, 1961), pp. 45–46. Originally published 1855.

2. Pettigrew is quoted in James W. Patton, "Facets of the South in the 1850's," *Journal of Southern History,* 23 (February–November 1957), 22. *Charleston Mercury,* April 30, 1861, printed in Frank Moore, ed., *The Rebellion Record,* I (New York: G. P. Putnam, 1861), "Rumors & Incidents," 67. See also extract from *Daily Delta* (New Orleans), p. 68.

3. There are many works on Calhoun. Richard N. Current's *John C. Calhoun* is a useful introduction (New York: Washington Square Press, 1963). The case of William L. Yancey is also interesting. See Austin L. Venable, "William L. Yancey's Transition from Unionism to States Rights," *Journal of Southern History,* 10 (February–November 1944), 331–342.

4. An idea of European interest in America may be gathered from Henry

Steele Commager, ed., *America in Perspective: The United States through Foreign Eyes* (New York: New American Library, n.d.).

5. On slavery in the Revolution and the early national period see John Richard Alden, *The South in the Revolution, 1763–1789,* vol. III of *A History of the South,* ed. Wendell Holmes Stephenson and E. Merton Coulter (n.p.: Louisiana State University Press, 1957), and R. S. Cotterill, *The Old South* (Glendale, Calif.: Arthur H. Clark, 1936), pp. 108ff. Thomas P. Abernethy's contribution to *A History of the South* (*The South in the New Nation,* published in 1961) is not good on the slavery issue.

Numerous writers, including W. J. Cash in *The Mind of the South* (New York: Knopf, n.d.), p. 63, have suggested that Southerners felt guilt about slavery. A fair attempt at documentation is made by Charles Grier Sellers, Jr., in "The Travail of Slavery," in *The Southerner as American,* ed. Charles Grier Sellers, Jr. (New York: E. P. Dutton, 1966), pp. 40–71. That there was ever much anti-slavery sentiment in the South has been questioned by Gordon E. Finnie in "The Antislavery Movement in the Upper South before 1840," *Journal of Southern History,* 35 (August 1969), 319–342.

The point that the defense of slavery began before outside abolitionist attacks is made in, for example, Stanley M. Elkins, *Slavery: A Problem in American Institutional and Intellectual Life* (New York: Grosset & Dunlap, 1963), p. 207. The standard work on the closing of the Southern mind to criticism of slavery is Clement Eaton's *The Freedom-of-Thought Struggle in the Old South* (New York: Harper & Row, 1964).

6. Increasing Southern resentment of the North, on economic and moral grounds, is discussed in Avery Craven, *The Coming of the Civil War* (Chicago: University of Chicago Press, 1966). On the economic independence movement see P. L. Rainwater, "Economic Benefits of Secession: Opinions in Mississippi in the 1850's," *Journal of Southern History,* 1 (February–November, 1935), 459–474.

7. An interesting personal case of how nullification created sectionalism is described in John W. Higham, "The Changing Loyalties of William Gilmore Simms," *Journal of Southern History,* 9 (February–November 1943), 210–224.

8. On the problem of whether slavery was profitable see Alfred H. Conrad and John R. Meyer, "The Economics of Slavery in the Ante-Bellum South," *Journal of Political Economy,* 66 (April 1958), 95–130; Thomas P. Govan, "Was Plantation Slavery Profitable?" *Journal of Southern History* 8.4 (1942), 513–535; Charles W. Ramsdell, "The Natural Limits of Slavery Expansion," *Mississippi Valley Historical Review,* 16 (June–March 1929–30), 151–171; and Robert William Fogel and Stanley L. Engerman, *Time on the Cross: The Economics of American Negro Slavery,* 2 vols. (Boston: Little, Brown, 1974).

Featherstonhaugh is quoted in Katharine M. Jones, *The Plantation South* (New York: Bobbs-Merrill, 1957), pp. 121–122.

9. See Harvey Wish, ed., *Ante-Bellum: Writings of George Fitzhugh and Hinton Rowan Helper on Slavery* (New York: Capricorn Books, 1960).

10. A solid study of the romantic mood in the South is Rollin G. Osterweis, *Romanticism and Nationalism in the Old South* (Gloucester, Mass.: Peter Smith, 1964). William R. Taylor's *Cavalier & Yankee: The Old South and American National Character* (Garden City, N.Y.: Doubleday, 1963) is particularly good on the Tidewater.

11. The ideas in this paragraph are condensed from *Cavalier & Yankee,* esp. pp. xvi–xviii, and Cash's *Mind of the South,* chap. 3.

12. Cash, *Mind of the South,* chap. 3.

13. Cash, *Mind of the South,* p. 64, for the comment on the defense mechanism. On the middling sort see Frank L. Owsley, *Plain Folk of the Old South* (n.p.: Louisiana State University Press, 1949), esp. pp. 1–9 and 133–149. A. N. J. Den Hollander presents an interesting discussion of the white trash myth in "The Tradition of the 'Poor Whites,' " in *Culture in the South,* ed. W. T. Couch (Chapel Hill: University of North Carolina Press, 1935), pp. 403–431. Recent medical findings on dirt-eating are given in Robert W. Twyman, "The Clay Eater: A New Look at an Old Southern Enigma," *Journal of Southern History,* 37 (August 1971), 439–448.

14. Clement Eaton, *A History of the Old South,* 2d. ed. (New York: Macmillan, 1966), pp. 389 and 414. Peter F. Walker, *Vicksburg: A People at War, 1860–1865* (Chapel Hill: University of North Carolina Press, 1960), pp. 18–20.

15. David Donald notes the humble birth of some who propagated the myth in "The Proslavery Argument Reconsidered," *Journal of Southern History,* 37 (February 1971), 3–18. See also Eaton, *History of the Old South,* pp. 241–297.

16. Jane H. Pease, "A Note on Patterns of Conspicuous Comsumption among Seaboard Planters, 1820–1860," *Journal of Southern History,* 35 (August 1969), 381–393.

17. On planter houses see, for instance, Clement Eaton, *The Growth of Southern Civilization, 1790–1860* (New York: Harper & Row, 1963), p. 121. The conclusions drawn by Eaton, who is among the most careful scholars in the field, are to be trusted more than those of say, Francis Butler Simkins, who draws an undocumented picture of planters living in baronial splendor. See his *A History of the South* (New York: Knopf, 1953), pp. 133–134.

18. De Bow is quoted in Frederick Law Olmsted, *The Cotton Kingdom,* ed. Arthur M. Schlesinger (New York: Knopf, 1962), p. 541. Hinton Rowan Helper, *The Impending Crisis of the South: How to Meet It* (New York: Collier Books, 1963), p. 321.

19. This thesis is argued persuasively by Clement Eaton in chapter 4 of his *History of the Old South.*

20. On the development of the Yankee figure in the popular mind see Richard M. Dorson, *American Folklore* (Chicago: University of Chicago Press, 1959), pp. 40–41. A wealth of Southern and western tales about Yankees is provided in Thomas D. Clark, *The Rampaging Frontier: Manners and Humors*

of Pioneer Days in the South and the Middle West (Bloomington: Indiana University Press, 1964), esp. pp. 302–303, 308–310, 317.

21. J. L. McConnel, *Western Characters or Types of Border Life* (New York: Redfield, 1853), p. 276. John Bernard, *Retrospections of America, 1797–1811*, ed. Boyle Bernard (New York: Harper & Brothers, 1887), pp. 42–43 and 45.

22. On Southerners believing that Yankees were all traders see Harriet Martineau, *Society in America*, I, (New York: AMS Press, 1966), 187. Originally published 1837.

23. The journal is quoted in Chester Forrester Dunham, *The Attitude of the Northern Clergy toward the South, 1860–1865* (Toledo: Gray, 1942), p. 89.

The significance of poor communications in this period is suggested by Howard R. Floan in the preface to his study of New York and New England writers, *The South in Northern Eyes, 1831–1861* (Austin: University of Texas Press, 1958), p. viii. Floan has many useful insights but he overstates the difference in viewpoint between writers of the two areas.

24. The apparently anonymous traveler is quoted in J. Frazer Smith, *White Pillars: Early Life and Architecture of the Lower Mississippi Valley* (New York: Bramhall House, 1941), p. 17.

25. Olmsted is quoted in Owsley, *Plain Folk*, p. 2. George Wilson Pierson, *Tocqueville in America* (Garden City, N.Y.: Doubleday, 1959), p. 369. Compare John Winston Coleman, Jr., *Slavery Times in Kentucky* (Chapel Hill: University of North Carolina Press, 1940), p. 6.

26. Frances Trollope, *Domestic Manners of the Americans*, ed. Donald Smalley (New York: Knopf, n.d.), p. 226. Even on the national level the stereotype of the Southerner as gentle by birth was not truly accurate. Eaton points out that Andrew Jackson, Calhoun, Alexander H. Stephens, George McDuffie, Joseph E. Brown, and Andrew Johnson came from the yeoman class. *History of the Old South*, p. 297.

27. Wilkie is quoted in William Fletcher Thompson, Jr., *The Image of War: The Pictorial Reporting of the American Civil War* (New York: Thomas Yoseloff, 1960), p. 87.

28. Willis' comments were made in his book *Health Trip to the Tropics* (New York, 1853), quoted in William J. Chute, ed., *The American Scene: 1600–1860. Contemporary Views of Life and Society* (New York: Bantam Books, 1964), pp. 390–393, and Jones, *Plantation South*, p. 339.

29. Bayrd Still, ed., "Observations of Henry Barnard on the West and South of the 1840's," *Journal of Southern History*, 8.2 (1942), 256, letter of April 4, 1843. Van Buren is quoted in Jones, *Plantation South*, p. 371. Larry Gara, ed., "A New Englander's View of Plantation Life: Letters of Edwin Hall to Cyrus Woodman, 1837," *Journal of Southern History*, 18 (August 1952), 347, letter of March 24, 1837.

30. Martineau, *Society in America,* p. 31. Gorgas is quoted in Patton, "Facets of the South," p. 13.

31. Note Hawthorne's comment that "the weaknesses and defects, the bad passions, the mean tendencies, and the moral diseases which lead to crime are handed down from one generation to another, by a far surer process of transmission than human law has been able to establish." *The House of the Seven Gables* (New York: Airmont, 1963), pp. 112–113. Note also the contrast with "the splendid generosity of character" of one branch of the Pyncheon family that had emigrated to Virginia, p. 65.

De Forest's comments are in *Miss Ravenel's Conversion from Secession to Loyalty,* ed. Gordon S. Haight (New York: Holt, Rinehart & Winston, 1955), p. 17.

32. Francis A. Walker, *College Athletics: An Address before the Phi Beta Kappa Society, Alpha, of Massachusetts at Cambridge, June 29, 1893* quoted in George M. Fredrickson, *The Inner Civil War: Northern Intellectuals and the Crisis of the Union* (New York: Harper & Row, 1968), p. 223.

33. Dana's comments are on p. 11 of his book *Two Years before the Mast* (New York: Airmont, 1965). Parkman created *The Oregon Trail* from his experience.

34. Henry David Thoreau lived in the woods at Walden Pond for almost two years. Thomas Wentworth Higginson (1823–1911), a minister, led a mob to rescue a fugitive slave in Boston. In the Civil War he commanded a black regiment.

35. These are well-known arguments regarding the history of the period. See, for instance, John Richard Alden, *Rise of the American Republic* (New York: Harper & Row, 1963), pp. 277–279.

36. On distaste for Lincoln see chapters 3, 4, and 6 below.

37. Dixon Ryan Fox, *The Decline of Aristocracy in the Politics of New York, 1801–1840,* ed. Robert V. Remini (New York: Harper & Row, 1965), pp. 5–6, 274, and 352ff.

38. James Fenimore Cooper, *The American Democrat* (New York: Vintage Books, 1956), esp. pp. 92–102, 148, 154–160 and 180–181. Consult also Cooper's novel *Home as Found* (1838).

39. Fox, *Decline of Aristocracy,* p. 369. Glyndon G. Van Deusen, *William Henry Seward* (New York: Oxford University Press, 1967), pp. 56 and 62.

40. Francis J. Grund, *Aristocracy in America* (New York: Harper & Brothers, 1959), pp. 13–16. Originally published 1839. John MacGregor, *Our Brothers and Cousins* (London: Seeley, Jackson, and Halliday, 1859), pp. 122–124 and 139. Some of the electioneering techniques that troubled gentlemen of the old school are described in Robert V. Remini, *The Election of Andrew Jackson* (Philadelphia: J. B. Lippincott, 1963). Richard Hofstadter makes some useful comments on the decline of the gentleman as a public figure in

Anti-Intellectualism in American Life (New York: Random House, 1962), pp. 145–171.

41. *Harper's Weekly,* January 3, 1857, p. 1.

42. *Harper's Weekly,* January 17, 1857, p. 37; February 28, 1857, p. 129; March 21, 1857, p. 177; October 10, 1857, p. 642; March 26, 1859, p. 194; April 28, 1860, p. 258.

43. There is a good discussion of theories regarding the rise and fall of empires in Stow Persons, *American Minds: A History of Ideas* (New York: Holt, Rinehart and Winston, 1958), p. 121ff. For a view that differs from my own in seeing the period as one of almost complete optimism about the future see Fred Somkin, *Unquiet Eagle: Memory and Desire in the Idea of American Freedom, 1815–1860* (Ithaca, N.Y.: Cornell University Press, 1967), esp. p. 64.

44. On violence during the Revolution see, for instance, Hiller B. Zobel, *The Boston Massacre* (New York: W. W. Norton, 1971).

45. Leo Marx has dealt with American attitudes to technological change in *The Machine in the Garden: Technology and the Pastoral Idea in America* (New York: Oxford University Press, 1964). There is no better introduction to nineteenth-century concern regarding both materialism and technological change than Henry David Thoreau's *Walden: Or, Life in the Woods* (1854), esp. the chapters on "Economy" and "Sounds."

46. *Fashion,* act V. The play is printed in Myron Matlaw, ed., *The Black Crook and Other Nineteenth-Century American Plays* (New York: E. P. Dutton, 1967).

47. Leonard L. Richards, *"Gentlemen of Property and Standing": Anti-Abolition Mobs in Jacksonian America* (New York: Oxford University Press, 1971), p. 60.

48. Marvin Meyers points out in his *The Jacksonian Persuasion: Politics and Belief* (Stanford: Stanford University Press, 1960), pp. 59 and 233, that the Jacksonians, like their opponents, often felt they were defending traditional values. The association of Jackson with the ugliness of popular politics came in large part from the techniques used during the presidential campaign of 1828. See Remini, *The Election of Andrew Jackson.* Margaret Bayard Smith, *The First Forty Years of Washington Society,* ed. Gaillard Hunt (New York: Scribner's, 1906), pp. 295–297.

49. On the class background of leading abolitionists see David Donald, *Lincoln Reconsidered: Essays on the Civil War Era,* 2d. ed. (New York: Random House, 1961), pp. 19–36. On opposition to the abolitionists see Richards, *"Gentlemen of Property."* Martineau, *Society in America,* III,31–32. Also, Thomas Colley Grattan, *Civilized America,* I (London: Bradbury and Evans, 1859), 188–216.

50. Channing is quoted in Martineau, *Society in America,* III, 40–41.

51. Interesting interpretations of Parkman's experience in the west will be found in Henry Nash Smith, *Virgin Land: The American West as Symbol and Myth* (New York: Knopf, n.d.), pp. 54–55, and Howard Doughty, *Francis*

Parkman (New York: Macmillan, 1962), pp. 117–126. Also p. 39 for Parkman's concern about the state of political life.

Ralph Waldo Emerson, *English Traits,* in *The Complete Prose Works of Ralph Waldo Emerson,* 6th ed. (London: Ward, Lock, Bowden, n.d.), p. 247.

52. Erasmus Darwin Keyes, *Fifty Years' Observation of Men and Events Civil and Military* (New York: Scribner's, 1884), p. 346.

53. Flint's comments on the Kentuckian are in Thomas D. Clark, *A History of Kentucky* (Lexington: John Bradford, 1960), pp. 275–276. Preface to *The Personal Narrative of James O. Pattie, of Kentucky* (Cincinnati: J. H. Wood, 1831), quoted in James K. Folsom, *Timothy Flint* (New York: Twayne, 1965), p. 27.

54. Quoted in William H. Townsend, *Lincoln and the Bluegrass: Slavery and Civil War in Kentucky* (Lexington: University of Kentucky Press, 1955), p. 248. Though Kentucky did not secede from the Union and large numbers of her population did not see themselves as Southern, "Chivalric Kentuckians" were generally regarded as members of the Southern gentleman class.

55. For the Southern rationale of slavery see note 11 above.

56. Whipple's comment, written in his diary on November 25, 1843, is in Jones, *Plantation South,* p. 157. Amelia M. Murray, *Letters from the United States, Cuba and Canada* (New York: G. P. Putnam, 1856), pp. 196–197.

57. Joseph G. Baldwin, *The Flush Times of Alabama and Mississippi* (New York: Hill & Wang, 1957), esp. pp. 59–65. Originally published 1853.

58. Norton's book titled *Considerations on Some Recent Social Theories* (Boston, 1853), is cited in Fredrickson, *Inner Civil War,* p. 32.

59. George Templeton Strong, *The Diary of George Templeton Strong,* vol. II: *The Turbulent Fifties 1850–1859,* ed. Allan Nevins and Milton Halsey Thomas (New York: Macmillan, 1952), p. 275.

60. Herman Melville, *The Confidence Man* (New York: Airmont, 1966), p. 39. Originally published 1857. Grattan, *Civilized America,* II, 223.

61. Francis Pulszky and Theresa Pulszky, *White, Red, Black: Sketches of Society in the United States,* III (London: Trübner, 1853), 5.

62. Frederick Douglass, *Narrative of the Life of Frederick Douglass* (New York: New American Library, 1968), pp. 52–53 and xii.

63. For examples of reports of Southern violence see *Harper's Weekly,* March 26, 1859, p. 196; April 9, 1859, p. 119. The piece on Atchison is from the *Chicago Tribune,* July 15, 1856, quoted in Bernard A. Weisberger, *Reporters for the Union* (Boston: Little, Brown, 1953), p. 34.

64. Clement Eaton, "Mob Violence in the Old South," *Mississippi Valley Historical Review,* 29 (June 1942–March 1943), 366. Catherine Cooper Hopley, *Life in the South: from the Commencement of the War.* (London: Chapman and Hall, 1863), pp. 6–9. Also, Lord Newton, *Lord Lyons: A Record of British Diplomacy* (London: Thomas Nelson & Sons, n.d.), pp. 18–19.

65. *Harper's Weekly,* September 27, 1862, pp. 612, 618, and 616–617.

66. On Legree's character see *Uncle Tom's Cabin,* chap. 35.

67. *The Octoroon,* esp. act I. The play is printed in Matlaw, ed., *American Plays.*

68. A. De Puy Van Buren, quoted in Jones, *Plantation South,* p. 370.

2. The Plantation and the Garrison

1. These are, of course, universal military qualities that, with some modifications for time and place, could be applied to the discussion of most eras before our own technological age. Notes on the minutiae of army life will be found in Jack Coggins, *Arms and Equipment of the Civil War* (Garden City, N.Y.: Doubleday, 1962), and Philip Van Doren Stern, *Soldier Life in the Union and Confederate Armies* (Greenwich, Conn.: Fawcett, 1961).

2. Harriet Martineau, *Society in America,* III (New York: AMS Press, 1966), pp. 11–12, and [Henry Cogswell Knight], *Letters from the South and West,* by Arthur Singleton (Boston, 1824), pp. 125–127, quoted in Charles L. Sanford, ed., *Quest for America 1810–1824* (Garden City, N.Y.: Doubleday, 1964), pp. 314–315.

3. J. S. Buckingham, *The Slave States of America,* I (London: Fisher, Son, [1842]), pp. 74–75 and 556–557.

4. Frances Anne Kemble, *Journal of a Residence on a Georgian Plantation in 1838–1839,* ed. John A. Scott (London: Jonathan Cape, 1961), pp. 93, 325–326, 332, and 353.

5. Frederick Law Olmsted, *The Cotton Kingdom,* ed. Arthur M. Schlesinger (New York: Knopf, 1962), pp. 555 and 314.

6. Olmsted, *Cotton Kingdom,* p. 334.

7. On the carrying of arms see, for example, [Joseph H. Ingraham], *The South West,* by a Yankee, quoted in W. S. Tryon, ed., *My Native Land: Life in America 1790–1870* (Chicago: University of Chicago Press, 1961), pp. 158 and 160–161; J. S. Buckingham, *America,* I (London: Fisher, Son, [1841]), 357–359; and Charles Dickens, *American Notes and Reprinted Pieces* (London: Chapman & Hall, n.d.), p. 71. Olmsted, *Cotton Kingdom,* p. 275. Frederick Hawkins Piercy, *Route from Liverpool to Great Salt Lake Valley,* ed. Fawn M. Brodie (Cambridge, Mass.: Harvard University Press, 1962), p. 81. Also, Tryon, ed., *My Native Land,* p. 205.

8. On the song see John William Ward, *Andrew Jackson: Symbol for An Age* (New York: Oxford University Press, 1962), pp. 3–29. Note also Gilbert J. Hunt, *The Historical Reader* (New York, 1819), pp. 208–209, quoted in Sanford, ed., *Quest for America,* pp. 267–269. The citizen soldier's remarks are in John William De Forest, "Charleston Under Arms," *Atlantic Monthly,* 7 (April, 1861), p. 502.

9. The first quotation is from Isabella Lucy Bird, *The Englishwoman in America* (Madison: University of Wisconsin Press, 1966), p. 126. First published 1856. Frederick Marryat, *A Diary in America: With Remarks on Its Institutions* (New York: Knopf, 1962), pp. 245 and 248. First published 1839.

A. De Puy Van Buren, quoted in Katharine M. Jones, *The Plantation South* (New York: Bobbs-Merrill, 1957), pp. 368–369. Edwin B. Bronner, ed., "A Philadelphia Quaker Visits Natchez, 1847," *Journal of Southern History,* 27 (February–November, 1961), 519.

10. See Chapter 1 above.

11. De Forest, "Charleston Under Arms," p. 490.

12. Herman Melville, *White Jacket,* in *The Works of Herman Melville,* VI (New York: Russell & Russell, 1963), p. 176.

13. Daniel Robinson Hundley, *Social Relations in Our Southern States* (New York: H. B. Price, 1860), pp. 49–50. Oliver Otis Howard, *Autobiography of Oliver Otis Howard,* I (New York: Baker & Taylor, 1908), 105. The officer who resigned was Daniel Tyler of Connecticut. His case is cited in Marcus Cunliffe, *Soldiers and Civilians: The Martial Spirit in America 1775–1865* (Boston: Little, Brown, 1968), p. 342.

14. Thomas Jefferson, *Notes on the State of Virginia* (New York: Harper & Row, 1964), pp. 155–156. The diary of Catherine Deveraux, cited in Clarence Poe, ed., *True Tales of the South at War* (Chapel Hill: University of North Carolina Press, 1961), p. 103.

15. Mary Boykin Chesnut, *A Diary from Dixie,* ed. Ben Ames Williams (Boston: Houghton Mifflin, 1949), entry for April 27, 1861, p. 47. Also speech by Sam Houston, May 10, 1861, in Frank Moore ed., *The Rebellion Record,* I (New York: G. P. Putnam, 1861), document 185, pp. 266–267.

16. John W. Higham, "The Changing Loyalties of William Gilmore Simms," *Journal of Southern History,* 9 (February–November 1943), 211. See also John Hope Franklin, "As For Our History . . . ," in Charles Grier Sellers, Jr., ed., *The Southerner as American* (New York: E. P. Dutton, 1966), pp. 3–18. On the War of 1812 see, for instance, Frances Wright, *Views of Society and Manners in America,* ed. Paul R. Baker (Cambridge, Mass.: Harvard University Press, 1963), pp. 183–185. Wright, an English radical, visited America in 1818 and absorbed the current views on the war. A later, typically Southern view, is the speech by Robert Hayne of South Carolina in *Congressional Debates,* 21st Cong., 1st Sess., vol. VI, pt. I (1829–1830), pp. 50–53.

17. J. F. H. Claiborne, *Life and Correspondence of John A. Quitman,* I (New York: Harper & Brothers, 1860), pp. 316–317. Also, John Hope Franklin, *The Militant South 1800–1861* (Boston: Beacon Press, 1964), p. 9.

18. On the relation between martial pride and the idea of a Cavalier South see Rollin G. Osterweis, *Romanticism and Nationalism in the Old South* (Gloucester, Mass.: Peter Smith, 1964), esp. pp. 48, 55, and 125–127.

The exchange in Congress nearly caused a duel between Bissell and Jefferson Davis—described in Donald Fred Tingley, "The Jefferson Davis–William H. Bissell Duel," *Mid America,* 38.3 (1956), 146–155. For the military background to the incident see Lew Wallace, *An Autobiography,* I (New York: Harper and Brothers, 1906), 164–192.

Erasmus Darwin Keyes, *Fifty Years' Observation of Men and Events Civil and Military* (New York: Scribner's, 1884), p. 158. Philo Tower, *Slavery Unmasked* (Rochester: E. Darrow & Brother, 1856), p. 366.

19. Olmsted, *Cotton Kingdom,* pp. 621–622.

20. Quoted in Thomas D. Clark, *A History of Kentucky* (Lexington: John Bradford, 1960), pp. 276–277.

21. The remarks on blue-lights and blue-bellies are in Thomas D. Clark, *The Rampaging Frontier: Manners and Humors of Pioneer Days in the South and the Middle West* (Bloomington: Indiana University Press, 1964), pp. 301–302. The former term apparently referred to the supposed activities of New Englanders in traitorously signaling to British ships at night with blue lights. New England was also attacked in John Armstrong, *Notices of the War of 1812,* II (New York: Wiley & Putnam, 1840), pp. 13–14 and 194–195.

J. Frost, *The Mexican War and Its Warriors* (New Haven: H. Mansfield, 1849). Also, *The Rough and Ready Annual; or Military Souvenir* (New York: D. Appleton, 1848).

22. Hal Bridges, "D. H. Hill's Anti-Yankee Algebra," *Journal of Southern History,* 22 (February–November 1956), 220–222.

23. For the earlier discussion of New England self-doubt see Chapter 1 above. Oliver Wendell Holmes, *Elsie Venner* (1861), quoted in Sam S. Baskett and Theodore B. Strandness, *The American Identity: A College Reader* (Boston: D. C. Heath, 1962), pp. 599–601.

24. Holmes, *The Autocrat of the Breakfast-Table* (London: Ward, Lock, n.d.), p. 277.

25. Mason Wade, ed., *The Journals of Francis Parkman,* I (London: Eyre & Spottiswoode, n.d.), entry for December 24, 1843, p. 125. In writing about the consumptive wretch, Parkman may have had in mind the mild Wm. Ellery Channing, a leading Unitarian. Parkman was refreshed to hear an Episcopalian sermon in which God was treated as a man of war. Wade, ed., *Journals,* I, entry for July 17, 1842, 48.

26. The use of the label abolitionist to describe men as diverse as Henry David Thoreau, Theodore Parker, and William Lloyd Garrison, involves an oversimplification. But it is the best blanket term available.

27. Charles Sumner, *Report on the War with Mexico* (1847), printed in *Old South Leaflets,* VI (Boston: Directors of the Old South Work, Old South Meeting House, n.d.), no. 132, pp. 138–167. Also, James Russell Lowell's *Biglow Papers* in *The Complete Poetical Works of James Russell Lowell* (London: Harrap, n.d.), pp. 173–175. Henry David Thoreau, *Walden and Other Writings,* ed. Brooks Atkinson (New York: Random House, 1950), pp. 635–659. Derogatory comments on New Englanders who took part in the war will also be found in Theodore Parker's 1848 lecture on American character— Perry Miller, ed., *The American Transcendentalists: Their Prose and Poetry* (Garden City, N.Y.: Doubleday, 1957), pp. 356–357. On the military and fugitive slaves see the remark of Richard Henry Dana, legal counsel for Anthony Burns, in Robert F. Lucid, ed., *The Journal of Richard Henry Dana, Jr.,* II

(Cambridge, Mass.: Harvard University Press, 1968), entry for May 27, 1854, p. 629.

28. Henry Steele Commager, ed., *Theodore Parker: An Anthology* (Boston: Beacon Press, 1960), pp. 283–284.

29. Lowell, "An Interview with Miles Standish," *Poetical Works,* pp. 81–82.

30. Octavius Brooks Frothingham, *Gerrit Smith: A Biography* (New York: G. P. Putnam's Sons, 1909), pp. 196–197. Also Dana's speech on the utilitarian spirit in Lucid, ed., *Journal of Dana,* II, 651. Whittier, "The Pine Tree," *The Poetical Works of John Greenleaf Whittier* (London: Frederick Warne, n.d.), p. 177.

31. Thoreau, "A Plea for Captain John Brown," *Walden,* p. 695.

32. Harold Underwood Faulkner, *American Economic History,* 8th ed. (New York: Harper & Row, 1960), p. 336.

33. Franklin, *Militant South,* pp. vii & 129–192. The military review was reported in *Harper's Weekly,* September 24, 1859, p. 615.

34. Cunliffe, *Soldiers and Civilians,* pp. 355–356 & 360–369.

35. Cunliffe, *Soldiers and Civilians,* p. 351.

36. Albert K. Weinberg, *Manifest Destiny: A Study of Nationalist Expansionism in American History* (Chicago: Quadrangle Books, 1963), esp. p. 101. Charles Winslow Elliott, *Winfield Scott: The Soldier and the Man* (New York: Macmillan, 1937), pp. 336–366.

37. Walter Lord, *A Time to Stand* (London: Transworld, 1964), pp. 31–36. Weinberg, *Manifest Destiny,* p. 171.

38. On the new regiments see Marilyn McAdams Sibley, "Robert E. Lee to Albert Sidney Johnston, 1857," *Journal of Southern History,* 29 (February–November, 1963), pp. 100–107; and Fitzhugh Lee, *Makers of American History: General Lee* (New York: University Society, 1905), pp. 54–55.

39. Fairfax Downey, *Clash of Cavalry: The Battle of Brandy Station, June 9, 1863* (New York: David McKay, 1959), pp. 15–18. The officer is quoted in Fred Harvey Harrington, *Fighting Politician Major General N. P. Banks* (Philadelphia: University of Pennsylvania Press, 1948), p. 63. The statistics are based on Russell F. Weigley, *History of the United States Army* (New York: Macmillan, 1967), p. 221. I assumed in making the calculation that the North had a human population of roughly 21,000,000.

40. Faulkner estimates in his *Economic History* that only 16.1 percent of the whole population were city dwellers by 1860. On the amount of unfarmed land in North and South see Frank L. Owsley, *Plain Folk of the Old South* (n.p.: Louisiana State University Press, 1949), p. 48ff. New Orleans is analyzed in Ward, *Jackson,* pp. 1–29.

41. LeRoy H. Fischer, *Lincoln's Gadfly, Adam Gurowski* (Norman: University of Oklahoma Press, 1964), pp. 72–73. William Harlan Hale, *Horace Greeley: Voice of the People* (New York: Collier Books, 1961), p. 37. W. A. Swanberg, *Sickles the Incredible* (New York: Scribner's, 1956), p. 34. Arthur

M. Schlesinger, Jr., *The Age of Jackson* (Boston: Little, Brown, n.d.), p. 210.
L. A. Gobright, *Recollection of Men and Things at Washington, During the Third of a Century* (Philadelphia: Claxton, Remsen & Haffelfinger, 1869), pp. 135–138.

The standard works on affairs of honor are uniformly disappointing in that they do not attempt to get beyond stereotypes of North and South. The majority rely on recounting a few famous duels such as that between Andrew Jackson and Charles Dickinson and all accept unquestioningly the hackneyed argument that dueling died out in the North as a result of revulsion at the death of Alexander Hamilton. They do not explain, for example, why men like Senator Benjamin Wade of Ohio would fight when challenged. See Harnett Thomas Kane, *Gentlemen, Swords and Pistols* (New York: William Morrow, 1951); Robert Baldick, *The Duel: A History of Duelling* (New York: Clarkson N. Potter, 1965); and William Oliver Stevens, *Pistols at Ten Paces: The Story of the Code of Honor in America* (Boston: Houghton Mifflin, 1940).

42. Swanberg, *Sickles*, pp. 5, 10–11, 63–64, and 97 for the Butterworth, Murphy, and Sickles incidents. The plea of temporary insanity, entered at Sickles' trial, was apparently the first such in the history of American jurisprudence.

Harper's Weekly, March 13, 1858, p. 162. As late as December 7, 1872, *Harper's* reported the killing of a man in New York on grounds of honor (p. 946). For the dangers of burglary and common assault on the streets of New York, see the cartoons on pp. 528 and 544, August 22, 1857.

There are many examples of violence among Northerners outside New York. The New York *Tribune*, February 19, 1861, noted that Congressman Kellog of Illinois had beaten up a newspaperman (p. 4). Earlier, during the Speakership contest of 1855–56 both sides carried guns. One man estimated that on an average day there were 300 loaded weapons on the floor and in the galleries of the House of Representatives. Harrington, *Banks*, p. 30.

Few wild young men of the South can have outdone Philip Spencer, son of John C. Spencer of New York, secretary of war, who was hanged for mutiny aboard the brig Somers in 1842. While Spencer may not have been fully guilty of the charge, he had talked of mutiny. His earlier record included excessive drinking, hitting a superior, abusing and challenging a British officer to fight. Harrison Hayford, ed., *The Somers Mutiny Affair* (Englewood Cliffs, N.J.: Prentice-Hall, 1959).

43. George Templeton Strong, *Diary of the Civil War, 1860–1865,* ed. Allan Nevins (New York: Macmillan, 1962), p. 4.

44. Buckingham, *Slave States*, I, 183; Olmsted, *Cotton Kingdom*, p. 44; Clement Eaton, *The Freedom-of-Thought Struggle in the Old South* (New York: Harper & Row, 1964), pp. 177 and 237. He also notes that a surprising number of men in the South continued to think independently (p. 268).

One is inclined to suspect that the lack of discussion about the evils of slavery in the South was sometimes due as much to consensus as to intimidation.

45. On the 1830s mobs see Leonard L. Richards, *"Gentlemen of Property and Standing": Anti-Abolition Mobs in Jacksonian America* (New York: Oxford University Press, 1971). The Garrison and Phillips mobs are noted in Irving H. Bartlett, *Wendell Phillips: Brahmin Radical* (Boston: Beacon Press, 1961), pp. 35–36 and 226–231. Higginson's exploit is in his *Cheerful Yesterdays* (Boston: Houghton Mifflin, 1899), pp. 147–160. Philip Regis De Trobriand, *Four Years With the Army of the Potomac,* trans. George K. Dauchy (Boston: Ticknor, 1889), p. 33, for the Wisconsin affair. On the convention see Alice Felt Tyler, *Freedom's Ferment: Phases of American Social History from the Colonial Period to the Outbreak of the Civil War* (New York: Harper & Row, 1962), p. 455, and Dixon Ryan Fox, *The Decline of Aristocracy in the Politics of New York 1801–1840,* ed. Robert V. Remini (New York: Harper & Row, 1965), p. 279 for the burning of the house. The violence in Rhode Island is described in Schlesinger, *Jackson,* pp. 411–412. Also p. 219 for another mob action. On intolerance in the northwest see Keith Huntress, "The Murder of Joseph Smith," in Marvin S. Hill and James B. Allen, eds., *Mormonism and American Culture* (New York: Harper & Row, 1972), pp. 74–86. Norton's book is referred to in Chapter 1 above.

46. Wallace, *Autobiography,* I, 219.

47. The Bull Run statistics are dealt with in Chapter 4 below.

48. On the ignorance of Southerners regarding their own region note the surprise recorded by a Virginian on finding that the Deep South was not full of violence. Herbert A. Kellar, ed., "A Journey through the South in 1836: Diary of James B. Davidson," *Journal of Southern History,* 1 (February–November, 1935), 367.

3. Prelude

1. Perhaps the best study of Northern thought during the Secession Crisis is Kenneth M. Stampp, *And the War Came: The North and the Secession Crisis, 1860–1861* (Chicago: University of Chicago Press, 1964). David M. Potter's *Lincoln and His Party in the Secession Crisis* (New Haven: Yale University Press, 1962), is also useful.

2. The events at Sumter are described in most general histories of the war. Bruce Catton has a detailed account in *The Centennial History of the Civil War,* I: *The Coming Fury* (New York: Pocket Books, 1967).

The problems encountered by the War Department are noticed in Erwin Stanley Bradley, *Simon Cameron: Lincoln's Secretary of War* (Philadelphia: University of Pennsylvania Press, 1966); and A. Howard Meneely, *The War Department, 1861: A Study in Mobilization and Administration* (New York: Columbia University Press, 1928).

3. Henry Villard, *Memoirs of Henry Villard,* I (Boston: Houghton Mifflin, 1904), 159–160.

4. Robert Barnwell Rhett, a leading South Carolina secessionist, was

reputed to have said that he would eat the bodies of everyone killed in a civil war—E. Merton Coulter, *The Confederate States of America, 1861–1865,* vol. VII of *A History of the South,* ed. Wendell Holmes Stephenson and E. Merton Coulter (n.p.: Louisiana State University Press, 1950), pp. 14–15. William Howard Russell, *My Diary North and South,* ed. Fletcher Pratt (New York: Harper & Row, 1965), pp. 38–40.

5. New York *Times,* April 16, 1861, quoted in George Winston Smith and Charles Judah, eds., *Life in the North during the Civil War: A Source History* (Albuquerque: University of New Mexico Press, 1966), p. 39. Also, quotation from New York *Tribune,* pp. 39–40. George Ticknor, *Life, Letters, and Journals,* II, 5th ed. (New York: Johnson Reprint, 1968), letter of April 12, 1861, p. 433. See also Georgeanna Muirson (Woolsey) Bacon, ed., *Letters of a Family during the War for the Union, 1861–1865,* I (n.p.: Printed for private distribution, 1899), pp. 66–71.

6. New York *Tribune,* April 19, 1861, quoted in Frank Moore, ed., *The Rebellion Record,* I (New York: G. P. Putnam, 1861), "Rumors & Incidents," p. 28. See also Sacramento (Calif.) *Bee,* quoted on p. 109, in which an unarmed Yankee sea captain makes a South Carolinian holding a pistol back down during an argument over Northern character.

7. The *Liberator,* August 10, 1855, quoted in Irving H. Bartlett, *Wendell Phillips: Brahmin Radical* (Boston: Beacon Press, 1961), p. 200.

8. Bartlett, *Phillips,* pp. 139, 94–95, 155–156. On the Brown raid see Wendell Phillips, *Speeches, Lectures and Letters,* first series (Boston: Lee and Shepard, 1892), speech on November 1, 1859, pp. 274–275. On the Secession Crisis see "Disunion," a lecture delivered on January 20, 1861, *Speeches,* pp. 343–347 and 358. On the probability of Southern military victory see Moore, ed., *Rebellion Record,* I, "Diary of Events," 38.

9. Phillips, "Under the Flag," lecture given on April 12, 1861, *Speeches,* first series, pp. 396–397.

10. A selection of statements in opposition to the war is given in Horace Greeley, *The American Conflict,* I (Hartford, Conn.: O. D. Case, 1864), pp. 455–457.

President Buchanan was among those who felt anti-slavery agitation was responsible for the crisis. See his Fourth Annual Message to Congress in U.S., Congress, Senate, *Executive Documents,* doc. 1, 36th Cong., 2d sess., vol I, p. 3ff. The New York *Herald* continued to blame "nigger worshippers" well into the war: Carl Sandburg, *Abraham Lincoln,* II: *The War Years, 1861–1864* (New York: Dell, 1959), 122–124. Threats of war against the Republicans will be found in Lew Wallace, *An Autobiography,* I (New York: Harper and Brothers, 1906), 257–259; and Wood Gray, *The Hidden Civil War: The Story of the Copperheads* (New York: Viking Press, 1964), pp. 46–47.

The most obvious application of State Rights philosophy in the North was the adoption of personal liberty laws in defiance of the Federal Fugitive Slave Act. The single best source for ideas on the nature of the Union is Paul C.

Nagel, *One Nation Indivisible: The Union in American Thought, 1776–1861* (New York: Oxford University Press, 1964). Useful comments on localism will also be found in Daniel Boorstin, *The Genius of American Politics* (Chicago: University of Chicago Press, 1958), pp. 125–126; Frank E. Vandiver, "The Civil War as an Institutionalizing Force," in Vandiver, ed., *Essays on the American Civil War* (Austin: University of Texas Press, 1968); and Richard O. Curry, "The Union as It Was: A Critique of Recent Interpretations of the 'Copperheads,'" *Civil War History*, 13.1 (1967), 25–39.

11. This paradox in Northern thought is brought out by Stampp in *And the War Came,* esp. pp. 37–57.

12. Joseph Pearson Farley, *West Point in the Early Sixties* (Troy, N.Y.: Pafraets, 1902), p. 25. R. S. Ewell, *The Making of a Soldier. Letters of General R. S. Ewell,* ed. Piercy Gatling Hamlin (Richmond: Whittet & Shepperson, 1935), p. 97.

13. Edward J. Nichols, *Toward Gettysburg: A Biography of General John F. Reynolds* ([University Park]: Pennsylvania State University Press, 1958), letter of December 23, 1859, p. 68. William Tecumseh Sherman, *Home Letters of General Sherman,* ed. M. A. DeWolfe Howe (New York: Scribner's, 1909), letter of November 29, 1860, p. 185. Emerson Gifford Taylor, *Gouverneur Kemble Warren: The Life and Letters of an American Soldier, 1830–1882* (Boston: Houghton Mifflin, 1932), p. 50.

14. James Longstreet, *From Manassas to Appomattox: Memoirs of the Civil War in America* (Bloomington: Indiana University Press, 1960), p. 29. Abner Doubleday, *Reminiscences of Forts Sumter and Moultrie in 1860–'61* (New York: Harper & Brothers, 1876), pp. 18–19, 32, 37–39, and 126. Compare Anderson's letter of April 8, 1861, in *The War of the Rebellion: A Compilation of the Official Records of the Union and Confederate Armies,* series I, vol. I (Washington: Government Printing Office, 1880), p. 294. Hereafter cited as O.R.

15. Doubleday, *Sumter and Moultrie,* pp. 137–138. Cf. Erasmus Darwin Keyes, *Fifty Years' Observation of Men and Events Civil and Military* (New York: Scribner's, 1884), p. 318.

16. Critics of West Point are discussed in T. Harry Williams, "The Attack upon West Point during the Civil War," *Mississippi Valley Historical Review,* 25 (March 1939), 491–504. Williams' view differs from my own in that he gives little credence to the charge of aristocratic influence.
Russell, *My Diary North and South,* April 12, 1861, p. 46.

17. Jacob Dolson Cox, *Military Reminiscences of the Civil War,* I (New York: Scribner's, 1900), pp. 205–206.

18. Butler's troubles are recorded in Benjamin F. Butler, *Private and Official Correspondence of Gen. Benjamin F. Butler during the Period of the Civil War,* ed. Jessie Ames Marshall, I (n.p.: Privately issued, 1917), 37–41 and 76–77. Also of interest is Butler's exchange with the War Department on the treatment of runaway slaves, pp. 186–188 and 201–203.

19. Joseph W. Revere, *Keel and Saddle: A Retrospect of Forty Years of Military and Naval Service* (Boston: James R. Osgood, 1872), pp. 269–271.

20. Sarah Norton and M. A. DeWolfe Howe, *Letters of Charles Eliot Norton*, I (Boston: Houghton Mifflin, 1913), letter of April 10, 1861, pp. 230–231. George Templeton Strong, *Diary of the Civil War, 1860–1865*, ed. Allan Nevins (New York: Macmillan, 1962), entry for April 5, 1861, p. 114. Shame at the failure of the North to actively resent secession was also expressed by the historian John Lothrop Motley. George William Curtis, ed., *The Correspondence of John Lothrop Motley* (New York: Harper & Brothers, 1889), letter of February 9, 1861, p. 358.

21. New York *Tribune*, May 8, 1861, p. 4. Martha Perry Lowe, "To Arms," quoted in Moore, ed., *Rebellion Record*, I, "Poetry & Incidents," 31.

22. W. W. Howe, "The New Birth," New York *Tribune*, quoted in Moore, ed., *Rebellion Record*, I, "Poetry & Incidents," 31. "The Rising of the North," *Madison State Journal*, also in Moore, "Rumors & Incidents," pp. 123–124; and *Vanity Fair*, p. 141. See also "Redemption" and Bayard Taylor, "To the American People," "Rumors & Incidents," pp. 61 and 104.

23. Moore, "Rumors & Incidents," p. 94. Also p. 109 on Yankee tin peddlers. There are some interesting comments on Northern brokers putting duty before profit in the *National Republican* (Washington), April 22, 1861.

24. Bliss Perry, *Life and Letters of Henry Lee Higginson* (Boston: Atlantic Monthly Press, 1921), letter of April 22, 1861, p. 142. Also, Curtis, ed., *Motley*, letter of June 14, 1861, pp. 375–376; Daniel Aaron, *The Hales and the "Great Rebellion"* (Northampton, Mass.: Smith College, 1966), diary entry for April 19, 1861, p. 15; and Jordan D. Fiore, *Massachusetts in the Civil War*, II: *The Year of Trial and Testing 1861–1862* (Boston: Massachusetts Civil War Centennial Commission, 1961), 10 and 13.

On the repair of the engine see Moore, ed., *Rebellion Record*, I, "Rumors & Incidents," New York *Times*, 55 and *Newburyport Herald* (Mass.), p. 80. The incident is described by Benjamin F. Butler in *Butler's Book* (Boston: A. M. Thayer, 1892), pp. 201–202.

25. The *Watchman and Reflector* is quoted in Moore, ed., *Rebellion Record*, I, doc. 128, p. 184. *Harper's Weekly*, May 11, 1861, p. 290.

26. "Better Than Dollars," *Harper's Weekly*, April 20, 1861, p. 242. Also, *Philadelphia Intelligencer*, quoted in Moore, ed., *Rebellion Record*, I, "Rumors & Incidents," p. 115.

27. Strong, *Diary, 1860–1865*, entry for May 9, 1861, p. 141.

28. Mrs. Clement C. Clay, Jr., *A Belle of the Fifties* (New York: Doubleday, Page, 1905), p. 152. On predictions of defeat: Cox, *Reminiscences*, I, 27.

29. The offer of command is in Douglas Southall Freeman, *R. E. Lee*, I (New York: Scribner's, 1942), pp. 432 and 436–437. Scott's comment is in Charles Winslow Elliott, *Winfield Scott: The Soldier and the Man* (New York: Macmillan, 1937), pp. 712–713.

30. Warlike activities were reported by, for instance, William Tecumseh

Sherman of Ohio who was then superintendent of a military academy in Louisiana. See Sherman, *Home Letters,* letter of October 29, 1859, p. 163; and John Sherman and William Tecumseh Sherman, *The Sherman Letters: Correspondence between General and Senator Sherman from 1837–1891,* ed. Rachel Sherman Thorndike (New York: Scribner's, 1894), letter of February 1860, p. 80.

31. Examples of accusations against the Cabinet will be found in Moore, ed., *Rebellion Record,* I, "Rumors & Incidents," 9 and 11–12. Most Buchanan biographies mention the charges. See Philip Shriver Klein, *President James Buchanan* (University Park, Pa.: Pennsylvania State University Press, 1962), pp. 374–378 and 397; Philip Gerald Auchampaugh, *James Buchanan and His Cabinet on the Eve of Secession* (Boston: J. S. Canner, 1965), pp. 90–91. Stampp's argument is in *And the War Came,* esp. pp. 46–57. Compare also Lincoln's inaugural address with Buchanan's draft of an answer to Governor Pickens' demand for the surrender of Fort Sumter, December 20, 1860, in James Buchanan, *The Works of James Buchanan,* ed. John Bassett Moore, XI (New York: Antiquarian Press, 1960), 72.

32. The atmosphere in the capital is vividly described in Margaret Leech, *Reveille in Washington, 1860–1865* (New York: Grosset & Dunlap, n.d.), pp. 4–48. On the secessionist cockades see John W. Stepp and I. William Hill, *Mirror of War: The Washington Star Reports the Civil War* (Englewood Cliffs, N.J.: Prentice-Hall, 1961), p. 16.

33. Most Lincoln biographies mention the assassination rumors. See, for instance, Benjamin P. Thomas, *Abraham Lincoln: A Biography* (New York: Knopf, 1952), pp. 242–244. Some typical plot stories are in a letter to Lincoln from his friend Charles Ballance, in Harry E. Pratt, ed., *Concerning Mr. Lincoln* (Springfield: Abraham Lincoln Association, 1944), pp. 42–43.

34. Hinton Rowan Helper, *The Impending Crisis of the South: How to Meet It* (New York: Collier Books, 1963), pp. 131, 159–160, and 261–269. There are useful comments on the susceptibility to rumor of people in crisis, in Gordon W. Allport and Leo Postman, *The Psychology of Rumor* (New York: Russell & Russell, 1965). Some general insights are also given in Richard Hofstadter's *The Paranoid Style in American Politics and Other Essays* (New York: Random House, 1967). Using Hofstadter's thesis and Donald's analysis of abolitionist backgrounds (Chapter 1, note 48 above), David Brion Davis has written *The Slave Power Conspiracy and the Paranoid Style* (Baton Rouge: Louisiana State University Press, 1969). Samples of abolitionist plot theories are given in John L. Thomas, *Slavery Attacked: The Abolitionist Crusade* (Englewood Cliffs, N.J.: Prentice-Hall, 1965), pp. 70–75, and 148–152.

35. The statistics are from Russell F. Weigley, *History of the United States Army* (New York: Macmillan, 1967), p. 199.

36. On the claim that Northern officers would not fight, see New York *Tribune,* February 26, 1861, p. 8.

John Sherman and William Tecumseh Sherman, *Sherman Letters,* May

30, 1861, pp. 116–117. Also John Hay, "Letters of John Hay and Extracts from Diary" (Washington: Printed but not published, 1908), diary entry for April 21, 1861, p. 17.

The accusation about blank cartridges was made by Fitz Henry Warren in the New York *Tribune,* quoted by Louis M. Starr in *Reporting the Civil War: The Bohemian Brigade in Action, 1861–65* (New York: Collier Books, 1962), p. 28. On the protection of property see Abner R. Small, *The Road to Richmond: The Civil War Memoirs of Maj. Abner R. Small,* ed. Harold Adams Small (Berkeley: University of California Press, 1959), pp. 15–16; and McDowell's comments in the O.R., first series, I, 654–655 and 743–744.

37. Nathaniel Beverley Tucker, *The Partisan Leader,* ed. Carl Bridenbaugh (New York: Knopf, 1933), esp. pp. vii, xiv, xviii, xxx, xxxiii–iv, 31–32, 36–38, and 120–121. See also note 40 below for a Northern speech in which the book was used as evidence of a plot.

38. Seward is quoted on the plot thesis in Russell, *My Diary North and South,* pp. 35–36. On regulars' distaste for civil war see, for instance, Ethan Allen Hitchcock, *Fifty Years in Camp and Field,* ed. W. A. Croffut (New York: G. P. Putnam's Sons, 1909), pp. 428–429. Nichols, *Reynolds,* letter of June 11, 1861, p. 73. Also, Peter Smith Michie, *Life and Letters of Emory Upton* (New York: D. Appleton, 1885), p. 30; and David D. Porter, *Incidents and Anecdotes of the Civil War* (New York: D. Appleton, 1885), p. 7.

39. P. H. Sheridan, *Personal Memoirs of P. H. Sheridan,* I (London: Chatto & Windus, 1888), pp. 121–122.

40. John Jay, "The Great Conspiracy," quoted in Moore, ed., *Rebellion Record,* I, doc. 254, esp. pp. 381–388.

41. Schenck's report and that of the officer opposed to him are in the O.R., first series, I, 126 and 128–129. The quotation is from R. H. Beatie, Jr., *Road to Manassas* (n.p.: Cooper Square, 1961), pp. 68–69 and 122. The absurdity of the masked battery business was seen clearly by the Polish expatriate Adam Gurowski, whose impressions are recorded in his *Diary from March 4, 1861, to November 12, 1862* (Boston: Lee and Shepard, 1862), p. 58.

42. For a typical description of the South as ruled by a military aristocracy with the advantages of that form of government see *Harper's Weekly,* June 29, 1861, p. 402.

43. Moore, ed., *Rebellion Record,* I, doc. 249, pp. 366–367; doc. 263, pp. 413–414.

44. Keyes, *Fifty Years' Observation,* pp. 330 and 338.

45. Stepp and Hill, *Mirror of War,* p. 45; and Charles A. Ingraham, *Elmer E. Ellsworth and the Zouaves of '61* (Chicago: University of Chicago Press, 1925), p. 135.

46. Theodore Winthrop, "Washington as a Camp," *Atlantic Monthly,* 8 (July 1861), pp. 106 and 109. See also the comments in Henry T. Tuckerman, *The Rebellion: Its Latent Causes and True Significance* (New York: James G. Gregory, 1861), p. 48.

47. Chase is quoted in Elliott, *Scott,* p. 686; Everett in Stampp, *And the War Came,* p. 73; Barlow in Allan Nevins, *The War for the Union,* I: *The Improvised War, 1861–1862* (New York: Scribner's, 1959), 210–211.

48. Stanton's remarks are in Buchanan, *Works,* XI, letter of April 11, 1861, p. 179. Oliver Otis Howard, *Autobiography of Oliver Otis Howard,* I (New York: Baker & Taylor, 1908), 137–138. Edward Bates, *The Diary of Edward Bates, 1859–1866,* ed. Howard K. Beale, Annual Report of the American Historical Association for the Year 1930, vol. IV (Washington: Government Printing Office, 1933), 185–186. Gurowski, *Diary from 1861 to 1862,* April 1861, p. 33, and May 1861, p. 44.

49. On the North's organizational efforts see note 2 above; and Nevins, *War for the Union,* I, chaps. four and five. There is much material on Lincoln's policy. See, for instance, Richard N. Current, *Lincoln and the First Shot* (Philadelphia: J. B. Lippincott, 1963); and Richard Hofstadter, *The American Political Tradition and the Men Who Made It* (New York: Knopf, n.d.), pp. 120–124.

50. Before becoming President, Lincoln had served only one term in Congress. His military experience is noted in Thomas, *Lincoln,* pp. 30–34.

51. On Lincoln's problems with office seekers, Thomas, *Lincoln,* pp. 252–253; and Sandburg, *Lincoln,* II, 48–50. On his seeming lack of polish, see the comment of a Kentuckian in William H. Townsend, *Lincoln and the Bluegrass: Slavery and Civil War in Kentucky* (Lexington: University of Kentucky Press, 1955), p. 266; views of Washingtonians in Leech, *Reveille in Washington,* pp. 35–36 and 49; and the selections from Northern newspapers in Courtlandt Canby, ed., *Lincoln and the Civil War: A Profile and a History* (New York: Dell, 1958), pp. 226–228. The bad feeling created by Lincoln's joke telling is apparent in Villard, *Memoirs,* I, 143–144. The height contest is in Sandburg, *Lincoln,* II, 14. Lincoln apparently forced the unhappy Senator Charles Sumner into a similar bout; see *The Diary of a Public Man* (New Brunswick: Rutgers University Press, 1946). On Lincoln as seemingly indecisive see William Harlan Hale, *Horace Greeley: Voice of the People* (New York: Collier Books, 1961), p. 248; Glyndon G. Van Duesen, *William Henry Seward* (New York: Oxford University Press, 1967), pp. 280–281; and David Donald, *Lincoln Reconsidered: Essays on the Civil War Era,* 2d. ed. (New York: Random House, 1961), pp. 128–130.

For contrast, note the comments on Jefferson Davis in Clay, *A Belle of the Fifties,* p. 68; and Almira R. Hancock, *Reminiscences of Winfield Scott Hancock by His Wife* (New York: Charles L. Webster, 1887), pp. 45–46.

52. *Southern Literary Messenger,* 30 (June 1860), 401–409, and 31 (November 1860), 346–347. *Mobile Advertiser,* February 12, 1861, printed in Moore, ed., *Rebellion Record,* I, "Rumors & Incidents," 22.

There are many works on the South and Secession. Those of general interest include Avery Craven, *The Growth of Southern Nationalism, 1848–1861,* vol. VI of *A History of the South,* esp. pp. 349–390; Dwight Lowell

Dumond, *The Secession Movement, 1860–1861* (New York: Octagon Books, 1963); Ralph A. Wooster, *The Secession Conventions of the South* (Princeton: Princeton University Press, 1962); and Dumond's *Southern Editorials on Secession* (Gloucester, Mass.: Peter Smith, 1964).

53. On Southern anxiety about the west, see for instance Thomas Cooper DeLeon, *Four Years in Rebel Capitals* (New York: Collier Books, 1962), pp. 138–139.

54. On the Yankee craze see Moore, ed., *Rebellion Record*, I, "Rumors & Incidents," *Richmond Examiner*, May 3, 1861, pp. 79 and 137–138; *Charleston Mercury*, May 8, 1861, p. 81; *Charleston Courier, Mobile Advertiser*, and *Charleston Evening News*, May 7, 1861, p. 70.

The "Old Ben" story is quoted in Greeley, *American Conflict*, I, 508. It was attributed to the *Picayune* (New Orleans) but this paper denied authorship; see Moore, ed., *Rebellion Record*, I, "Rumors & Incidents," 128.

55. On Southern confidence see Moore, ed., *Rebellion Record*, I, "Rumors & Incidents," *Charleston Mercury*, June 2, 1861, 114; *New Orleans Crescent*, p. 83; and feelings of Southerners recorded by Russell in *My Diary North and South*, e.g., pp. 64, 72, 82, and 157. Beauregard is quoted in T. Harry Williams, *P. G. T. Beauregard: Napeoleon in Gray* (New York: Collier Books, 1962), p. 88.

56. L. H. Sigourney, "Seceding Virginia," printed in Moore, ed., *Rebellion Record*, I, "Rumors & Incidents," 116. Walt Whitman, "Virginia—The West," *Leaves of Grass* (New York: New American Library, 1954), p. 241. Also, Aaron, *The Hales and the Rebellion*, p. 21; and Morris Schaff, *The Spirit of Old West Point, 1858–1862* (Boston: Houghton Mifflin, 1907), p. 210.

4. The Penalties of Defeat

1. There is a vast amount of material on Civil War strategic questions. Chapters one to three in Walter Millis, *Arms and Men: A Study in American Military History* (New York: New American Library, 1958), give a good introduction to the nature of war in the period. On the relative advantages of the two sides see David Donald, ed., *Why the North Won the Civil War* (New York: Collier Books, 1962). On the numerical line-up see Thomas Schoonover, "Manpower, North and South, in 1860," *Civil War History*, 6.2 (1960), 170–173.

2. One of the clearest accounts of the battle is R. H. Beatie, Jr., *Road to Manassas* (n.p.: Cooper Square, 1961). Francis F. Wilshin provides a useful short summary in his *Manassas National Battlefield Park, Virginia* (Washington: Government Printing Office, 1962).

3. Adam Gurowski, *Diary from March 4, 1861, to November 12, 1862* (Boston: Lee and Shepard, 1862), July 1861, pp. 74 and 78–79. Cf. note 41, chapter 3 above. Also, New York *World* report quoted by Frank Moore in *The Rebellion Record*, I (New York: G. P. Putnam, 1861), docs., p. 87.

4. For Russell's view of the battle see *My Diary North and South*, ed. Fletcher Pratt (New York: Harper & Row, 1965), pp. 224–230 and 232–234; and his letter to the London *Times* in Moore, ed., *Rebellion Record*, I, docs., pp. 58–59. Walt Whitman, *Specimen Days* (New York: New American Library, 1961), pp. 38–40.

5. Benjamin F. Butler, *Private and Official Correspondence of Gen. Benjamin F. Butler during the Period of the Civil War*, ed. Jessie Ames Marshall, I (n.p.: Privately issued, 1917), letter of July 27, 181–182. Edward M. Emerson, *Life and Letters of Charles Russell Lowell* (Boston: Houghton Mifflin, 1907), letter of August 5, p. 217.

6. William Harlan Hale, *Horace Greeley: Voice of the People* (New York: Collier Books, 1961), pp. 253–254 and 258. The headline was from the New York *Evening Post*, July 26, printed in Moore, ed., *Rebellion Record*, II (New York: G. P. Putnam, 1864), "Rumors & Incidents," p. 5. See *Wilkes' Spirit of the Times*, September 21, 1861, p. 35, for a prediction that the North would win next time.

7. Washington Chauncey Ford, ed., *A Cycle of Adams Letters 1861–1865*, I (Boston: Houghton Mifflin, 1920), letters of July 23, pp. 22–23, and August 27, p. 38. Edward Cary, *George William Curtis* (Boston: Houghton Mifflin, 1894), letter of July 29, pp. 148–149.

8. Billings, *Hardtack and Coffee*, reprinted in Philip Van Doren Stern, *Soldier Life in the Union and Confederate Armies* (Greenwich, Conn.: Fawcett Publications, 1961), p. 178. DeLeon, *Four Years in Rebel Capitals* (New York: Collier Books, 1962), p. 159. Bruce Catton, *The Penguin Book of the American Civil War* (Harmondsworth, Middlesex: Penguin Books, 1966), p. 55. James A. Rawley, *Turning Points of the Civil War* (Lincoln: University of Nebraska Press, 1966), pp. 57 and 67. Nevins, *The War for the Union*, vol. I: *The Improvised War, 1861–1862* (New York: Scribner's, 1959), p. 223.

9. O.R., first series, I, 75–76 and 912–913.

10. On the fear of rebel cavalry see Fairfax Downey, *Clash of Cavalry. The Battle of Brandy Station, June 9, 1863* (New York: David McKay, 1959), pp. 10–12; and Bruce Catton, *Mr. Lincoln's Army* (New York: Pocket Books, 1964), p. 75. *Wilkes' Spirit of the Times*, November 2, 1861, p. 137.

11. The action at Fairfax Court House was reported in the O.R., first series, I, 60. My view of Stuart's charge is based on Beatie, *Road to Manassas*, pp. 171–172. On the Black Horse Cavalry see Downey, *Clash of Cavalry*, pp. 10–12; and James Ralph Johnson, Alfred Hoyt Bill, and Hirst Dillon Milhollen, *Horsemen Blue and Gray* (New York: Oxford University Press, 1960), p. 13.

12. Carl Schurz, *The Reminiscences of Carl Schurz*, II (New York: McClure, 1907), pp. 229–231.

13. On the cavalry with McDowell see Beatie, *Road to Manassas*, pp. 122–123 and 191. The evidence given by the generals is in U.S., Congress, Senate, Joint Committee on the Conduct of the War, *Report*, 37th Cong., 3d

sess., S. Rep. Com. 108, vol. II, pt. 1, 1863, pp. 113–115, 119, 124, 139, and 152–153. The officers were J. B. Richardson, S. P. Heintzelman, Wm. B. Franklin, Irvin McDowell, and M. C. Meigs.

14. William T. Lusk, *War Letters of William Thompson Lusk* (New York: Privately printed, 1911), p. 79.

15. E. Kirby Smith, *To Mexico with Scott: Letters of Captain E. Kirby Smith to His Wife* (Cambridge, Mass.: Harvard University Press, 1917), pp. 151–152. John Sedgwick, *Correspondence of John Sedgwick*, I (New York: Printed for C. & E. B. Stoeckel, by the DeVinne Press, 1902–1903), letter of November 23, 1846, p. 39.

16. Charles Winslow Elliott, *Winfield Scott: The Soldier and the Man* (New York: Macmillan, 1937), pp. 718–719. On McDowell's view see Russell, *My Diary North and South,* p. 193, and Beatie, *Road to Manassas,* pp. 66–67.

There are some interesting comments regarding the rebel failure to attack Washington in R. L. Dabney, *Life of Lieut.-Gen. Thomas J. Jackson,* I (London: James Nisbet, 1864), 268–277. Cf. Joseph E. Johnston, *Narrative of Military Operations* (Bloomington: Indiana University Press, 1959; New York: Kraus Reprint, 1969), pp. 59–65. Examples of friction in the Southern service will be found in Ellsworth Eliot, Jr., *West Point in the Confederacy* (New York: G. A. Baker, 1941), pp. 20–21; and Russell, *My Diary North and South,* pp. 58 and 63–64.

17. Henry Villard, *Memoirs of Henry Villard,* I (Boston: Houghton Mifflin, 1904), p. 199. George Meade, *The Life and Letters of George Gordon Meade,* I (New York: Scribner's, 1913), 233. Edward J. Nichols, *Toward Gettysburg: A Biography of General John F. Reynolds* ([University Park]: Pennsylvania State University Press, 1958), pp. 78–79.

18. General Philip Kearny's Letters, 1861/2, Library of Congress, Manuscript Division, letters of August 29, 1861, to Courtlandt Parker, and January 13, 1862, to Parker.

19. Butler, *Correspondence,* I, letter of Fisher A. Hildreth to Butler, August 19, 1861, p. 220. James Harrison Wilson, *Under the Old Flag,* I (New York: D. Appleton, 1912), p. 60.

20. On Miles and Tyler see Beatie, *Road to Manassas,* pp. 166–167.

21. On discipline in the rebel army see, for instance, George Cary Eggleston, *A Rebel's Recollections* (Bloomington: Indiana University Press, 1959), pp. 69–73.

22. New York *Tribune,* August 12, 1861, "The Two Armies," p. 4. Benjamin P. Thomas, *Abraham Lincoln: A Biography* (New York: Knopf, 1952), p. 266. The figures are from Thomas L. Livermore, *Numbers & Losses in the Civil War* (New York: Kraus Reprint, 1969), p. 77.

23. *Harper's Weekly,* November 9, 1861, "Wanted—A Little Pluck," p. 706.

24. William W. Hassler, ed., *The General to His Lady: The Civil War Letters of William Dorsey Pender to Fanny Pender* (Chapel Hill: University of North Carolina Press, 1965), p. 16. Also, for instance, DeLeon, *Rebel Capitals*, pp. 37–51.

25. Richard Taylor, *Destruction and Reconstruction. Personal Experiences of the Late War*, ed. Richard B. Harwell (New York: Longmans, Green, 1955), pp. 7–8; Frank E. Vandiver, *Ploughshares into Swords: Josiah Gorgas and Confederate Ordnance* (Austin: University of Texas Press, 1952), pp. 55 and 60; Fred Albert Shannon, *The Organization and Administration of the Union Army, 1861–1865*, I (Gloucester, Mass.: Peter Smith, 1965), for the number of rifles in U.S. arsenals.

26. Ashley Halsey, Jr., "South Carolina Began Preparing for War in 1851," *Civil War Times Illustrated*, 1.1 (1962), 8–13. The references to the Virginia troops are in the O.R., first series, I, 26–27, 851–852, and 800.

27. On Northerners who began preparing for war see Jacob Dolson Cox, *Military Reminiscences of the Civil War*, I (New York: Scribner's, 1900), 7–8; and Lew Wallace, *An Autobiography*, I (New York: Harper and Brothers, 1906), 242–245.

28. Abner R. Small, *The Road to Richmond: The Civil War Memoirs of Maj. Abner R. Small*, ed. Harold Adams Small (Berkeley: University of California Press, 1959), p. 26.

29. Wade is quoted in T. Harry Williams, *Lincoln and the Radicals* (Madison: University of Wisconsin Press, 1965), p. 36. *Wilkes' Spirit of the Times*, September 14, 1861. Also, September 21, 1861, p. 35; and Edward Bates, *The Diary of Edward Bates, 1859–1866*, ed. Howard K. Beale, Annual Report of the American Historical Association for the Year 1930, IV (Washington: Government Printing Office, 1933), September 30, 1861, 194.

30. *Harper's Weekly*, August 3, 1861, "Our Institutions on Their Trial," p. 482.

31. William Tecumseh Sherman, *Home Letters of General Sherman*, ed. M. A. DeWolfe Howe (New York: Scribner's, 1909), October 29, 1859, pp. 162–163; John Sherman and William Tecumseh Sherman, *The Sherman Letters: Correspondence between General and Senator Sherman from 1837 to 1891*, ed. Rachel Sherman Thorndike (New York: Scribner's, 1894), February 1860, p. 80.

There is an interesting chapter on Sherman's background in Edmund Wilson, *Patriotic Gore: Studies in the Literature of the American Civil War* (New York: Oxford University Press, 1966). The standard biographies of Sherman are Lloyd Lewis, *Sherman: Fighting Prophet* (New York: Harcourt, Brace & World, 1932), and B. H. Liddell Hart, *Sherman: Soldier, Realist, American* (London: Stevens & Sons, 1960).

32. William Tecumseh Sherman, *Memoirs of General William T. Sherman*, I (Bloomington: Indiana University Press, 1957), 166–172.

33. Sherman, *Home Letters,* January 5, 1861, pp. 189–190; December 18, 1860, p. 187; January 1861, p. 188; John Sherman and William Tecumseh Sherman, *Sherman Letters,* February 1860, p. 80; January 18, 1861, p. 106.

34. Sherman, *Home Letters,* July 3, 1861, p. 200; July 19, 1861, pp. 201–202; John Sherman and William Tecumseh Sherman, *Sherman Letters,* pp. 111–112; and April 22, 1861, p. 113.

35. Sherman, *Home Letters,* July 24, 1861, pp. 203–204; July 28, 1861, pp. 209–210; and August 3, 1861, p. 211.

36. The analysis of Sherman's behavior is based on John Sherman and William Tecumseh Sherman, *Sherman Letters,* September 9, 1861, pp. 128–129, and October 5, 1861, pp. 132–133; Lewis, *Sherman,* pp. 189–191 and 197; Villard, *Memoirs,* I, 210–211. For a different view of Sherman at this time see Liddell Hart's book, which suggests that Sherman did not lose his perspective.

5. One Man's Role

1. Kenneth P. Williams, *Lincoln Finds a General: A Military Study of the Civil War,* I (New York: Macmillan, 1957). T. Harry Williams, *Lincoln and His Generals* (New York: Knopf, 1964). Treatments favorable to McClellan are Warren W. Hassler, Jr., *General George B. McClellan: Shield of the Union* (Baton Rouge: Louisiana State University Press, 1957); and William Star Myers, *A Study in Personality: General George Brinton McClellan* (New York: D. Appleton-Century, 1934).

2. O.R., first series, II, 205–209.

3. G. B. McClellan, *McClellan's Own Story* (New York: Charles L. Webster, 1887), letters of August 2, 1861, p. 82, and October 31, 1861, p. 172; Williams, *Lincoln and His Generals,* p. 44.

4. Williams, *Lincoln Finds a General,* I, 105–112; and Nevins, *War for the Union,* I, 225.

5. A typical attack on Stone is to be found in *Report,* 37th Cong., 3d. sess., S. Rep. Com. 108, vol. III, pt. 2., pp. 267ff. McClellan's role is described in T. Harry Williams, *Lincoln and the Radicals* (Madison: University of Wisconsin Press, 1965), pp. 94–104. On Manassas see Allan Nevins, *The War for the Union,* II: *War Becomes Revolution* (New York: Scribner's, 1960), 46–47.

6. All the McClellan biographies deal with the choice of route. Williams gives a succinct treatment in chapter 4 of *Lincoln and His Generals.*

7. McClellan, *Own Story,* April 23, 1862, p. 313; and Williams, *Lincoln Finds a General,* I, 164.

8. The best short narrative of the campaign is probably again Williams, *Lincoln and His Generals,* chaps. 5 and 6.

9. On Jackson's Valley campaign see G. F. R. Henderson, *Stonewall Jackson and the American Civil War* (New York: David McKay, 1961), esp. chap. 12.

10. Quoted in Louis M. Starr, *Reporting the Civil War: The Bohemian Brigade in Action, 1861–65* (New York: Collier Books, 1962), p. 113.

11. Antietam is well described in Nevins, *War for the Union*, II, 215–231; and Bruce Catton, *Mr. Lincoln's Army* (New York: Pocket Books, 1964), chap. 5.

12. On the Crimean War experience see Richard P. Weinert, "The Year McClellan Studied War in Europe," *Civil War Times Illustrated*, II (May 1963), 38–41. The influence of Jomini is discussed in David Donald, *Lincoln Reconsidered: Essays on the Civil War Era*, 2d. ed. (New York: Random House, 1961), pp. 82–102, and T. Harry Williams, "The Military Leadership of North and South," in David Donald, ed., *Why the North Won the Civil War* (New York: Collier Books, 1962), pp. 33–54.

13. McClellan's comment on Sebastopol is in his *Own Story*, p. 313.

14. McClellan's comments on August 16, 1861, and June 22, 1862, are in his *Own Story*, pp. 87 and 407. On the March report see Williams, *Lincoln and His Generals*, p. 50; and Williams, *Lincoln Finds a General*, I, 154–155. Also, p. 164 for Magruder's numbers. In giving McClellan only 91,000 men in the last week of June 1862, I allow him the benefit of the doubt: Ralph Newman and E. B. Long estimate, for example, that he had 100,000. *The Civil War Digest* (New York: Grosset & Dunlap, 1960), p. 18. It is usual to give McClellan approximately 87,000 effectives and Lee 51 to 55,000 at Antietam. However, Frederick Tilberg maintains that straggling had actually cut Lee's force to 41,000 effectives. *Antietam National Battlefield Site, Maryland* (Washington: Government Printing Office, 1961), p. 45.

15. Myers, *McClellan*, p. 211. Harnett T. Kane, *Spies for the Blue and Gray* (New York: Ace Books, n.d.), p. 91. Charles Winslow Elliott, *Winfield Scott: The Soldier and the Man* (New York: Macmillan, 1937), p. 735. Thomas, *Lincoln*, p. 287. Williams, *Lincoln Finds a General*, I, 127–129. O.R., first series, V, 613–614.

16. Alonzo H. Quint, *The Potomac and the Rapidan* (Boston: Crosby and Nichols, 1864; New York: O. S. Felt, 1864), p. 34. McClellan, *Own Story*, pp. 4 and 39.

17. On the fact that McClellan never did admit he had made mistakes see his attempt to cover the gross mistakes regarding enemy numbers in his *Own Story*, pp. 75–76. See also Allan Pinkerton's blunt denial of error in *The Spy of the Rebellion* (Toronto: Rose Publishing, n.d.), p. viii.

18. McClellan's background and tastes are summarized in Margaret Leech, *Reveille in Washington, 1860–1865* (New York: Grosset & Dunlap, n.d.), p. 119; and Myers, *McClellan*, pp. 1–2.

19. McClellan, *Own Story*, pp. 39–40.

20. Adam Gurowski, *Diary from March 4, 1861, to November 12, 1862* (Boston: Lee and Shepard, 1862), entry for October 6, 1861, p. 107. Thomas Kearny, *General Philip Kearny: Battle Soldier of Five Wars* (New York: G. P.

Putnam's Sons, 1937), letter of May 28, 1862, p. 251. Thomas W. Hyde, *Following the Greek Cross or, Memories of the Sixth Army Corps* (Boston: Houghton Mifflin, 1895), p. 46.

21. G. B. McClellan, *The Mexican War Diary of George B. McClellan,* ed. William Star Myers (Princeton: Princeton University Press, 1917), entries for December 1846, p. 18, January 4, 1847, p. 43, and April 18, 1847, p. 80. McClellan, *Own Story,* p. 87.

22. Compare comments of John F. Reynolds, chapter 4 above.

23. McClellan, *Own Story,* letter of August 16, 1861, p. 87.

24. The stopping of recruiting is dealt with in Benjamin P. Thomas and Harold M. Hyman, *Stanton: The Life and Times of Lincoln's Secretary of War* (New York: Knopf, 1962), pp. 201–202. The snubbing episode is in Williams, *Lincoln and His Generals,* p. 45.

25. On rebel problems with the elective principle see David Donald, "Died of Democracy," in Donald, ed., *Why the North Won the Civil War,* pp. 79–90.

26. Williams, *Lincoln Finds a General,* I, 123–124 and 153–155 for the Quaker guns.

27. *Cincinnati Gazette* quoted in Washington *National Republican,* November 17, 1862.

28. Bellows' background and philosophy are considered in George M. Fredrickson, *The Inner Civil War: Northern Intellectuals and the Crisis of the Union* (New York: Harper & Row, 1968), esp. pp. 100–101 and 108–109. The address was extensively reported in the newspapers, including the Washington *National Republican,* October 29, 1862.

29. George Templeton Strong, *Diary of the Civil War, 1860–1865,* ed. Allan Nevins (New York: Macmillan, 1962), entry for October 17, 1862, pp. 266–267. *National Republican,* October 29, 1862.

30. *National Republican,* November 17, 1862. The Southern press gleefully picked up Bellows' address. See, for instance, *Southern Literary Messenger,* September–October 1862, pp. 586–587, and November–December 1862, pp. 698–699.

31. Edward Bates, *The Diary of Edward Bates, 1859–1866,* ed. Howard K. Beale, Annual Report of the American Historical Association for the Year 1930, IV (Washington: Government Printing Office, 1933), March 13, 1862, 239–240.

32. Willoughby M. Babcock, Jr., *Selections from the Letters and Diaries of Brevet-Brigadier General Willoughby Babcock* (New York: Division of Archives and History of the University of the State of New York, 1922), letter of July 15, 1862, pp. 106–108. General Philip Kearny's Letters, 1861/2, Library of Congress, Manuscript Division, July 31, 1862.

33. *Tribune,* September 5, 1862, p. 4.

34. E. H. Derby, "Resources of the South," *Atlantic Monthly* (October 1862), p. 506.

35. Fairfax Downey, *Clash of Cavalry: The Battle of Brandy Station, June 9, 1863* (New York: David McKay, 1959), pp. 44 and 46. McClellan tried to blame this problem, as he did others, on numbers. See his *Own Story*, telegram of October 21, 1862, p. 640.

36. Bates, *Diary*, June 4, 1862, p. 261.

37. David Hunter Strother, *A Virginia Yankee in the Civil War*, ed. Cecil D. Eby, Jr. (Chapel Hill: University of North Carolina Press, 1961), March 13, 1862, pp. 13–14; March 28, 1862, p. 22; June 13, 1862, p. 58; and June 25, 1862, p. 62.

38. Gurowski, *Diary from 1861 to 1862*, July 4, 1862, p. 236. Georgeanna Muirson (Woolsey) Bacon, ed., *Letters of a Family during the War for the Union, 1861–1865*, I (n.p.: Printed for private distribution, 1899), 478. James Fowler Rusling, *Men and Things I Saw in Civil War Days* (New York: Eaton & Mains, 1899), letter of August 27, 1862, p. 271.

39. Hyde, *Following the Greek Cross*, p. 36. Alexander Hays, *Life and Letters of Alexander Hays*, ed. George Thornton Fleming (Pittsburg: n.p., 1919), p. 194. For contrast, see the comment of the civilian Stanton to Charles A. Dana, on January 24, that the Potomac "army has got to fight or run away;" and that "the champagne and oysters on the Potomac must be stopped." McClellan apparently enjoyed serving these dishes to visitors. Charles A. Dana, *Recollections of the Civil War* (New York: Collier Books, 1963), pp. 27–28.

40. Warren Lee Goss, *Recollections of a Private. A Story of the Army of the Potomac* (New York: Thomas Y. Crowell, 1890), pp. 92–93. Oliver Otis Howard, *Autobiography of Oliver Otis Howard*, I (New York: Baker & Taylor, 1908), 271.

41. On Hooker's view of McClellan see Walter H. Hebert, *Fighting Joe Hooker* (New York: Bobbs-Merrill, 1944), pp. 80 and 83. Kearny's comments are in his Letters, April 18, 1862, and Kearny, *General Kearny*, pp. 199 and 212. Jacob Dolson Cox, *Military Reminiscences of the Civil War*, I (New York: Scribner's, 1900), 371.

42. Prince de Joinville, *The Army of the Potomac: Its Organization, Its Commander, and Its Campaign*, trans. William Henry Hulbert (New York: Anson D. F. Randolph, 1863), pp. 8–10.

43. Joinville, *Army of the Potomac*, pp. 11–17 and 71–72.

44. Joinville, *Army of the Potomac*, pp. 18–19.

45. Cox, *Reminiscences*, I, 370–371.

6. Desperate Measures

1. John Beatty, *Memoirs of a Volunteer, 1861–1863*, ed. Harvey S. Ford (New York: Norton, 1946), p. 115. John Hope Franklin, *The Emancipation Proclamation* (Garden City, N.Y.: Doubleday, 1965), p. 129.

2. Alexis de Tocqueville, *Democracy in America*, ed. Richard D. Heffner (New York: New American Library, 1956), pp. 37, 120–121, and 90–91.

3. *North American Review*, 84 (January 1862), 155. *Harper's Weekly*, March 1, 1862, pp. 130–131.

4. George Meade, *The Life and Letters of George Gordon Meade*, I (New York: Scribner's, 1913), January 26, 1862, 243–244. James Buchanan, *The Works of James Buchanan*, ed. John Bassett Moore, XI (New York: Antiquarian Press, 1960), March 29, 1862, 264, and April 2, 1862, 265–267.

5. [Rose O'Neal] Greenhow, *My Imprisonment and the First Year of Abolition Rule at Washington* (London: Richard Bentley, 1863), pp. 104–105. William Harlan Hale, *Horace Greeley: Voice of the People* (New York: Collier Books, 1961), pp. 261–262 and 278–279.

6. Committee on the Conduct of the War, *Report*, 37th Cong., 3d. sess., S. Rep. Com. 108, vol. II, pt. 1, pp. 139 and 155. Edward L. Pierce, *Memoir and Letters of Charles Sumner*, IV: *1860–1874* (London: Sampson Low, Marston, 1893), 43–44 and 47.

7. Nathaniel Hawthorne, letter of May 26, 1861, in *Harper's Weekly*, February 17, 1883, p. 99. T. Harry Williams, *Lincoln and the Radicals* (Madison: University of Wisconsin Press, 1965), p. 192.

8. An article in the *Atlantic Monthly* for April, 1862, while delicately phrased, clearly envisioned some kind of race war after emancipation. It suggested that a week after freedom was declared slaves in the Southern interior would know "what their rights are, and will, where opportunity offers, prepare to take them" (p. 509). See also, for instance, John W. Forney's editorial, in the July 30, 1862, issue of the *Philadelphia Press*, considered to be an administration house journal. That Lincoln envisioned potential race conflict is clear from the Proclamation which noted that slaves might use violence in "necessary self-defence." On Southern belief that black resistance was one aim of emancipation see the cartoon by Adalbert John Volck in Harnett T. Kane, *Gone Are the Days: An Illustrated History of the Old South* (New York: E. P. Dutton, 1960), p. 320.

9. Grant's character is discussed more fully in chapter 8 below.

10. See note 49, Chapter 1 above.

11. On the dictatorship see note 15 below.

12. *North American Review*, 94 (January 1862), 154–156. On the charges against McClellan see, for instance, G. B. McClellan, *McClellan's Own Story* (New York: Charles L. Webster, 1887), p. 38; Williams, *Lincoln and the Radicals*, pp. 47, 77–78, and 82; Hale, *Greeley*, p. 263. The confrontation with Mr. Lincoln is described in McClellan, *Own Story*, pp. 195–196.

13. McClellan, *Own Story*, p. 85. Jacob Dolson Cox, *Military Reminiscences of the Civil War*, I (New York: Scribner's, 1900), 364.

14. McClellan, *Own Story*, p. 160. Also Edward Bates, *The Diary of Edward Bates, 1859–1866*, ed. Howard K. Beale, Annual Report of the American Historical Association for the Year 1930, IV (Washington: Government Printing Office, 1933), April 22, 1862, 253; and Orville Hickman Browning,

The Diary of Orville Hickman Browning, ed. Theodore C. Pease and James G. Randall, I (Springfield, Ill.: n.p., 1927), April 2, 1862, 538.

15. McClellan, *Own Story,* p. 407.

16. McClellan, *Own Story,* letters of May 1, 1862, p. 316; July 22, 1862, pp. 453–454; and July 31, 1862, p. 460. David Homer Bates, *Lincoln in the Telegraph Office* (New York: Century, 1907), pp. 103–104.

17. John Sedgwick, *Correspondence of John Sedgwick,* II (New York: Printed for C. & E. B. Stoeckel, by the DeVinne Press, 1902–1903), letter of April 27, 1862, 44–45.

18. Custer's life at West Point is described in Jay Monaghan, *Custer: The Life of General George Armstrong Custer* (Boston: Little, Brown, 1959), pp. 29, 32, 35, 37 and 39. For his relations with McClellan see p. 68. The piano incident is in Frederick Whittacker, *A Complete Life of Gen. George A. Custer* (New York: Sheldon, 1876), p. 128. George Edward Pickett, *Soldier of the South: General Pickett's War Letters to His Wife,* ed. Arthur Crew Inman (Boston: Houghton Mifflin, 1928), letter of June 1, 1862, p. 15.

19. Porter's background is described in Otto Eisenschiml, *The Celebrated Case of Fitz-John Porter: An American Dreyfus Affair* (New York: Bobbs-Merrill, 1950), p. 18. Porter's comments are on pp. 34–35 and in T. Harry Williams, *Lincoln and His Generals* (New York: Knopf, 1964), p. 148.

20. Fitz-John Porter, Fitz-John Porter Papers, Library of Congress, Manuscript Division, vol. III, letter of July 17, 1862. Also, M. C. Meigs, "General M. C. Meigs on the Conduct of the Civil War," *American Historical Review,* 26.2 (1921), 293–294 for treasonous talk among McClellan's officers at Harrison's Landing.

21. Emerson Gifford Taylor, *Gouverneur Kemble Warren: The Life and Letters of an American Soldier, 1830–1882* (Boston: Houghton Mifflin, 1932), pp. 80 and 90–91.

22. *O.R.,* first series, vol. XII, pt. 3, pp. 473–474. Williams, *Lincoln and His Generals,* p. 123.

23. *O.R.,* first series, vol. XII, pt. 2, pp. 50ff. Marsena Rudolph Patrick, *Inside Lincoln's Army: The Diary of Marsena Rudolph Patrick, Provost Marshal General, Army of the Potomac,* ed. David S. Sparks (New York: Thomas Yoseloff, 1963), pp. 108 and 120.

24. Quoted in Jacob D. Cox, *The Second Battle of Bull Run* (Cincinnati: Peter G. Thomson, 1882), pp. 73–74 and 75–76.

25. Herman Haupt, *Reminiscences of General Herman Haupt* (Milwaukee: Wright & Jays, 1901), pp. 82–83.

26. Carl Schurz, *The Reminiscences of Carl Schurz,* II (New York: McClure, 1907), 382. McClellan, *Own Story,* letter of July 22, 1862, p. 454. Williams, *Lincoln and His Generals,* p. 157.

27. The reporter is quoted in Franklin, *Emancipation Proclamation,* p. 75. Cox, *Reminiscences,* I, 358–361. See George Winston Smith and Charles

Judah, eds., *Life in the North during the Civil War: A Source History* (Albuquerque: University of New Mexico Press, 1966), pp. 90–91, for another example of civilians urging McClellan to ignore the government.

28. Charles S. Wainwright, *A Diary of Battle: The Personal Journals of Colonel Charles S. Wainwright,* ed. Allan Nevins (New York: Harcourt, Brace & World, 1962), p. 125. John Gibbon, *Personal Recollections of the Civil War* (New York: G. P. Putnam's Sons, 1928), pp. 92–93 and 98. Allan Nevins, *The War for the Union,* II: *War Becomes Revolution* (New York: Scribner's, 1960), 231, for the plan to march on Washington.

29. John Hay, "Letters of John Hay and Extracts from Diary" (Printed but not published, 1908), p. 60. Gideon Welles, *Diary of Gideon Welles,* ed. Howard K. Beale, I (New York: W. W. Norton, 1960), 104 and 116. Salmon P. Chase, *Inside Lincoln's Cabinet: The Civil War Diaries of Salmon P. Chase,* ed. David Donald (New York: Longmans, Green, 1954), p. 119.

30. Edward L. Pierce, *Memoir and Letters of Charles Sumner,* IV: *1860–1874* (London: Sampson Low, Marston, 1893), 83. Benjamin F. Butler, *Private and Official Correspondence of Gen. Benjamin F. Butler during the Period of the Civil War,* II (n.p.: Privately issued, 1917), letter of September 28, 1862, 334. *Wilkes' Spirit of the Times,* September 13, 1862, 24–25.

There were also periodic fears of a military dictatorship in the Confederacy but the mistrust never reached the same debilitating proportions. See John B. Jones, *A Rebel War Clerk's Diary,* ed. Earl Schenck Miers (New York: Sagamore Press, 1958), p. 225.

31. Schurz, *Reminiscences,* II, 392–393. S. E. Finer, *The Man on Horseback: The Role of the Military in Politics* (London: Pall Mall Press, 1962), pp. 6–11 and 142–144.

32. The review is in the New York *Tribune,* January 25, 1861, p. 3.

33. Antebellum violence is dealt with in chapters 1 and 2 above. Marcus Cunliffe makes some interesting comments on assassination attempts in *American Presidents and the Presidency* (n.p.: Fontana/Collins, 1972), chap. 5. On Lincoln and the intellectuals see Lorraine A. Williams, "Northern Intellectual Reaction to Military Rule during the Civil War," *Historian,* 27 (November–August 1964–65), 334–349. On Kentucky see E. Merton Coulter, *The Civil War and Readjustment in Kentucky* (Gloucester, Mass.: Peter Smith, 1966). Vallandigham is sympathetically treated in Frank L. Klement, *The Copperheads in the Middle West* (Chicago: University of Chicago Press, 1960).

34. Catherine S. Crary, ed., *Dear Belle: Letters from a Cadet and Officer to His Sweetheart, 1858–1865* (Middletown, Conn.: Wesleyan University Press, 1965), letter of November 12, 1862, p. 167.

35. Sedgwick, *Correspondence,* I, 80–81.

36. Cornelia McDonald, *A Diary With Reminiscences of the War and Refugee Life in the Shenandoah Valley, 1860–1865* (Nashville: Cullom & Ghertner, 1934), entry for May 22, 1862, p. 67. It is interesting that Wilkins chose to unburden himself on Mrs. McDonald, a Southerner whose husband

served in the Confederacy. Perhaps he felt that a Southerner would understand his contempt for the amateur in war.

37. Warren W. Hassler, Jr., *General George B. McClellan: Shield of the Union* (Baton Rouge: Louisiana State University Press, 1957), pp. 113–115. McClellan, *Own Story,* letter of May 25, 1862, p. 396.

38. John Sherman and William Tecumseh Sherman, *The Sherman Letters: Correspondence between General and Senator Sherman from 1837 to 1891,* ed. Rachel Sherman Thorndike (New York: Scribner's, 1894), September 22, 1862, pp. 162–163.

39. Edward J. Nichols, *Toward Gettysburg: A Biography of General John F. Reynolds* ([University Park]: Pennsylvania State University Press, 1958), p. 137. Walter H. Hebert, *Fighting Joe Hooker* (New York: Bobbs-Merrill, 1944), p. 133.

40. Wainwright, *Diary,* October 29, 1862, pp. 117–118. For background on the desertion question see Ella Lonn, *Desertion during the Civil War* (New York: Century, 1928), p. 227; and Joseph L. Eisendrath, Jr., "Was Lincoln Really Lenient with Deserters and Sleeping Sentries," *Lincoln Herald,* 60 (Fall 1958), 94.

41. Wainwright, *Diary,* January 4, 1863, p. 156.

42. General Philip Kearny's Letters, 1861/2, Library of Congress, Manuscript Division, July 20, 1862. Southern problems with desertion are dealt with in Lonn, *Desertion.* On the popular election of junior officers see David Donald, "Died of Democracy," in David Donald, ed., *Why the North Won the Civil War* (New York: Collier Books, 1962), pp. 79–90.

43. David Hunter Strother, *A Virginia Yankee in the Civil War,* ed. Cecil D. Eby, Jr. (Chapel Hill: University of North Carolina Press, 1961), July 4, 1862, p. 66; September 24, 1862, pp. 116–117.

44. Wainwright, *Diary,* October 29, 1862, p. 117; January 19, 1862, p. 10. Beecher is quoted in George H. Gordon, *A War Diary of Events in the War of the Great Rebellion, 1863–1865* (Boston: James R. Osgood, 1882), p. 7.

45. Browning, *Diary,* I, 583–584.

46. Butler, *Correspondence,* II, letter of July 3, 1862, 41. Also, letter of R. George to Butler, July 3, 1862, pp. 44–45. Georgeanna Muirson (Woolsey) Bacon, ed., *Letters of a Family during the War for the Union, 1861–1865,* I (n.p.: Printed for private distribution, 1899), 483–484. U. S. Grant, *Personal Memoirs of U. S. Grant,* I (New York: Charles L. Webster, 1885–86), 406.

47. *Wilkes' Spirit of the Times,* July 19, 1862, p. 312. Stephen E. Ambrose, *Halleck: Lincoln's Chief of Staff* (Baton Rouge: Louisiana State University Press, 1962), p. 87. Butler, *Correspondence,* II, Richard S. Fay to Butler, p. 291.

48. George Alfred Townsend, *Rustics in Rebellion: A Yankee Reporter on the Road to Richmond, 1861–65* (Chapel Hill: University of North Carolina Press, 1950), pp. 164 and 189–190.

A good example of the prewar image of Southern indolence, as opposed to

Northern energy is the treatment of St. Clare in *Uncle Tom's Cabin:* the character is aware that slavery is wrong but he has long since given up taxing his mental resources with questions about how to abolish the evil. One of the few pieces published during the war that employed the stereotype of indolence was "On Picket Duty" in Louisa May Alcott's *On Picket Duty, and Other Tales* (Boston: James Redpath, 1864).

49. Chase, *Diary*, September 13, 1862, p. 139. Gordon, *War Diary*, pp. 7–8.

50. Bacon, *Letters*, I, letter of Abby Howland Woolsey, July 5, 1862, 441–442.

51. Wendell Phillips, *Speeches, Lectures and Letters,* first series (Boston: Lee and Shepard, 1892), pp. 448–463. See also Wm. C. Beecher and Samuel Scoville assisted by Mrs. H. W. Beecher, *A Biography of Rev. Henry Ward Beecher* (New York: Charles L. Webster, 1888), pp. 230–231.

52. Hans Christian Heg, *The Civil War Letters of Colonel Hans Christian Heg,* ed. Theodore Christian Blegen (Northfield, Minn.: Norwegian-American Historical Association, 1936), letter of July 19, 1862, p. 110. *Harper's Weekly,* September 20, 1862, p. 594.

53. Lincoln is quoted in Franklin, *Emancipation Proclamation,* p. 32.

54. Phillips, *Speeches,* first series, pp. 550–551.

55. Epes Sargent, "The Cabalistic Words," *Atlantic Monthly* (November 1862), pp. 612–613. There is something of the same magical quality about Whittier's "What Gives the Wheat Fields Blades of Steel?" in his *The Poetical Works of John Greenleaf Whittier* (London: Frederick Warne, n.d.), pp. 241–242.

7. Fighting for Defeat

1. Darius N. Couch, "Sumner's 'Right Grand Division' " in Robert Underwood Johnson and Clarence Clough Buel, eds., *Battles and Leaders of the Civil War,* III (New York: Century, 1884–1888), 120. Wilson, *Under the Old Flag,* I (New York: Appleton, 1912), 127.

2. The fact that books by Southerners about Confederate leaders were published in the North during 1863 is brought out in Douglas Southall Freeman, *The South to Posterity* (Port Washington, N.Y.: Kennikat Press, 1964), pp. 15–16. Freeman comments that as these books "made the utmost of Southern generalship and often disparaged Federal leaders" there was a "definite risk" to Northern morale.

"Barbara Frietchie," in Whittier, *The Poetical Works of John Greenleaf Whittier* (London: Frederick Warne, n.d.), pp. 250–251. See also references to Jackson's death in note 47 below.

3. John Chipman Gray and John Codman Ropes, *War Letters, 1862–1865* (Boston: Houghton Mifflin, 1927), letter of Gray to Ropes, December 2, 1862, pp. 33–34.

4. Almira R. Hancock, *Reminiscences of Winfield Scott Hancock by His Wife* (New York: Charles L. Webster, 1887), p. 46. John M. Schofield, *Forty-Six Years in the Army* (New York: Century, 1897), p. 15. Wilson, *Patriotic Gore: Studies in the Literature of the American Civil War* (New York: Oxford University Press, 1966), p. 331ff. John Esten Cooke, *Wearing of the Gray: Being Personal Portraits, Scenes and Adventures of the War* (Bloomington: Indiana University Press, 1959), pp. 357–359.

5. Northern insecurity about losing the tradition of Washington was nicely illustrated at the beginning of the war when a rumor that the rebels intended to remove Washington's remains from Mount Vernon and take them South caused a great deal of anguish. The loss would have been both literal and symbolic.

6. On radical distaste for Burnside see T. Harry Williams, *Lincoln and the Radicals* (Madison: University of Wisconsin Press, 1965), p. 197.

7. Chapter 4 of Edward J. Stackpole's *Drama on the Rappahannock: The Fredericksburg Campaign* (Harrisburg, Pa.: Military Service Publishing Company, 1957) proved a useful introduction to Burnside's plan of campaign.

8. Burnside's remark is quoted in Newton Martin Curtis, *From Bull Run to Chancellorsville* (New York: G. P. Putnam's Sons, 1906), p. 224. On the general lack of confidence in Burnside's plan see the comment by Swinton of the New York *Times* in Francis Winthrop Palfrey, *Campaigns of the Civil War,* V: *The Antietam and Fredericksburg* (New York: Scribner's, 1882), 184; testimony of John Cochrane, the Union General, before the Committee on the Conduct of the War, in the *Report* of the Committee, II, 744; and comment of an enlisted man in Bruce Catton, *Glory Road* (New York: Pocket Books, 1964), p. 43.

9. Martin Schenck, "Burnside's Bridge," *Civil War History*, 2 (December 1956), quoted in Stackpole, *Fredericksburg*, p. 253.

10. On Burnside's background and the 1862 expedition see Bruce Catton, *Mr. Lincoln's Army* (New York: Pocket Books, 1964), pp. 267ff.

11. For Burnside's comment on the superiority of McClellan see Curtis, *From Bull Run to Chancellorsville,* p. 225. His report is quoted in Stackpole, *Fredericksburg,* p. 65.

12. Palfrey, *Campaigns,* p. 140, quotes Burnside and gives the position of Jackson at the time. See also pp. 179–180 for an example of a Federal officer overestimating rebel numbers at Fredericksburg. The old excuse for Burnside's behavior—that he was ruined by the failure of the pontoons to arrive—is successfully refuted in Wesley Brainerd, "The Pontoniers at Fredericksburg," Johnson and Buel, eds., *Battles and Leaders,* III, 121–122.

13. James Buchanan, *The Works of James Buchanan,* ed. John Bassett Moore, XI (New York: Antiquarian Press, 1960), letter of February 14, 1863, 329–330. The poem is in Frank Moore, ed., *The Rebellion Record,* VI (New York: G. P. Putnam, 1864), "Poetry & Incidents," 27–28. Greeley is quoted in William Harlan Hale, *Horace Greeley: Voice of the People* (New York: Collier Books, 1961), pp. 274–275.

14. Goss, *Recollections of a Private* (New York: Thomas Y. Crowell,

1890), pp. 134–136. Oliver Wendell Holmes, Jr., *Touched With Fire: Civil War Letters and Diary of Oliver Wendell Holmes, Jr., 1861–1864*, ed. Mark DeWolfe Howe (Cambridge, Mass.: Harvard University Press, 1947), December 20, 1862, pp. 79–80.

15. Frankl's philosophy is advanced in *Man's Search for Meaning: An Introduction to Logotherapy* (New York: Washington Square Press, 1963). George M. Fredrickson has some interesting comments on the ideas of Civil War soldiers in his *The Inner Civil War: Northern Intellectuals and the Crisis of the Union* (New York: Harper & Row, 1968), esp. pp. 85–87 and 166–169.

16. Hays, *Life and Letters of Alexander Hays,* ed. George Thornton Fleming (Pittsburg: n.p., 1919), December 26, 1862, p. 288, and January 28, 1863, pp. 306–307.

17. Hooker is quoted in Louis M. Starr, *Reporting the Civil War: The Bohemian Brigade in Action, 1861–65* (New York: Collier Books, 1962), p. 160, and Walter H. Hebert, *Fighting Joe Hooker* (New York: Bobbs-Merrill, 1944), p. 164. See also Lincoln's letter of appointment to Hooker, dated January 26, 1863, in which the President noted Hooker's talk of a dictator and, in a masterful way, chided him for it while promising the general his full support. Lincoln's firm yet kindly handling of Hooker touched the latter and no doubt encouraged his activities in the months before Chancellorsville. Roy P. Basler, ed., *The Collected Works of Abraham Lincoln,* VI (New Brunswick, N.J.: Rutgers University Press, 1953), 78–79.

Wade's remarks are in Orville Hickman Browning, *The Diary of Orville Hickman Browning,* ed. Theodore C. Pease and James G. Randall, I (Springfield, Ill.: n.p., 1927), 597. It was still the contention of many radicals like Wade that the North needed a man with "ideas" at the head of the army. See speech of Representative Julian, February 18, 1863, in U.S., 37th Cong., 3rd. sess., 1862–63, *Congressional Globe,* new series no. 67, pp. 1068–1069.

18. The Democrat is quoted in Gurowski, *Diary from November 18, 1862, to October 18, 1863* (New York: Carleton, 1864), pp. 150–151. Washington Chauncey Ford, ed., *A Cycle of Adams Letters 1861–1865,* I (Boston: Houghton Mifflin, 1920), letter of January 23, 1863, 238. William T. Lusk, *War Letters of William Thompson Lusk* (New York: Privately printed, 1911), December 16, 1862, pp. 244–245, and December 22, 1862, p. 256. Lincoln's message is in the O.R., first series, XXI, 67–68. Charles S. Wainwright, *A Diary of Battle: The Personal Journals of Colonel Charles S. Wainwright,* ed. Allan Nevins (New York: Harcourt, Brace & World, 1962), December 25, 1862, pp. 149–150, and January 4, 1863, pp. 155–156. Also p. 134 on Washington using Porter as a scapegoat.

19. John Beatty, *Memoirs of a Volunteer, 1861–1863,* ed. Harvey S. Ford (New York: Norton, 1946), December 21, 1862, pp. 149–150. William Tecumseh Sherman, *Home Letters of General Sherman,* ed. M. A. DeWolfe Howe (New York: Scribner's, 1909), January 28, 1863, pp. 237–239; John Sherman and William Tecumseh Sherman, *The Sherman Letters: Corre-*

spondence between General and Senator Sherman from 1837 to 1891, ed. Rachel Sherman Thorndike (New York: Scribner's, 1894), February 18, 1863, pp. 191–192. See also U.S., 37th Cong., 3rd sess., 1862–63, *Congressional Globe,* new series no. 46, speech of Senator Sherman, February 5, 1863, p. 735.

20. U.S., 37th Cong., 3rd sess., 1862–63, *Congressional Globe,* new series no. 77, p. 1220.

21. *Harper's Weekly,* December 27, 1862, p. 818. On the actual problem of the press see J. G. Randall, "The Newspaper Problem in Its Bearing upon Military Secrecy during the Civil War," *American Historical Review,* 23 (January 1918), 303–323; and "Federal Generals and a Good Press," *American Historical Review,* 39 (January 1934), 284–297.

22. *How a Free People Conduct a Long War: A Chapter from English History* (Philadelphia: William S. & Alfred Martien, 1863).

23. In his *Diary from 1862 to 1863* Gurowski recorded the common opinion that Northerners were not a military people (p. 129). Stillé, *Free People,* pp. 6 and 30. Biographical material on Stillé will be found in George Templeton Strong, *Diary of the Civil War, 1860–1865,* ed. Allan Nevins (New York: Macmillan, 1962), p. lii. See pp. 282 and 288 for the influence of Stillé's work.

24. Stillé, *Free People,* esp. pp. 5, 7–8, 10–11, 18–19, and 21.

25. Other pieces besides Stillé's which may have had some influence in reviving Northern spirits included Francis Wayland's "No Failure for the North," *Atlantic Monthly,* II (April 1863), 500–514. Wayland's essential argument was that people expected too much in the beginning but they were now too despondent. It would take time to beat the South, he said, because Northerners were not a violent people. "The report of the revolver was not heard in our streets, nor was the glitter of the bowie-knife seen in our bar-rooms."

26. Jay Monaghan, *Custer: The Life of General George Armstrong Custer* (Boston: Little, Brown, 1959), p. 115. Oliver Otis Howard, *Autobiography of Oliver Otis Howard,* I (New York: Baker & Taylor, 1908), 347–348.

27. On the corps badges see remarks by John D. Billings in Philip Van Doren Stern, *Soldier Life in the Union and Confederate Armies* (Greenwich, Conn.: Fawcett, 1961), 180–191; Darius N. Couch, "The Chancellorsville Campaign," *Battles and Leaders,* III, 154; and Curtis, *From Bull Run to Chancellorsville,* p. 229. See also p. 227 for Hooker's order assuming command.

28. *Reports* of the Committee, II, February 17, 1863, pp. 753–754.

29. The Fitzhugh Lee incident, which took place on February 24, 1863, is in Hebert, *Hooker,* p. 186; his instructions to Stoneman are printed in Curtis, *From Bull Run to Chancellorsville,* pp. 230–231.

30. Alfred Pleasanton, "The Successes and Failures of Chancellorsville," *Battles and Leaders,* III, 175. A second spirited action is described on pp. 179 and 183–188. In explaining the change in fortune of the Union cavalry at this time account must also be taken of the increasing physical disadvantage of the rebels—the quality and number of horses, the type of firearm, etc. It was during this period that the North's material preponderance began to tell. Nevertheless,

the improvement in performance was so swift as to indicate that Hooker's influence, with its direct impact, was the key factor. Cf. Ray P. Stonesifer, Jr., "The Union Cavalry Comes of Age," *Civil War History*, 2.3 (1965), 274–283.

31. Couch's article was reprinted in *Battles and Leaders*. See note 28 above.

32. Useful treatments of the Chancellorsville campaign include Abner Doubleday, *Chancellorsville and Gettysburg* (New York: Scribner's, 1882), and Edward J. Stackpole, *Chancellorsville: Lee's Greatest Battle* (Harrisburg: Stackpole, 1958). Hooker's comments are on p. 146.

33. For the claim that Lee understood Hooker's intentions see R. E. Colston, "Lee's Knowledge of Hooker's Movements," in *Battles and Leaders*, III, 233. The arguments against Colston are summarized in Stackpole, *Chancellorsville*, pp. 129–130. See also pp. 144–145 for Meade's remarks to Slocum.

34. Pleasanton, "Chancellorsville," pp. 174–175.

35. Couch, "Chancellorsville," pp. 159 and 161.

36. Couch, "Chancellorsville," p. 170. Hebert, *Hooker*, p. 199.

37. There are some interesting remarks on Lee's grasp of the situation in Stackpole, *Chancellorsville*, pp. 203–207.

38. John Hay, "Letters of John Hay and Extracts from Diary" (Printed but not published, 1908), diary entry for September 9, 1863, pp. 95–96. Couch, "Chancellorsville," p. 157.

39. Couch, "Chancellorsville," p. 161. Emerson Gifford Taylor, *Gouverneur Kemble Warren: The Life and Letters of an American Soldier, 1830–1882* (Boston: Houghton Mifflin, 1932), letter of May 8, 1863. On the feeling in favor of McClellan see Wainwright, *Diary*, pp. 201, 211, and 229; Marsena Rudolph Patrick, *Inside Lincoln's Army: The Diary of Marsena Rudolph Patrick, Provost Marshal General, Army of the Potomac*, ed. David S. Sparks (New York: Thomas Yoseloff, 1963), p. 263.

40. John Sherman and William Tecumseh Sherman, *Sherman Letters*, letter of May 7, 1863, pp. 203–205. Greeley is quoted in Hebert, *Hooker*, p. 219, and Hale, *Greeley*, p. 278. Alfred Lacy Hough, *Soldier in the West: The Civil War Letters of Alfred Lacy Hough*, ed. Robert G. Athearn (Philadelphia: University of Philadelphia Press, 1956), letter of May 28, 1863, p. 96. See also confident comments by western soldiers in Bell Irvin Wiley, *The Life of Billy Yank: The Common Soldier of the Union* (New York: Bobbs-Merrill, 1962), p. 94.

41. Philip Regis de Trobriand, *Four Years With the Army of the Potomac*, trans. George K. Dauchy (Boston: Ticknor, 1889), pp. 471 and 480. Catton, *Glory Road*, pp. 264 and 276.

42. Patrick, *Inside Lincoln's Army*, June 13, 1863, p. 258; and June 19, 1863, p. 261. See also gloom expressed in George H. Gordon, *A War Diary of Events in the War of the Great Rebellion, 1863–1865* (Boston: James R. Osgood, 1882), p. 114.

43. John Gibbon, *Personal Recollections of the Civil War* (New York:

G. P. Putnam's Sons, 1928), pp. 128–129. George Meade, *The Life and Letters of George Gordon Meade*, I (New York: Scribner's, 1913), letter of June 23, 1863, 386–387. Partly, the antagonism toward "Dutchmen" was a product of the apparent failure of the predominantly German Eleventh Corps at Chancellorsville. H. M. M. Richards, "Citizens of Gettysburg in the Union Army," *Battles and Leaders*, III, 289, defends the people of Pennsylvania against the charges.

The discharged officer was a Major Haller, whose case is cited in Michael Jacobs, *Notes on the Rebel Invasion of Maryland and Pennsylvania and the Battle of Gettysburg* (Philadelphia: J. B. Lippincott, 1864), pp. 12–13.

44. Alpheus S. Williams, *From the Cannon's Mouth: The Civil War Letters of General Alpheus S. Williams*, ed. Milo M. Quaife (Detroit: Wayne State University Press, 1959), letter of June 29, 1863, pp. 221–222.

45. Jacobs, *Notes on the Invasion*, pp. 15–16. Wainwright, *Diary*, July 1, 1863, p. 236. Meade's circular is in Catton, *Glory Road*, p. 277.

46. On the soldiers' faith in Jackson and the optimism he had inspired see John Esten Cooke, *Stonewall Jackson and the Old Stonewall Brigade*, ed. Richard B. Harwell (Charlottesville: University of Virginia Press, 1954), a series of articles written early in 1863. Northern relief on the death of Jackson is recorded in Gideon Welles, *Diary of Gideon Welles*, ed. Howard K. Beale, I (New York: Norton, 1960), p. 297; Ford, ed., *A Cycle of Adams Letters*, I, 56–58; and Mary Boykin Chesnut, *A Diary from Dixie*, ed. Ben Ames Williams (Boston: Houghton Mifflin, 1949), p. 341, which gives a description of a Northern cartoon showing Jackson flanking his way into Heaven. Northern opinion of Jackson seems to have softened somewhat with his death.

47. Jackson's comment is in John Bell Hood, *Advance and Retreat: Personal Experiences in the United States and Confederate States Armies*, ed. R. N. Current (Bloomington: Indiana University Press, 1959), p. 49. Pickett's remarks are in his *Letters*, June 24, 1863, p. 43. See also comment of a rebel officer on reconstructing the Union in Edwin H. Fay, *"This Infernal War": The Confederate Letters of Sgt. Edwin H. Fay*, ed. Bell Irvin Wiley assisted by Lucy E. Fay (Austin: University of Texas Press, 1958), p. 282.

48. Arthur James Lyon Fremantle, *The Fremantle Diary*, ed. Walter Lord (New York: Capricorn Books, 1960), entries for June 3, 1863, p. 133, and July 1, 1863, p. 205.

49. Fremantle, *Diary*, July 4, 1863, pp. 219–220. The question of Longstreet's culpability has been hashed over many times. The essential arguments are in Johnson and Buel, eds., *Battles and Leaders*, III, 339–354 and 355–356. The artillery barrage is detailed in Fairfax Downey, *The Guns at Gettysburg* (New York: Collier Books, 1962), p. 153ff. On Lee's belief in the invincibility of the Southern soldier see Hood, *Advance and Retreat*, p. 53.

50. On Southern opinion about who won the battle see Glenn Tucker, *High Tide at Gettysburg: The Campaign in Pennsylvania* (New York: Bobbs-Merrill, 1964). Ford, ed., *A Cycle of Adams Letters*, I, July 22, 1863, 53.

51. Meade's address is quoted in T. Harry Williams, *Lincoln and His Generals* (New York: Knopf, 1964), p. 265.

52. Williams, *Lincoln and His Generals,* pp. 266–267.

53. Patrick, *Inside Lincoln's Army,* entries for October 12, 1863, p. 298, and July 14, 1863, p. 271.

54. Ford, ed., *A Cycle of Adams Letters,* I, 55–57. Welles, *Diary,* I, July 7, 1863, 363; July 11, 1863, 368; July 14, 1863, 370; July 18, 1863, 379. Also Hay, "Letters," remarks on July 14, 1863, p. 86 for Lincoln's disgust with the tenor of Meade's congratulatory address, and p. 88 for Wadsworth's remarks. See also Gurowski, *Diary from 1862 to 1863,* July 16, 1863, p. 272.

55. Hays, *Letters,* July 18, 1863, p. 418, and August 10, 1863, p. 477. Gray and Ropes, *Letters,* November 2, 1863, p. 254.

56. Printed in Stern, ed., *Soldier Life,* pp. 42–43.

57. For a typical view that Gettysburg did mark the turning point in the war see Joseph B. Mitchell, *Decisive Battles of the Civil War* (New York: G. P. Putnam's Sons, 1955), p. 129. Noah Brooks, *Washington, D.C., in Lincoln's Time,* ed. Herbert Mitgang (New York: Collier Books, 1962), p. 83.

58. Quoted in Catton, *Glory Road,* pp. 267–268.

59. *Southern Literary Messenger,* January–December, 1863, pp. 572–574. Also, Thomas Cooper DeLeon, *Four Years in Rebel Capitals* (New York: Collier Books, 1962), p. 289.

8. War in Earnest

1. Fuller's work is referred to in notes 3 and 4 below. Before beginning the discussion proper, I should point out that I do not mean to claim that Grant was alone responsible for winning the war. Much credit must be given to President Lincoln, who probably helped shape Grant's thinking and sustained him to the end. Some of Grant's subordinates, particularly Sherman, played key roles and I have included a section on Sherman's victory in the chapter. I do not apologize for this digression away from Virginia because Sherman's case is intriguing enough to warrant a diversion. He was the only Union general to suffer acutely from inferiority feelings and yet achieve a significant offensive mentality.

2. U. S. Grant, *Personal Memoirs of U. S. Grant,* II (New York: Charles L. Webster, 1885–86), 167.

3. Grant's faulty plan is dealt with in J. F. C. Fuller, *The Generalship of Ulysses S. Grant* (London: John Murray, 1929), p. 215.

4. The best outline of the strategy is in J. F. C. Fuller, *Grant and Lee: A Study in Personality and Generalship* (Bloomington: Indiana University Press, 1957), pp. 206ff.

5. Butler's role in the latter part of the war is discussed in Robert S. Holzman, *Stormy Ben Butler* (New York: Collier Books, 1961), chap. 10. Banks' campaign is dealt with in Fred Harvey Harrington, *Fighting Politician Major*

General N. P. Banks (Philadelphia: University of Pennsylvania Press, 1948).

6. Marsena Rudolph Patrick, *Inside Lincoln's Army: The Diary of Marsena Rudolph Patrick, Provost Marshal General, Army of the Potomac,* ed. David S. Sparks (New York: Thomas Yoseloff, 1963), p. 294.

7. Otto Eisenschiml, ed., *Vermont General: The Unusual War Experiences of Edward Hastings Ripley, 1862–1865* (New York: Devin-Adair, 1960), entry for November 21, 1863, pp. 169–170.

8. Committee on the Conduct of the War, *Reports,* II, 410–411. Stephen E. Ambrose, *Halleck: Lincoln's Chief of Staff* (Baton Rouge: Louisiana State University Press, 1962), p. 149.

9. Cf. Bruce Catton, *U. S. Grant and the American Military Tradition* (Boston: Little, Brown, 1954), pp. 118–119.

10. There is a reasonable account of the fighting in Bruce Catton, *A Stillness at Appomattox* (New York: Pocket Books, 1958), p. 63ff.

11. Sylvanus Cadwallader, *Three Years with Grant,* ed. Benjmin P. Thomas (New York: Knopf, 1955), pp. 18–19. Horace Porter, *Campaigning with Grant* (New York: Century, 1906), pp. 69–70.

12. Porter, *Campaigning with Grant,* pp. 46–47.

13. Washington Chauncey Ford, ed., *A Cycle of Adams Letters, 1861–1865,* I (Boston: Houghton Mifflin, 1920), p. 156.

14. Quoted in Bruce Catton, *Grant Moves South* (Boston: Little, Brown, 1960), p. 119.

15. Grant, *Memoirs,* I, 191–192.

16. On Grant's background see Ulysses S. Grant, III, *Ulysses S. Grant: Warrior and Statesman* (New York: William Morrow, 1969), pp. 15–16.

17. On the working relationship between Lincoln and Grant see T. Harry Williams, *Lincoln and His Generals* (New York: Knopf, 1964), chap. 12 and 13.

18. Fuller, *Grant & Lee,* pp. 272–274.

21. Noah Brooks, *Washington, D.C., in Lincoln's Time,* ed. Herman Mitgang (New York: Collier Books, 1962), p. 150. Martindale's comments are in Benjamin F. Butler, *Private and Official Correspondence of Gen. Benjamin F. Butler during the Period of the Civil War,* V (n.p.: Privately issued, 1917), August 5, 1864, 5. Phillips' views are in Irving H. Bartlett, *Wendell Phillips: Brahmin Radical* (Boston: Beacon Press, 1961), p. 269.

22. Gurowski, *Diary from October 19, 1863, to Nov. 10, 1864* (Washington: W. H. & O. H. Morrison, 1865), June 24, 1864, pp. 107–108. Butler, *Correspondence,* IV, June 19, 1864, 418.

23. John L. Ransom, *John Ransom's Diary* (New York: Dell, 1964), p. 211. Butler, *Correspondence,* IV, July 28, 1864, 553–554.

24. For general descriptions of Union wartime propaganda see George Winston Smith, "Union Propaganda in the American Civil War," *Social Studies,* 35 (January 1944), 26–32; William B. Hesseltine, "The Propaganda Literature of Confederate Prisons," *Journal of Southern History,* 1.1 (1935),

56–66; and William Fletcher Thompson, Jr., *The Image of War: The Pictorial Reporting of the American Civil War* (New York: Thomas Yoseloff, 1960), chap. 7. Parker is quoted in Butler, *Correspondence,* IV, 553–554.

25. On the sense of humiliation attendant on Early's raid see Edward Bates, *The Diary of Edward Bates, 1859–1866,* ed. Howard K. Beale, Annual Report of the American Historical Association for the Year 1930, IV (Washington: Government Printing Office, 1933), July 31, 1864, 392 and Gideon Welles, *Diary of Gideon Welles,* ed. Howard K. Beale, II (New York: Norton, 1960), July 11, 1864, 73.

26. Lincoln is quoted in P. H. Sheridan, *Personal Memoirs of P. H. Sheridan,* I (London: Chatto & Windus, 1888), 347. On Sheridan's background see Frank A. Burr & Richard J. Hinton, *The Life of General Philip H. Sheridan* (Providence: J. A. & R. A. Reid, 1888). George Hughes Hepworth, *The Whip, Hoe, and Sword: Or the Gulf-Department in '63* (Boston: Walker, Wise, 1864), pp. 287–288.

27. Sheridan, *Memoirs,* I, 386–387.

28. Theodore Lyman, *Meade's Headquarters, 1863–1865: Letters of Colonel Theodore Lyman from the Wilderness to Appomattox,* ed. George R. Agassiz (Boston: Atlantic Monthly Press, 1922), May 24, 1864, p. 125.

29. Wilson, *Patriotic Gore: Studies in the Literature of the American Civil War* (New York: Oxford University Press, 1966), pp. 181 and 188. Otto Eisenschiml, "Sherman: Hero or War Criminal?", *Civil War Times Illustrated,* 2.9 (1964), 7, 29.

30. Sherman, *Home Letters of General Sherman,* ed. M. A. DeWolfe Howe (New York: Scribner's, 1909), pp. 305, 308. The statistics on actual troops numbers are drawn from Mark Mayo Boatner, III, *The Civil War Dictionary* (New York: David McKay, 1959), p. 33.

31. Sherman, *Home Letters,* October 27, 1864, p. 315.

32. John Sherman and William Tecumseh Sherman, *The Sherman Letters: Correspondence between General and Senator Sherman from 1837 to 1891,* ed. Rachel Sherman Thorndike (New York: Scribner's, 1894), August 3, 1863, p. 212.

33. Quoted in James Harrison Wilson, *Under the Old Flag,* II (New York: D. Appleton, 1912), 17.

34. Sherman, *Memoirs of General William T. Sherman,* I (Bloomington: Indiana University Press, 1957), 258, 338; II, 144, 152.

35. Sherman, *Memoirs,* I, 337–338 and *Home Letters,* pp. 342–343, 346.

36. On Sherman and the destruction of the Southern ruling class see, for instance, his letter to Sheridan, written just before the Atlanta campaign, and quoted in Wilson, *Patriotic Gore,* p. 181.

37. Quoted in Wilson, *Patriotic Gore,* pp. 180–181, 199–200.

38. In the language of the psychologist, it might be said that Sherman had passed over his "threshold" of frustration.

39. Sherman, *Home Letters,* p. 305.

40. Sherman, *Home Letters,* p. 295.

41. Custer's later conduct is described in Wilson, *Patriotic Gore,* p. 313.

42. Alexander Hays, *Life and Letters of Alexander Hays,* ed. George Thornton Fleming (Pittsburg: n.p., 1919), April 17, 1864, p. 583. On mass killing see Orville Hickman Browning, *The Diary of Orville Hickman Browning,* ed. Theodore C. Pease and James G. Randall (Springfield, Ill.: n.p., 1927), I, 697; II, 21. David Hunter Strother, *A Virginia Yankee in the Civil War,* ed. Cecil D. Eby, Jr. (Chapel Hill: University of North Carolina Press, 1961), pp. 235, 254–255.

43. Harvey Reid, *The View from Headquarters: Civil War Letters of Harvey Reid,* ed. Frank L. Byrne (Madison: State Historical Society of Wisconsin, 1965), p. 203. James A. Connolly, *Three Years in the Army of the Cumberland: The Letters and Diary of Major James A. Connolly,* ed. Paul M. Angle (Bloomington: Indiana University Press, 1959), pp. 298, 324.

44. Earl Schenck Miers, ed., *Sherman's Civil War* (New York: Collier Books, 1962), pp. 419–420.

45. James T. Ayers, *The Diary of James T. Ayres: Civil War Recruiter,* ed. John Hope Franklin (Springfield: Occasional Publications of the Illinois State Historical Society, no. 50, 1947), p. 98. Welles, *Diary,* II, April 7, 1865, 276–277. James F. Rusling, "The Yankee as a Fighter," *United States Service Magazine,* 4.1 (1865), 27–43. James Russell Lowell, "Ode Recited at the Harvard Commemoration, July 21, 1865," *Atlantic Monthly,* 16 (September 1865), 369.

46. Robinson is quoted in Chester Forrester Dunham, *The Attitude of the Northern Clergy toward the South, 1800–1865* (Toledo: Gray, 1942), p. 88. *Harper's Weekly* (July 8, 1865), p. 418. The resolution regarding the corps badges is in E. D. Townsend, *Anecdotes of the Civil War in the United States* (New York: D. Appleton, 1884), pp. 195–196.

47. George H. Hepworth, *The Criminal; The Crime; The Penalty* (Boston: Walker, Fuller, 1865), pp. 15–16.

48. George H. Hepworth, *Two Sermons Preached in the Church of the Unity, April 23, 1865. I: On the Death of Abraham Lincoln. II: Duties Suggested by the National Grief* (Boston: Printed for the Society, by John Wilson and Son, 1865), pp. 16–17. Hepworth, *Criminal,* pp. 5, 7, 9.

49. *Wilkes' Spirit of the Times,* April 15, 1865, p. 104.

50. On Appomattox, compare the matter-of-fact description of Grant's dress given by Horace Porter in "The Surrender at Appomattox Court House," in Johnson and Buel, eds., *Battles and Leaders,* IV, 737–738, and the symbolic interpretation given to the incident by Lloyd Lewis in *Myths after Lincoln* (New York: Grosset & Dunlap, n.d.), pp. 3–4. The cursing incident is in Burke Davis, *To Appomattox: Nine April Days, 1865* (New York: Rinehart, 1959), p. 397.

51. Henry Kyd Douglas, *I Rode With Stonewall: Being Chiefly the War Experiences of the Youngest Member of Jackson's Staff* (Greenwich, Conn.: Fawcett, 1961), pp. 318–319. See also Hooker's admiring remarks about the steadiness and efficiency of Lee's infantry in Committee on the Conduct of the War, *Reports,* II, March 11, 1865, 113.

52. Graham is quoted in Davis, *Appomattox,* p. 149. Henry Robinson Berkeley, *Four Years in the Confederate Artillery. The Diary of Private Henry Robinson Berkeley,* ed. William H. Runge (Chapel Hill: University of North Carolina Press, 1961), p. 137. Charles S. Wainwright, *A Diary of Battle. The Personal Journals of Colonel Charles S. Wainwright,* ed. Allan Nevins (New York: Harcourt, Brace & World, 1962), pp. 520–521.

There is a great deal of material on the failure of Confederate morale. Two accessible pieces are Stephen E. Ambrose, "Yeoman Discontent in the Confederacy," *Civil War History,* 8.3 (1962), 259–268; and Frank L. Owsley, "Defeatism in the Confederacy," *North Carolina Historical Review,* 3.3 (1926).

53. Wilson, *Under the Old Flag,* I, 402–403. See also, Grant, *Memoirs,* II, 291–292. Thomas W. Hyde, *Following the Greek Cross or, Memories of the Sixth Army Corps* (Boston: Houghton Mifflin, 1895), p. 180.

54. The quotation is from Clarence Edward Macartney, *Grant and His Generals* (New York: McBride, 1953), p. 33. The officer's comment is in Wilson, *Under the Old Flag,* I, 403.

55. Augustus Meyers, *Ten Years in the Ranks U.S. Army* (New York: Stirling Press, 1914), p. 320. Goss, *Recollections of a Private* (New York: Thomas Y. Crowell, 1890), p. 311.

56. Oliver Wendell Holmes, Jr., *Touched with Fire: Civil War Letters and Diary of Oliver Wendell Holmes, Jr., 1861–64,* ed. Mark DeWolfe Howe (Cambridge, Mass.: Harvard University Press, 1947), pp. 149–150. John William De Forest, *A Volunteer's Adventures: A Union Captain's Record of the Civil War,* ed. James H. Craushore (New Haven: Yale University Press, 1946), letter of August 8, 1864, p. 165. Wainwright, *Diary,* June 9, 1864, p. 412.

57. Cf. the perceptive comment by Adam Gurowski in his *Diary from 1863 to 1864,* entry for May 7, 1864, p. 92.

58. On Jomini see David Donald, *Lincoln Reconsidered: Essays on the Civil War Era,* 2d. ed. (New York: Random House, 1961), pp. 87ff., and David Donald, ed., *Why the North Won the Civil War* (New York: Collier Books, 1962), pp. 37ff.

59. On the belief that McClellan had achieved as much as Grant see the extensive comment in Wainwright, *Diary,* entry for June 15, 1864, p. 419.

60. Meade's thoughts are recorded in Patrick, *Inside Lincoln's Army,* p. 284; and Lyman, *Meade's Headquarters,* p. 188.

61. Dana is quoted in Bruce Catton, *The Centennial History of the Civil War,* III (New York: Pocket Books, 1967), 284–285. Noah Brooks, *Washing-*

ton, D.C. *in Lincoln's Time,* ed. Herbert Mitgang (New York: Collier Books, 1962), p. 130. Welles, *Diary,* I, 538–39; II, entry for April 20, 1864.

62. Wainwright, *Diary,* March 27, 1864, p. 338.

63. Lyman, *Meade's Headquarters,* pp. 152, 186–187, 207.

9. Losing the Peace

1. De Forest's war services are described in his *A Volunteer's Adventures: A Union Captain's Record of the Civil War,* ed. James H. Craushore (New Haven: Yale University Press, 1946).

2. De Forest, *Miss Ravenel's Conversion from Secession to Loyalty,* ed. Gordon S. Haight (New York: Holt, Rinehart & Winston, 1955), pp. 22–23.

3. De Forest, *Miss Ravenel's Conversion,* pp. 15, 19, 223.

4. De Forest, *Miss Ravenel's Conversion,* pp. 254–255, 335, 484.

5. Miss Ravenel's father says of Carter that he was the type of Southerner who drank heavily, gambled, and fought in bars or on the street. They were "deeply stained with the brutish forms of vice which flow directly from slavery." De Forest, *Miss Ravenel's Conversion,* pp. 188–189.

6. Wilson, *Patriotic Gore: Studies in the Literature of the American Civil War* (New York: Oxford University Press, 1966), pp. 703–705.

7. De Forest, "Chivalrous and Semi-Chivalrous Southrons," *Harper's New Monthly Magazine* (January 1869), pp. 192, 194–195.

8. De Forest, "Southrons," January 1869, pp. 192, 196–198; February, 1869, p. 346.

9. John Esten Cooke, *Wearing of the Gray: Being Personal Portraits, Scenes and Adventures of the War* (Bloomington: Indiana University Press, 1959), pp. 4, 249. George Cary Eggleston, *A Rebel's Recollections* (Bloomington: Indiana University Press, 1959), pp. 61–63, 69.

10. Cooke, *Wearing of the Gray,* p. xvi. Edward A. Pollard, *The Lost Cause: A New Southern History of the War of the Confederates* (New York: E. B. Treat, 1866), pp. 127–130. Sam R. Watkins, *"Co. Aytch": A Side Show of the Big Show* (New York: Collier Books, 1962), p. 244.

11. On the literary output of the South after the war see Paul H. Buck, *The Road to Reunion, 1865–1900* (Boston: Little, Brown, n.d.), esp. chap. 8.

12. Howard Melancthon Hamill, *The Old South: A Monograph* (Nashville: Confederate Veteran, 1905), pp. 7–11, 27–29, 78.

13. Trowbridge is quoted in Allan Nevins, *The Statesmanship of the Civil War,* 2d ed. (New York: Collier Books, 1962), p. 150. On Sherman see Wilson, *Patriotic Gore,* p. 205.

14. Browning, *The Diary of Orville Hickman Browning,* ed. Theodore C. Pease and James G. Randall, II (Springfield, Ill.: n.p., 1930), May 23, 1865, p. 29. Farley, *West Point in the Early Sixties* (Troy, N.Y.: Pafraets, 1902), p. 19.

15. The play is printed in Myron Matlaw, ed., *The Black Crook and Other Nineteenth Century American Plays* (New York: E. P. Dutton, 1967), p. 386 for the quotation.

16. Dana, *Recollections of the Civil War* (New York: Collier Books, 1963), p. 183.

17. John Chipman Gray and John Codman Ropes, *War Letters, 1862–1865* (Boston: Houghton Mifflin, 1927), August 21, 1864, pp. 375–376. Francis Winthrop Palfrey, *Campaigns of the Civil War, V: The Antietam and Fredericksburg* (New York: Scribner's, 1882), 135.

18. Harriet Beecher Stowe, *Men of Our Times: Or Leading Patriots of the Day* (Hartford: Hartford, 1868), pp. 12–13, 119–120.

19. On the lip service paid to Lincoln see the interesting article by Charles J. Stewart, "Lincoln's Assassination and the Protestant Clergy of the North," *Journal of the Illinois State Historical Society*, 54. 3 (1961), 268–293.

20. C. Vann Woodward, *The Burden of Southern History* (New York: Random House, n.d.), pp. 109–140. Although many historians talk of postwar corruption as a new phenomenon, the fact that contemporaries saw it as an old one is demonstrated by Mark Twain and Charles Dudley Warner's *The Gilded Age*. The book covers the corruption before and after the war and it makes no clear distinction between the two.

21. Henry Adams, *Democracy: An American Novel* (Leipzig: Bernhard Tauchmitz, 1882), p. 273.

22. Adams, *Democracy*, p. 20.

23. Ambrose Bierce, *In the Midst of Life and Other Tales* (New York: New American Library, 1961), pp. 10, 19.

24. Robert Penn Warren, *The Legacy of the Civil War: Meditations on the Centennial* (New York: Knopf, 1964), p. 73.

25. Wilbur R. Jacobs, ed., *Letters of Francis Parkman*, I (Norman: University of Oklahoma Press, 1960), September 4, 1861, 141.

26. Jacobs, ed., *Letters of Parkman*, I, October 14, 1862, 154–156, June 30, 1863, pp. 159–161.

27. De Forest, *Miss Ravenel's Conversion*, p. 484.

28. De Forest, "Southrons," January, 1869, p. 192.

29. Albion W. Tourgée, *A Fool's Errand: A Novel of the South during Reconstruction* (New York: Harper & Row, 1966). The author's biography is on pp. vii–xxv.

30. Tourgée, *A Fool's Errand*, p. 181.

31. Tourgée, *A Fool's Errand*, pp. 171, 323, 342. Another Northern radical whose respect for the South increased greatly was Whitelaw Reid, a journalist. He was at first a keen Reconstructionist but by 1870 he had decided that sympathy was due not to the black but the white, whose world was being remade. He wrote, "There was something inherently good and worth saving in that much laughed at chivalry." See Whitelaw Reid, *After the War: A Tour of*

the Southern States, 1865–1866, ed. C. Vann Woodward (New York: Harper & Row, 1965), esp. p. xx.

32. Higginson's case is cited in Buck, *Road to Reunion,* p. 235.

33. *Harper's Weekly,* October 7, 1865, p. 636.

34. T. Harry Williams, *P. G. T. Beauregard: Napoleon in Gray* (New York: Collier Books, 1962), pp. 336–337.

35. Quoted in Marshall W. Fishwick, *Lee after the War* (New York: Dodd, Mead, 1963), pp. 139, 199.

36. Theodore Lyman, *Meade's Headquarters, 1863–1865: Letters of Colonel Theodore Lyman from the Wilderness to Appomattox,* ed. George R. Agassiz (Boston: Atlantic Monthly Press, 1922), July 10, 1864, p. 187.

37. Homer Lea, *The Valor of Ignorance* (New York: Harper & Brothers, 1909), pp. 58–59. Lea somewhat resembled Parkman. Parkman had a weak constitution, and Lea was deformed and died early of a nervous disease. Both dreamed of military glory and in Lea's writings there is the identical concern with masculinity. Lea was able to gratify his martial desires after he found a military position with the Chinese. On Northern acceptance of Southern claims to superior marksmanship see the comment of General Palfrey in Theodore Ayrault Dodge, *A Bird's-Eye View of Our Civil War* (Boston: Houghton, Mifflin, 1883), pp. 116–117.

38. This and other works of the same type are covered in Thomas J. Pressly, *Americans Interpret Their Civil War* (New York: Free Press, 1965), pp. 53–77.

39. Pickett, *Soldier of the South: General Pickett's War Letters to His Wife,* ed. Arthur Crew Inman (Boston: Houghton Mifflin, 1928), September 17, 1861, p. 2. Farley, *West Point,* p. 23. Robert Bingham, "Sectional Misunderstandings," *North American Review,* 179 (September 1904), 357–370. See also Morris Schaff, *The Spirit of Old West Point, 1858–1862* (Boston: Houghton Mifflin, 1907), pp. 227–232.

40. Edgar S. Dudley, "Was Secession Taught at West Point? What the Records Show," *Century Illustrated Monthly Magazine,* 68 (August 1909), 630–635. Cf. Stephen E. Ambrose, *Duty, Honor, Country: A History of West Point* (Baltimore: Johns Hopkins Press, 1966), p. 187. James Kent, *Commentaries on American Law,* I (New York: O. Halsted, 1826), 195–196.

41. John Steinbeck, *America and Americans* (New York: Bantam Books, 1968), pp. 74–75.

42. Jay Luvaas, ed., *A Soldier's View: A Collection of Civil War Writings by Col. G. F. R. Henderson* (Chicago: University of Chicago Press, 1958), p. 31. Simkins, *A History of the South* (New York: Knopf, 1953), p. 222.

43. The marksmanship at Bull Run is detailed in Chapter 4 above. At Shiloh, every 1,000 rebels hit 252 of the enemy; the Union hit 162. At Wilson's Creek, August 10, 1861, 1,000 Union troops hit 214 rebels while every 1,000 rebels hit only 81. In the east, at Gaines' Mill for example, 1,000 Northerners hit 225 Southerners while 1,000 rebels hit only 112. At Mechanicsville, 1,000

Union hit 87 rebels; 1,000 Southerners hit only 16 Union men. Statistics computed from figures in Mark Mayo Boatner, III, *The Civil War Dictionary* (New York: David McKay, 1959).

44. On the running away of Northern veterans see John M. Schofield, *Forty-Six Years in the Army* (New York: Century, 1897), p. 145; and Philip Van Doren Stern, ed., *Soldier Life in the Union and Confederate Armies* (Greenwich, Conn.: Fawcett, 1961), p. 347. On lack of discipline in the Confederate army see Eggleston, *Recollections*, pp. 72–73; Thomas Cooper DeLeon, *Four Years in Rebel Capitals* (New York: Collier Books, 1962), p. 156; and Richard Taylor, *Destruction and Reconstruction: Personal Experiences of the Late War,* ed. Richard B. Harwell (New York: Longmans, Green, 1955), pp. 63–66.

45. On the qualifications of rebel generals see David Donald, "The Confederate as a Fighting Man," *Journal of Southern History,* 25 (May 1959), 189–191.

46. Eric L. McKitrick, "Party Politics and the Union and Confederate War Efforts," paper prepared for the Conference on American Political Party Development at Washington University, 1967. Also, Frank E. Vandiver, ed., *Essays on the American Civil War* (Austin: University of Texas Press, 1968), esp. p. 80.

47. Williams' thesis is presented in *Lincoln and His Generals* (New York: Knopf, 1964). The book is referred to in various parts of this work.

48. Catton, *The Penguin Book of the American Civil War* (Harmondsworth, Middlesex: Penguin Books, 1966), p. 33.

49. The statistics are from Grady McWhiney, "Who Whipped Whom? Confederate Defeat Reexamined," *Civil War History,* 2.1 (1965), 5–26. McWhiney maintains that the Confederacy actually defeated itself by attacking so often. This may be true to a certain extent, as in Lee's 1863 Pennsylvania campaign or Hood's defense of Alanta. But, on the whole, the spirit of the rebels appears to have been more of an asset that a liability, at least in the east. At Chancellorsville, for example, it was Lee's aggressive spirit and Hooker's lack of it that made the difference.

50. Franklin, *Militant South, 1800–1861* (Boston: Beacon Press, 1964), p. x.

51. James Warner Bellah, *The Valiant Virginians* (New York: Ballantine Books, 1968), "Note," n.p.

Index

A